Services Marketing Management

To Beatrice and Paul
– *Peter*

To Gervase, Phoebe and Hector
– *Angela*

Services Marketing Management

Third Edition

Peter Mudie and Angela Pirrie

AMSTERDAM • BOSTON • HEIDELBERG • LONDON • NEW YORK • OXFORD
PARIS • SAN DIEGO • SAN FRANCISCO • SINGAPORE • SYDNEY • TOKYO

Butterworth-Heinemann is an imprint of Elsevier

Butterworth-Heinemann is an imprint of Elsevier
Linacre House, Jordan Hill, Oxford OX2 8DP
30 Corporate Drive, Suite 400, Burlington, MA 01803, USA

First published as *The Management and Marketing of Services* 1993
Second edition 1999
Third edition 2006

British Library Cataloguing in Publication Data
A catalogue record for this book is available from the British Library

Library of Congress Cataloguing in Publication Data
A catalogue record for this book is available from the Library of Congress

ISBN-13: 978-0-7506-6674-9
ISBN-10: 0-7506-6674-9

For information on all Butterworth-Heinemann publications
visit our web site at http://books.elsevier.com

Typeset by Charon Tec Ltd, Chennai, India
www.charontec.com
Printed and bound in Great Britain

06 07 08 09 10   10 9 8 7 6 5 4 3 2 1

Working together to grow
libraries in developing countries

www.elsevier.com | www.bookaid.org | www.sabre.org

ELSEVIER   BOOK AID International   Sabre Foundation

Contents

Preface

Whilst largely retaining the overall structure of earlier editions, the third edition represents a thorough update and revamp of the content. For example, the impact of call centres, the significance of technology in the delivery of service and the trend toward the McDonaldization of services. Much more attention has been given to the importance of organizational climate and a completely new chapter has been devoted to relationship marketing. Greater prominence is attached to fundamental concepts, such as emotional labour, and techniques, for example, yield management. Service fairness and recovery and the law for services is the subject of extensive discussion in Chapter 12.

We continue to acknowledge, much more so in this edition, the difficulties and problems surrounding the management and marketing of services. Typical of this concern is reference to customer and employee feelings of frustration leading to acts of revenge and sabotage. We, therefore, challenge our readers to think more critically of the management of services, not least because of the growing reference to this area in our everyday lives. Finally, throughout the book we hope you remain conscious of the three parties to a service encounter – management, employees, customers – and all that may involve.

Peter Mudie
Angela Pirrie

Acknowledgements

Invaluable contributions were made to the presentation of the book by those organisations that kindly gave us permission to reproduce artwork or illustrations. In this context we would like to mention British Airways, Radisson SAS Hotels, Bain & Co., First Direct, Orange, The Cooperative Bank, Kwik-Fit, B&Q, Legal & General, Smile.co.uk and the English National Opera.

For granting copyright clearance we are grateful to the following: Bowling Green State University for Figure 2 from R Larsson and D E Bowen, 'Organisation and Customer: Managing Design and Coordination of Services', *Academy of Management Review*, Vol. 14, No. 2, 1989, © Bowling Green State University 1989; Harvard Business School Press for Exhibit 1 from G Lynn Shostack, 'Designing Services that Deliver', *Harvard Business Review*, Jan–Feb 1984, and for Figure 2 from F F Reicheld and W E Sasser Jr, 'Zero Defections: Quality Comes to Services' *Harvard Business Review*, Sep–Oct 1990, © Havard Business School Publishing; The American Marketing Association for Exhibit 3 from F F Reicheld 'Loyalty and the Renaissance of Marketing', *Marketing Management*, 1994, © American Marketing Association; Sage Publications Inc for Figure 3 from M Levine 'Placement and Misplacement of You-are-here Maps', *Environment and Behaviour*, Vol. 16, No. 2, 1984, © Sage Publications Inc 1984; Cornell HRA Quarterly for Exhibit 3 from W B Martin, 'Measuring and Improving your Service Quality' *Cornell HRA Quarterly*, May 1986, © Cornell HRA Quarterly 1986; Academic Press Inc (London) for Table 2 from G H Bower, J B Glack and T J Turner, *Scripts in Memory for Test, Cognitive Psychology II*, 1979, © Academic Press Inc (London) 1979; Pergamon Journals Ltd for Table 1, S D Ball, K Johnson and P Slattery, 'Labour Productivity in Hotels: An Empirical Analysis' *International Journal of Hospitality Management*, Vol. 5, No. 3, 1986, © Pergamon Journals Ltd 1986; Chartered Institute of Marketing for Figure 5 from R Brown, 'Marketing – a Function and a Philosophy', *The Quarterly Review of Marketing*, Vol. 12, Nos. 3 and 4, 1987, © Chartered Institute of Marketing 1987; MCB University Press Ltd for Figure 2 from G L Shostack 'How to Design a Service', *European Journal of Marketing*, Vol. 16, No. 1, 1982, © MCB University Press Ltd 1982; Marketing Management Association for Problem Impact Tree from R Rust *et al.* 'Making Complaints a Management Tool' *Journal of Marketing Management*, Vol. 1, No. 3, © Marketing Management Association; Production and Operations Management Society for R E Crandall and R E Markland, Figure 1, Demand Management – Today's Challenge For Service Industries, *Production and Operations Management*, Vol. 5, No. 2, 1996, © Production and Operations Management Society 1996; Continuum Books, London, for P Jones, Figure 3.4, Introduction to Hospitality Operations, 2002, © Continuum Books 2002; McGraw-Hill

Publishing for V A Zeithaml *et al.*, *Services Marketing* 5th edition Figure 11.5. Levels of Relationship Marketing © McGraw-Hill International; Emerald Group Publishing Ltd for J Haywood-Farmer, Figure 3, A Conceptual Model of Service Quality, *International Journal of Operations and Production Management*, Vol. 8, No. 6, 1987, © Emerald Group Publishing 1987; Tribune Media Services for R W Schmenner, Figure 1, 'How Can Businesses Survive and Prosper', *Sloan Management Review*, Spring, 1986, © Tribune Media Services 1986.

Invaluable contributions to the text were made by: Sholto Ramsay, Director, HelpMeGo for his contribution 'Technology and the future of services', Chapter 1. Janice Kirkpartick of Graven Images, Katherine Docherty of Farm 7, and Frazer Hay, Lecturer, Design and Media Arts, Napier University for contributing to Chapter 4; Jock Encombe of industrial psychologists YTS for his contribution on selection techniques in Chapter 7; David Stewart-David for his contribution to the section on Queuing in Chapter 8; Andy Ley of lawyers HBJ for his contribution on legal redress in relation to customer complaints in Chapter 12.

We would also like to thank Justine Storey of the Media Foundry, London for providing research by advertising agency Publicis on Petulant Britain; Catrin John, Head of Marketing of English National Opera for the seating plan in Chapter 8; Colin Shaw, CEO of Customer Experience Consultancy, Beyond Philosophy and Pain, Sunnak, Senior Account Executive, The SPA Way, London, for material on customer revenge in Chapter 1; Bill Taylor and Peter Morris of the Communication Workers Union for reports on Contact Centres; Rose Conroy, Press Officer, General and Municipal Boilermakers Union for the provision of a report on the electronic tagging of workers; Marianne Blaikie and Elizabeth McGregor-Smith of charteredbrands for their invaluable help and support in tracking down research reports, chasing permissions and much more besides; and to Karen Fisher of Napier University for her endless patience in typing the text from badly written hand written notes.

1

Introducing services

Introduction

Most organizations provide a service of some sort or another. For organizations such as airlines, trains, universities, car rental, health or government agencies service represents a major part of what they have to offer. They are known as service organizations. Others whose business is the manufacture of products, e.g. computers, mobile phones, washing machines, service is of lesser, albeit significant importance. There are particular problems and challenges in managing services, namely intangibility, inseparability, variability and perishability. In particular, services have to contend with uncertainties over customer involvement and what they expect. To address these and other problems service organizations have adopted an approach called 'McDonaldization', with increasing attention being given to efficiency and technology. Given the difficulties of providing a service, it is not surprising there is ongoing debate over the variability of its quality.

1.1 'What is this thing called service?'

The above question served as the title of an article by Nick Johns published in the *European Journal of Marketing*[1] in 1999. Whilst he noted that 'the word "service" has a great richness and diversity of meaning', there is also, it could be argued, an implicit recognition of the distinctiveness of service. It is equally a fitting introductory question for a text on services marketing management. Through the development of concepts and a body of knowledge services marketing and services management has become an area worthy of study in its own right. In arriving at this point, much of the detail has centred around the differences between service and manufacturing, giving rise to comment that 'it seems reasonable to expect that there are differences between managing an organization that produces something that can be seen, touched and held and managing an organization that produces something that is perceived, sensed, and

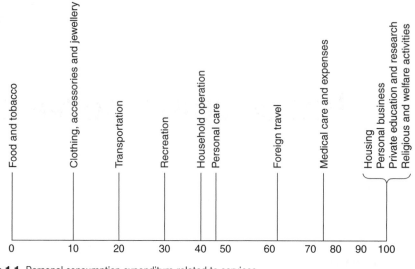

Figure 1.1 Personal consumption expenditure related to services
Source: Rathmell (1966)[3]

experienced'.[2] When asked to cite organizations or providers of services who or what might we mention? Answers could include plumbers, airlines, hair stylists, postal services, banks, child care, traffic wardens, estate agents. Although these businesses vary in size, scope and nature they are united by service as their major activity. To put the services/product distinction into perspective it is helpful to consider the goods–services continuum. In 1966 Rathmell[3] observed that most marketers have some idea of the meaning of the term 'goods'; they are tangible economic products that are capable of being seen and touched and may or may not be tasted, heard or smelled. As for services, Rathmell asserted that there was no clear understanding. He sought to change this by defining a good as a thing and service as an act, the former being an object, an article, a device or a material and the latter a deed, a performance, or an effort. Economic products were to be regarded as lying along a goods–services continuum with pure goods at one extreme and pure services at the other, but with most of them falling between these two extremes (Figure 1.1).

Some are primarily goods with service support, whereas others are primarily service with goods support. Most goods were seen as a complex of goods and facilitating services and most servers, a complex of services and facilitating goods. He applied the measuring rod of personal consumption to distinguish between goods and services. For the food and tobacco category, percentage personal consumption expenditure on the services was nil. For recreation it was 30 per cent and for religious and welfare activities, 100 per cent.

Sixteen years later Shostack[4] developed a refined version of the goods–services continuum and it remains a valuable perspective for understanding the nature of services (Figure 1.2). The essence of the continuum is that tangibility (ability to see, touch, smell, hear prior to purchase) decreases as one moves from left to right. Tangible entities are in evidence, such as equipment used by a nurse but, in general, they cannot be owned or possessed like salt or dog food. Every organization on the continuum delivers some degree of service as part of its total offer. However, it is the organizations to the right (of

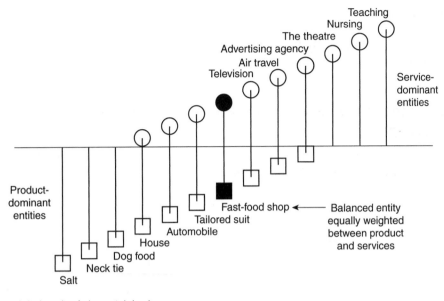

Figure 1.2 A scale of elemental dominance
Source: Shostack (1982)[4]

television) which deliver most in the way of service and can therefore truly bear the hallmark 'service organizations'. It is important to make a distinction between those for whom service is part of the overall offer (e.g. computer manufacturer, car dealer, fashion retailer) and those for whom service is the offer (e.g. bank, hotel, airline, accountant), as the latter exhibit particular characteristics that merit attention.

1.2 Characteristics of services

Services have the following four key distinguishing characteristics.

1.2.1 Intangibility

This is the most basic and often quoted difference between goods and services. Unlike tangible goods, services cannot generally be seen, tasted, felt, heard or smelled before being consumed. The potential customer is often unable to perceive the service before (and sometimes during and after) the service delivery. For many customers of car repair, for example, the service is totally intangible – they frequently cannot see what is being done and many are unable to evaluate what has been done. Rushton and Carson[5] asked a number of service organizations whether they consciously perceived a difference between the marketing of goods and services. Several respondents pointed to the intangibility of their products with comments such as:

We haven't got anything to show to customers like a can of baked beans.

It's more difficult trying to explain what they [the customers] get for their money.

Implications

To help a customer picture a service prior to usage a service organization needs to provide something tangible, e.g. computerized representation of hairstyles or a university prospectus.

1.2.2 Inseparability (or simultaneous production and consumption)

There is a marked distinction between physical goods and services in terms of the sequence of production and consumption:

Physical goods	Services
Production	Sold
↓	↓
Storage	Produced and consumed at the same time
↓	
Sold	
↓	
Consumed	

Whereas goods are first produced, then stored and finally sold and consumed, services are first sold, then produced and consumed simultaneously. For the production of many services (e.g. counselling, museums, hairdressing, rail travel, hotels), the customer must be physically present. Some services may be produced and delivered in circumstances where the customer's presence is optional, e.g. carpet cleaning, plumbing. Other services may rely more on written communication, e.g. distance learning course, or on technology, e.g. home banking. Whatever the nature and extent of contact, the potential for inseparability of production and consumption remains.

Implications

The involvement of the customer in the production and delivery of the service means that the service provider must exercise care in what is being produced and how it is produced. The latter task will be of particular significance. How teachers, doctors, bank tellers, lawyers, car mechanics, hairdressers conduct themselves in the presence of the customer may determine the likelihood of repeat business. Therefore, proper selection and training of customer contact personnel is necessary to ensure the delivery of quality.

1.2.3 Variability (or heterogeneity)

An unavoidable consequence of simultaneous production and consumption is variability in performance of a service. The quality of the service may vary depending on who provides it, as well as when and how it is provided. One hotel provides a fast efficient service and another, a short distance away, delivers a slow, inefficient service. Within a particular hotel, one employee is courteous and helpful while another is arrogant and obstructive. Even within one employee there can be variations in performance over the course of a day.

Implications

Reducing variability involves determining the causes. It may be due to unsuitable personality traits in an employee which are very difficult to detect at the selection stage. There is nothing much that can be done about this except hope that the employee decides to terminate his/her employment! However, there may be good sound reasons for variations in performance. For example, it could be due to poor training and supervision, lack of communication and information, and generally a lack of regular support.

Some have argued for a replacement of labour with automation and a production line approach to service operations. This would mean a reduction in employee discretion and an increase in standardization of procedures. The operation of McDonald's restaurants is put forward as an ideal model of service industrialization.

The other source of variability is, of course, the customer; Peters and Waterman[6] in their bestseller, *In Search of Excellence*, called for staying 'close to the customer'. Unfortunately, if we regard it as 'physical proximity' then, according to one view,[7] this is being 'steadily undermined by the zealots of increased productivity and back room operations. The customer is in danger of being controlled to the point where customer service is becoming just another stage in a systematic manufacturing process, McDonald's being the definitive example'.

1.2.4 Perishability

Services cannot be stored for later sales or use. Hotel rooms not occupied, airline seats not purchased and college places not filled cannot be reclaimed. As services are performances they cannot be stored. If demand far exceeds supply it cannot be met, as in manufacturing, by taking goods from a warehouse. Equally, if capacity far exceeds demand, the revenue and/or value of that service is lost.

Implications

Fluctuations in demand characterize service organizations and may pose problems where these fluctuations are unpredictable. Strategies need to be developed for producing a better match between supply and demand (see Chapter 8).

1.3 The '7 Ps' of services

Marketing activity is normally structured around the '4 Ps' – *product, price, promotion* and *place*. However, the distinctive characteristics of services requires the addition of three more Ps – *people, physical evidence* and *process*. As the additional three Ps figure prominently throughout the text, a brief description of each will suffice at this stage:

- People – the appearance and behaviour of service personnel
- Physical evidence – everything from the appearance, design, layout of the service setting, to brochures, signage, equipment (the 'tangibilizing' of the intangible)
- Process – how the service is delivered, the actual procedures and flow of activities.

Each of the three extra Ps is of central importance in services as each represents cues that customers rely on in judging quality and overall image.

1.4   Customer involvement and uncertainty

What makes a service really a service according to Teboul[8] is the interface: the front office, the dining room and the actual difference between a service and a manufacturing facility is the size of the interface. Teboul correctly identifies the main characteristics of the interface thus:

- The customer is physically present.
- The service and the delivery process are interdependent (simultaneous production and consumption).
- When the customer is in the interface he or she is visiting the factory – the place where the service is delivered. And the larger the interface the more visible the service is.

The physical presence of the customer is an important issue as it raises the questions:

- How much physical presence of the customer is necessary for the delivery of the service to take place?
- What is the nature of the customer contact and the implications for service management?

To say that a service cannot exist without simultaneous production and consumption is not strictly true. For example, a parcel delivery or data processing service is not consumed while it is being produced.

Finally, Teboul does not give an explanation of the 'size of the interface'. It could mean a number of things, e.g. physical space, amount of time, number of activities etc.

Teboul's view of service would seem to favour a counselling-type situation where the production, delivery and consumption occur simultaneously and are visible to all concerned. This is a very important view of service but it cannot be regarded as an exclusive explanation of what is meant by service.

Many organizations do, however, fall into a category similar to that outlined above. They can be portrayed as visible operational processes in which the customer is directly involved in some way. Unlike the purchase of a packet of soap powder, where it is fairly certain that it will do the job it is intended to, a stay in a hotel is potentially full of uncertainty in that so many things can go wrong.

Uncertainty about what the customer actually wants is a key factor for organizations whose major activity is providing a service. The uncertainty can occur before, during and after the service.

1.4.1   Before

The customer, as a major input to the service production process, is regarded as a major source of uncertainty.[9] Customers may bring with them their bodies, minds, goods or information to be serviced. The uncertainty for the service provider lies in not fully understanding these customer inputs, for example:

- Physical state of a body for a fitness clinic
- Mental state of mind for an education service
- State and complexity of a car for detecting faults during a service
- Capacity of clothing and carpet fabrics to withstand chemical treatment
- Amount and nature of customer information for a medical diagnosis.

In the above situations service providers are unsure about what to expect which in turn may affect their preparedness for creating and delivering an effective service.

1.4.2   During

Customers have been portrayed as posing problems for organizations by 'disrupting routines, ignoring offers of service, failing to comply with procedures and making exaggerated demands'.[10] The challenge for service organizations is the development of strategies to manage customer behaviour, hopefully in a way acceptable to both parties.

1.4.3   After

Intangibility of service means that the object of exchange is often an experience that can neither be touched nor possessed. Therefore, the customer may have difficulty understanding what has been obtained on receipt of a service. For example, what does the customer purchase when buying insurance? The more intangibility there is in a service, the greater this problem becomes. This is known as performance ambiguity.[11] As intangibility increases, the customer has less evidence available to assess the service.

1.5   Expectations and perceptions of a service

Before, during (if appropriate) and after consumption of a service two feelings are prominent, namely expectations and perceptions.

Expectations are usually formed prior to usage of a service but may also occur where a customer is actively involved in the delivery of a service. They reflect inclinations or beliefs as to what will or should happen. (See Chapter 5 for discussion.)

Perceptions can also develop during a service, but invariably materialize after usage. They represent the customer's evaluation of the service, particularly in relation to expectations.

Where perceptions match or exceed expectations the customer is said to be satisfied in accordance with the first law of service:[12]

$$\text{Satisfaction} = \text{Perception} - \text{Expectation}$$

(Reading Chapter 5 you will find the word 'quality' substituted for the word 'satisfaction'. Whilst it might appear confusing, the distinction can be explained. Satisfaction can arise where perception exceeds a modest level of customer expectations. Where customers seek quality, expectations will be set much higher.)

Measuring the customer's perception and expectations is vitally important. However, the following question must be asked of the service organization: 'What does it think of customer expectations and perceptions? To arrive at an answer, two variants of the original perceptions/expectations formula might be used. The objective is to determine whether or not any gaps exist between the customers' view and the service organization's perception of the customers' view.

A study that examined doctor–patient relationships[13] found that 'gaps can arise from inconsistent perceptions of expectations and experiences between patients and physicians'. This research was prefaced with a statement that should act as a continuing reminder for all service organizations:

> From a marketing perspective, the provider would design, develop, and deliver the service offering on the basis of his or her perceptions of client expectations. Likewise, modifications to the service offering would be affected by the provider's perceptions of client experiences. Whether these experiences exceed, match, or are below expectations can have a profound effect on future client/professional relationships.

To measure the gaps, doctors and patients were required to indicate their agreement/disagreement with a long list of statements (e.g. see Figure 1.3).

Not surprisingly, significant gaps were found. This is a profound problem for service organizations where the expectations/perceptions of one group are at odds with those of another. Why should this be the case? In terms of customer expectations service organizations may regard them as:

- Unrealistic
- Unprofitable
- Impractical
- Unreasonable.

And yet, by way of promises made, organizations contribute to rising expectations. To attract custom, organizations are often tempted to raise customer expectations. Promises are made to customers on aspects that customers are deemed to value. However, care must be exercised in making promises to customers. Consider the following sample of 'fuzzy over-promises' selected at random from the *Yellow Pages* directory:

> 'Number one for service and care'
> 'Fast and friendly service'
> 'Your satisfaction is our priority'

	Strongly agree	Agree	Neither	Disagree	Strongly disagree
Gap: Customer expectation – service organization's perception of customer expectations					
Example of statement: I expect my doctor to talk clearly, using words that I understand					
Gap: Customer experience – service organization's perception of customer experience					
Example of statement: My doctor spends enough time with me					

Figure 1.3 Gap analysis

'Quality of service you can depend on'
'You can't beat our service'

From the experience of one consultant, 'keeping the service promise is such a basic test that it is both surprising and frustrating that so many organizations fail to pass it'.[14]

Of course, over-promising is a risk-laden method for 'managing' customer expectations. Others see it in terms of altering expectations, plotting them in relation to what a firm can realistically deliver.[15] Various approaches are suggested, not least of which is that of shaping customer expectations in accordance with methods designed for the management of employee expectations. Overall, the emphasis (in managing expectations) centres round the need for clarity and focus in the service encounter.

1.6 Core and augmented service

The concept of core and augmented products is well established in marketing. 'What are consumers really buying?' expresses the core element. It was the late Charles Revson of Revlon who captured the essence of the core: 'In the factory we make cosmetics; in the drug store we sell hope.' In similar vein, a manufacturer of ball bearings is marketing anti-friction devices. As the core becomes perfected in the eyes of the customer, competitive pressures force organizations to offer additional benefits. This is the augmented product. It is ironic that much of these additional benefits are in the form of customer services: credit and financing, fast and reliable delivery, freephone helplines, and repair and maintenance.

Services are also in the business of providing a core benefit, e.g.:

- Rail travel – safe and reliable transportation
- Tax consultant – peace of mind

- Education course – career enhancement, self-actualization
- Hotel – hospitality, rest and recuperation
- Hairdresser – feel more attractive, confidence-booster.

In some cases, different market segments will perceive different core benefits from the same service, e.g. a keep-fit programme may be made up of people who wish to lose weight, get very fit or simply enjoy themselves.

The 'augmented product' for services is usually in the form of further services and these are also referred to as supplementary, peripheral and facilitating. A good example of augmentation is the introduction by British Airways of a speech recognition service to improve the efficiency of their customer flight and confirmation services while making it easier and more pleasant for customers to access flight information.[16] The airline industry is interesting as customers will take for granted that its core service, safety, is guaranteed. Consequently customers look for other benefits (reservation procedure, schedule convenience, on-board seating comfort and food quality) before selecting a particular airline. Similarly, in health services people will look beyond the core service, which they see as difficult to evaluate, to the 'little things' such as ease of making an appointment with a doctor or the quality of hospital food.

Services will vary in how much they need or resort to augmentation. Those that are low cost with no-frills (e.g. budget airlines) will offer far fewer 'extras' than those at the expensive, high-value end (e.g. exclusive hotels).

1.7   The 'McDonaldization' of services

Many writers have urged services to 'design and manage for efficiency'.[17] One of the earliest (1972, 1976) and most significant was Levitt.[18,19] He argued that services should be run like factories and believed that by adopting the predictability of the factory system, disruptions caused by people (employees and customers) in services would be minimized. 'Whenever people are involved', he argued, a key management issue is 'about how to control their personal behaviour and channel their choices'.[20] This type of thinking[21] and action is still prevalent today, arousing much in the way of controversy.

Over time, industrialization (of services) came to mean standardization, routinization and ultimately McDonaldization. Through the use of rules, regulations, scripts and technology, services sought to control the behaviour of employees and customers. Just as the production side of service (the back office) had been successfully 'industrialized', organizations have pursued a similar approach for managing the tensions and unpredictability on the consumption side (the front office). In 1992,[22] George Ritzer published a ground-breaking book on the 'McDonaldization of Society' (subsequent editions appearing in 1996 and 2004). For those interested in services marketing and management, the implications are of significance. Whilst acknowledging its many advantages he warns of its seductions and attractions.

Ritzer defines McDonaldization as 'the process by which the principles of the fast-food restaurant are coming to dominate more and more sectors of American society as well as the rest of the world'.[23] He attributes its success to four dimensions (efficiency, calculability, predictability and control) seemingly attractive to employees, customers and management. A brief account of the four dimensions follows.

Efficiency is regarded as the optimum method for getting from one point to another. The McDonald's restaurant offers the best available way to get from being hungry to being full. Customers see it as the quickest way to satisfy a need. Efficiency, then, for customers is obtaining something quickly with the minimum of effort, e.g. the Internet has increased shopping efficiency. Employees are also said to gain. By clearly defining what is to be done and how it is to be done, tasks are performed more rapidly and easily. For service management, efficiency means getting the most output from the least input, maximizing (where relevant) profitability. Sometimes customers are put to work (unpaid) in a drive for efficiency, e.g. putting petrol in your car and paying for it at the pump. The service literature refers to customers here as co-producers or part-time employees! Higher education offers up a futuristic view of efficiency: multiple choice exams (as the inane form of assessment) set and marked by computer and results delivered to students electronically within a short time period.

Calculability emphasizes calculating, counting, quantifying, e.g. how much time should a doctor spend with a patient. We live in a world 'completely overwhelmed by numbers and calculations'.[24] Services are not immune. Increasingly, management is asking, how many …, how often …, how much …, how soon …'. Steps in the service process are measured for the time they take and those that take the least are deemed the most efficient. Calculability, thus, makes it easier to determine efficiency.

Predictability means order, certainty, knowing what to expect. It suggests, for a service, that it can be pre-programmed/choreographed. Surprises are unlikely. The package tour is an apt illustration of a highly predictable service. Both customers and service provider know what is going to happen, where, when and how. In such circumstances predictability, as well as calculability, facilitates efficiency.

Control is the fourth dimension. It is exerted through the substitution of non-humans for human technology. A human technology (a screwdriver for example) is controlled by people; a non-human technology (the assembly line for instance) controls people. The ultimate stage in control is, of course, where people are replaced by machines. There is then no more uncertainty or unpredictability. It is also important to remember that control (of employees and customers) is exerted in many other ways in services, e.g. the use of scripts and uniforms, regulations and procedures, automated voice systems and the design of interior facilities.

1.8   The downside of McDonaldization

Ritzer acknowledges the benefits of efficiency, predictability, calculability and control. However, with the addition of a fifth dimension, the irrationality or rationality, he draws our attention to the negative aspects of McDonaldization. Through relentless standardization and numbing routines, both employees and customers can feel dehumanized and depersonalized. As employees are made to become more robotic-like in their behaviour, stress and a sense of loss of identity may follow. Customers feel as though they are part of an assembly line, a statistic to be processed. They regard tightly scripted procedures as fake or phoney. Frustration, for both parties, is a likely outcome with employees engaging in acts of sabotage and customers in acts of revenge (see Chapter 6). Moreover, trying to process many people and/or their possessions as quickly as possible with inadequate resources can have an adverse affect on service quality. So, a 'McDonaldized organization', for all its attractions, is not without problems.

1.9 Technology in services

As mentioned in the paragraph above, many services are faced with increasing demand and customer contact. To help address the problems services are turning to technology. The National Health Service is a good example. Struggling to cope with ever-increasing demands, the introduction of new technology will now play a much larger part in delivering medical care. In addition to the out-of-hours phone service (NHS24), patients will be diagnosed and monitored from afar by using telemedicine facilities and the Internet. With help and support from a health professional (not a doctor),the patient will play an increasing role in managing his/her own condition. Unlike the examples of the petrol pump or self-service in the supermarket, this example provides a more substantive, if controversial, illustration of the customer as part-time employee or co-producer of a service. Furthermore, the advance of technology not only enables services to transfer some of the work to customers but also allows organizations to vary according to customer type, the service received. With the advent of information technology, organizations can now amass a substantial amount of data on customers. Those seen as less worthy, less profitable or perceived to be a cause of inefficiency (e.g. elderly people blocking hospital beds) will need to serve themselves or simply go away.[25]

> Welcome to the new consumer apartheid. Those long lines and frustrating telephone trees aren't always the result of companies simply not caring about pleasing the customer anymore. Increasingly, companies have made a deliberate decision to give some people skimpy service because that's all their business is worth. Call it the dark side of the technology boom, where marketers can amass a mountain of data that gives them an almost Orwellian view of each buyer. Consumers have become commodities to pamper, squeeze, or toss away, according to Leonard L Berry, marketing professor at Texas A&M University. He sees 'a decline in the level of respect given to customers and their experiences'.[26]

The benefits of technology, for service organizations, are apparent in terms of productivity and cost savings. But what of the customer? After all, 'much of this technology delivered service is initiated and carried out by the consumer and involves no direct or indirect contact with representatives of the service provider'.[27] This is given further meaning by the view that 'across industries, technology is dramatically altering interpersonal encounter relationships, and in some instances, eliminating them altogether'.[28] So in this age of increasing technology-based service, what are the views of the customers? Dabholkar[29] studied a situation in a fast-food restaurant where customers could use a computerized touch screen to order a meal (technology-based self-service). The study found that feeling in control and the potential enjoyment from using this type of delivery, were important determinants of service quality. Reliability (error free), speed of delivery and ease of use were also found to be important. In an extensive study of consumers, Howard and Worboys[30] found that time-saving was seen as the biggest advantage of self-service. However, the findings also suggest that consumers still prefer the concept of human interaction rather than technological interfaces. Similar findings by Curry and Penman from the banking sector[31] indicate that the human element in the banker/customer relationship is more influential than the technology element. Equally they draw attention to differences between banks and their employees in the use of technology.

In a review of electronic government in the public sector, Hazlett and Hill[32] point to a 'lack of evidence to support the claim that the use of technology in service delivery results in less bureaucracy and increased quality'. They conclude that 'it is by no means certain that e-government can produce truly innovative, responsive public services, indeed it may merely exacerbate electronically, existing shortcomings'. It would appear that the overriding problem for technology in services is the willingness and ability of customers to use it. Parasuraman[33] has developed a scale called the technology readiness index designed to classify people in terms of their tendency to embrace and use new technology. The classification is arranged hierarchically with explorers at the top and laggards at the bottom. Not surprisingly, research indicates that those most favourably disposed to technology and heavy users are well educated, with a high income and younger. Those at the other end tend to be older, of a lower education level and income. What is intriguing is how far into the future this particular way of classifying people (in relation to technology use) will persist. Even more so, if you recall an earlier reference (Brady[25]) and with some worry, those at the lower or bottom end are the same group for whom technology will be the 'option' for accessing a range of services.

Technology not only appears in service provider/customer contacts. It is also present within the service organization's work environment. The aims are largely twofold: management control and efficiency. The following examples are simply illustrative. Ocado, an upmarket online grocer and a favourite with wealthier stay-at-home shoppers in London and the South East, has been the subject of a study[34] by the trade union GMB (General and Municipal Boilermakers). It centres on the company's practices at its distribution centre at Hatfield, where its warehouse workers, in company with an estimated 10 000 in all among other named firms (Tesco, Marks & Spencer, Sainsbury, B&Q, Boots and Homebase), are compelled to strap on chunky electronic surveillance tags that direct them to pick up goods for delivery. Professor Michael Blakemore of Durham University (the report author) says satellite and radio-based computer technology is turning some warehouses into 'battery farms' and creating 'prison surveillance'. Employers argue the union is over-reacting. They insist the system is not used to spy on workers but to make things easier and improve customer service. However, Paul Kenny, the union's acting General-Secretary, says: 'The GMB is not a Luddite organization, but we will not stand idly by to see our members reduced to robots with heartbeats.'

The other example involves a 2003 study of nurses working in three NHS trust hospitals who were required to use computer systems which produced detailed care plans for patients.[35] The stated aims of the projects were to improve nursing practice, to improve the quality of records, and to gain a better understanding of how nursing resources were used. Although surveillance was not principally intended, the systems were capable of linking any activity on the system to an identifiable user. Resistance did exist but what was at issue here was the standardization (or if you like McDonaldization) of nursing practice. Set against the nurses' aim of defending (or enhancing) their professional status and autonomy, the question then became one of what is nursing and how should it be done? What do these two brief examples signify? On the one hand there is management's need to control, to achieve efficiency goals. On the other hand there is the employee's loss of individuality, sense of self and the anxiety and stress brought on by monitoring.

(For a view on technology see the thoughts of Sholto Ramsay in Appendix 1.)

1.10   Call centres

The efficiencies of McDonaldization and advances in technology have given rise to the call centre (also known as customer contact centres). Many people work in them (see Chapter 9), and unless you are a hermit, your daily routine will regularly include some contact with call centres. They continue to be the subject of controversy with graphic accounts of employment conditions and customer experiences. Moore[36] portrays it thus:

> We all know what it feels like. You ring the bank or building society and an automated voice tells you to press a dozen buttons on your telephone keypad, then you listen to 'Greensleeves' for 10 minutes and finally hear the dreaded recorded message: 'You are held in a queue, your call will be answered shortly ...' By the time a human being answers, your stress levels are sky high.

> Now spare a thought for the person on the other end of the telephone. You could be the 500th disgruntled customer they have had to deal with today, while staring non-stop at a computer screen on long shifts without proper breaks and under constant surveillance.

> Call centres – where often huge teams of people handle a never-ending flow of customers' calls – have been described as '21st century sweat shops' and modern-day 'dark satanic mills', while their workers have been called 'battery hens' and 'galley slaves'. Horror stories, which have recently come to light, include tales of managers who threaten staff with wearing disposable nappies if they visit the toilet too often, and the worker who was disciplined for taking two six-second breaks between calls. It is no wonder some call centre staff report high levels of stress and anxiety.

Additionally, in a report by the Citizens Advice Bureau[37] evidence pointed to a number of common problems its clients have when dealing with call centres, whether provided by a government agency or a private company. These problems occurred across a wide range of services from access to benefits to provision of after-sales services (see Figure 1.4).

Comments and research on and about call centres have been widely discussed and contested. How far do they represent the reality of call centres? A useful starting point for reflection is to think of services as made up of a back office and front office (see Chapter 3). The back office has developed along the lines of a factory, inaccessible to the customer. In its traditional form the front office is open to the customer on terms of face-to-face interaction. There continues to be much debate over how much of a service should be back office and how much should be front office. Of course

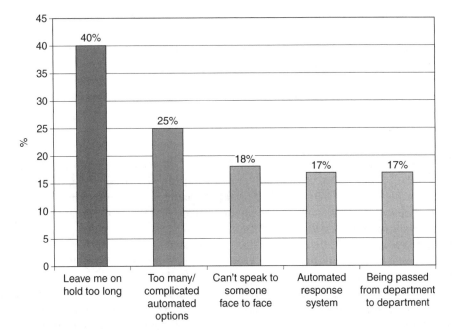

Figure 1.4 Most annoying aspects of call centres
Source: MORI survey commissioned by Citizens Advice. A nationally representative sample of 2253 adults (aged 15 years and over) were interviewed face-to-face throughout Great Britain by MORI between 8 and 13 July 2004

the nature of a service will partly determine the balance. However, the call centre represents a new kind of 'front-line' facility[38] redefined more in terms of a back office operation. Customers can experience difficulty in gaining access. Once obtained, contact may be with an automated response system. Frustration is inevitably felt. For employees in call centres it is a matter of being subject to some demanding working conditions.

It is to these working conditions that much of the comment/research has been directed. In the course of this debate reference is made to Frederick Winslow Taylor, author of the *Principles of Scientific Management*, published in 1911.[39] His objectives were to achieve:

- Efficiency, by increasing the output per worker and reducing 'underworking' by employees
- Standardization of job performance, by dividing tasks up into small and closely specified sub tasks
- Discipline, by establishing hierarchical authority and introducing a system whereby all management's policy decisions could be implemented.

Taylor was clearly obsessed with the achievement of efficiency, matching people to a task and then supervising, rewarding and punishing them in line with their performance. He believed there was no such thing as skill and all work could be analysed step-by-step as a series of unskilled operations that could then be constrained into any kind of job. Tasks specified what was to be done, how it was to be done and, importantly, the exact time allowed for doing it.

The routinization and fragmentation of tasks advocated by Taylor appear to be present in the call centre labour process.

> There is no question that the interaction of telephone and computer technologies, which defines the call centre, has produced new developments in the Taylorization of white-collar work.[40]

Operational efficiency is a key driving force and in order to maintain that employees are subject to electronic surveillance and monitoring by supervisors. The situation (for the employee) has been described as akin to having 'an assembly line in the head, always feeling under pressure and constantly aware that the completion of one task is immediately followed by another'.[41] Of course excessive and continuous control can be 'counterproductive' as employees become demotivated, demoralized and stressed out. Research by the Communication Workers Union suggests that staff turnover is in the region of 33%. The two most common factors cited for leaving are poor rates of pay and the intensity of the call centre environment. However, the buzz and vibrancy of the call centre atmosphere is also highlighted as one of the main features that staff like about their work.[42] On the subject of front-line call centre employee satisfaction, it would appear there is a general perception that it is not a measure seen to be critical.[43] What is vital is the performance of employees over a range of measures:

- The number of calls handled
- Time spent logging information
- Duration of calls
- Gaps between calls
- Numbers of calls waiting
- Numbers of calls abandoned.

These are all quantitative indicators designed to manage workforce productivity. Not so much in evidence are feedback mechanisms for the quality of service.

Successfully managing quantity and quality represents, in the view of some, a general dilemma that appears irresolvable:

> If operators are driven too hard with targets and quantitative output measurement, then the quality of service may suffer, as motivation and commitment are adversely affected. If on the other hand, there is an over-emphasis on informality with a relaxation of targets and surveillance, the centre may not turn over sufficient business.[44]

Moving toward employee empowerment and away from the traditional production line approach runs the risk of inconsistent quality of service due to the variability of both customers and employees.[45] The quality/quantity dilemma reflects a wider challenge beyond that of the call centre. In most service situations there are three parties involved: customers, management and employees. How can the needs of all three be satisfied? In other words, how does one create a win:win:win outcome?

Whatever one might think of call centres, they have attracted an enormous amount of academic and media attention in recent years, most of it projecting a very 'bleak picture of life at the sharp end of a technological treadmill'.[46] Other portrayals of the call centre are of 'dark satanic mills' and 'sweat shops'. Some have sought to inject a note of realism into the debate. Evidence collected does not always support these 'exaggerated claims'.[47]

1.11   The trouble with service ...

The literature on service provides knowledge on how to deliver quality and satisfy the customer. By applying a range of concepts, models and techniques the service provider should be in a position to deliver what the market wants. The everyday service reality experienced by customers and employees and often expressed through the media suggests something different. Why, then, is there such a discrepancy? A number of points are worthy of consideration:

- Probably at the top of any list should be efficiency, a word we hear much of today and one, according to a leading authority, that has a bad name.[48] Whether public or private, service organizations are seeking to obtain more and more output from fewer and fewer inputs (resources). Tight control and demanding use of resources is not necessarily a formula for delivering service quality.
- Front-line employees are regarded as pivotal for success by service organizations. That at least is the theory. The reality is that working conditions on the front line can be less than favourable: demanding management and customers, low pay and inadequate training. Consequently the resulting stress, frustration and lack of motivation impacts on performance.
- The ever-increasing use of technology frustrates those who equate service with personal service. Being served by a fellow human being is viewed by many as the hallmark of service. When the technology fails or is poorly designed from a user perspective, customer dissatisfaction is inevitable.
- 'All consumers are not created equal', as Hallberg observed.[49] Who you are (defined in terms of job status) and what you are worth to an organization (defined in terms of profitability) determines the quality of service received. In a study[50] of who gets the best service from British businesses, the customer's occupation was found to be significant. On the matter of profitability Zeithaml, Rust and Lemon[51] suggested that by sorting customers into profitability tiers or levels service can be tailored to achieve even higher profitability levels (see Chapter 11).
- We live in an environment of rising expectations with marketing promising better and better service. Competitive pressures are a major driving force. The trouble is that promises are not always matched with proper resources and commitment.

The above points may be contested and rightly so. Other reasons should be considered. In the course of such a discussion, two questions should be borne in mind:

- Who defines service?
- What constitutes good or bad service?

In addressing these questions you should consider, for the first question particularly, the three perspectives already mentioned in this chapter: management, employees, customers. For the second question, who or what is to be congratulated or to be blamed?

Summary

Managing a service requires knowledge and understanding of its four characteristics: intangibility, inseparability, variability and perishability. For each one there are important implications. Additionally there is a need to acknowledge that services possess three additional Ps (people, process and physical evidence) over and above the standard '4 Ps' of the marketing mix. Equally, the appearance of gaps between what consumers receive from a service (their perceptions) and what they hope for (their expectations) must be an ongoing concern. Furthermore, there may be differences of view between customers and the service organization over what to expect and what has been received. Another difficult area for services is customer involvement and the uncertainty that brings. To try to minimize the impact of this some services are operating more like a factory with the emphasis on standardization, efficiency measures and an increasing role for technology. This trend has engendered some criticism, particularly over the effect on service quality.

Appendix 1.1   Technology and the future of services

Technology, consumers' changing concerns and external factors will drive services marketing.

Key changes

1 Enterprises used to deliver services through humans – this was the services encounter. In the Internet-enabled future, enterprises will deliver service value through technologies: the Internet will be the 'point of contact'.
2 Customers will use their own technologies to delve into the enterprise's systems to achieve results when and how they choose. Those same technologies will enable customers to manage and mediate their service encounters.
3 Ubiquitous, connected technologies will change the perimeter and scope of enterprises. Enterprises will partner with customers and other commercial organizations seamlessly and rapidly so as to deliver value to customers.
4 Customers will become a core asset of companies. Enterprises will organize their services around 'marketspaces' rather than the concept of the market. Technologies enable enterprises of whatever size to gather together the resources and skills required to deliver within the marketspace.
5 Customers or other third parties will control the destinies of brands. Already customers are communicating together about services. On the Internet circuit, customers and concerned stakeholders will always get to the chicane first!

Key premises

1 Marketers will rely ever more heavily on technology to achieve success.
2 The affordability and ubiquity of information technologies is changing how consumers operate in the market. Once upon a time enterprises owned the powerful
   stuff, now consumers increasingly own and develop the innovative technologies.
   Think peer-to-peer file sharing or VOIP telephony.
3 The Internet is changing the value of IT for all agents in the market. Scale no
   longer has advantage.
4 Information technologies are creating an increasingly segmented market or rather
   technology can deliver service at new price points. Profit now exists at the long
   tail of the market rather than at the mass market.

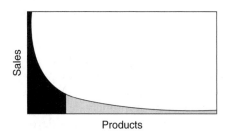

Figure A.1 Sales *vs* products

5 IT is reducing the 'information disparity' between consumers and marketers.
6 IT is 'empowering' consumers in many ways, but is also enabling new opportunities for corporate enterprises to add value in new and distinctive ways.

The last ten years of technology may not have radically changed marketing theory,
but it has certainly changed the practice of marketing. And if we might agree that
marketing theory remains essentially the same as before, technology has changed the
emphasis of marketing theory.

Marketing retains the key aim of 'satisfying customers' and the elements of marketing such as the marketing mix and the 4 Ps retain their hegemony, at least within the
minds of marketers. What has changed and continues to change is how these elements
are deployed and their relative value to the marketer. Marketers who can understand
these changes and grasp the new opportunities will be the winner in the future.

These changes reflect to a large extent the impact of technology on markets and
consumer behaviour and especially how the benefits of information technologies
have begun to flow to consumers and away from many corporate enterprises.

Understanding the Internet

At the heart of the changes is the Internet, which we can define as both a network of
computers (or mobile phones or cars) and a set of technologies that naturally connect
together all these disparate devices through public protocols. Most people experience
the Internet through their PC and therefore consider it a computer thing rather than
recognizing it is also a whole way of organizing communications networks.

The Internet is significant to marketers in a number of ways:

- The network is both increasingly connected and ubiquitous, connecting every-body in very immediate ways and in an information-rich fashion. It has the reach of mass media and yet can operate in a very local or niche fashion!
- The network is international and does not respect territories, long the basis for establishing different pricing regimes in different countries.
- Unlike previous marketing networks, such as television advertising, we can identify and potentially address each individual separately. This is the promise of segments of one.
- Information in the network flows in both directions and therefore allows for a range of interactions between enterprises and individual consumers. These can be conscious interactions such as customers engaging in online booking or they might be invisible interactions such as the measurement of consumer activities on web-sites by marketing analysts.
- Interactions take place in real time and as a result a whole range of interactions between a number of enterprises can take place 'at once'. When a consumer makes a request of one enterprise, the latter may poll other suppliers or partners in real time. The speed and immediacy of the encounter is hugely accelerated.
- The power of the network is underpinned by the sets of Internet technologies which are based on open and published standards. These technologies are designed to naturally inter-operate with each other in (increasingly) seamless ways. The analogy of the railways all agreeing a single standard gauge in the nineteenth century does not capture the way in which all industries have started to apply the Internet paradigm to their own industrial processes by creating open standards to their data. In the past, owning proprietary standards was a source of power: today it is a liability.
- The technologies upon which the Internet relies are themselves becoming ubiqui-tous and commoditized within the market. This can significantly reduce the cap-ital required to enter markets and significantly reduce the risks. This suggests that the Internet can impact not only at the level of marketing strategy, but also at higher level of corporate strategy where the individual themes of strategy as promulgated by Porter are increasingly subject to the same Internet forces.

The role of the Internet is changing the way that we conceptualize IT within the enterprise. Previously the role of IT was to apply control within the enterprise. The edge of the organization could be thought of as the end of the reach of the IT systems. Where enterprises did create data networks they were usually between businesses and not targeted at the end consumer. In the age of Internet we can understand the new IT in two ways:

- One way is to understand that IT is a delivery mechanism for a growing range of experiences and benefits which are being delivered as databits in a common lan-guage. These often combine products, information and services in new packages.
- The delivery mechanism is the Internet whether that be your PC or a mobile phone or even your car's GPS transponder.
- The common language is understood by a range of technologies which manage network protocols, for example, by translating data into audible music.

- Before the Internet, corporate technologies and consumer technologies had to be connected and enabled by humans; today consumers are increasingly able to manipulate corporate systems to achieve their goals. The one constant of services delivery, the human encounter, is being elided. For example, more and more people are booking holidays from the comfort of their own homes. They are querying travel business systems for information about holidays and availability, they are then paying for them online without once talking to a representative. Consumer bookings start a whole range of transactions between intermediaries and final suppliers.
- In the past marketers had an advantage: they had better IT than their customers. Increasingly this state is reversed. Furthermore, those consumers are using their skills and infrastructure to parallel marketing and sales channels that entirely avoid or ignore commercial channels.

We can think through some of these ideas by addressing them in the context of the themes of this book:

- Settings and structure
- Services delivery
- Relationships
- Performance and evaluation.

Settings and structure

Environmental uncertainty will play a large role in services marketing over the coming decade. This environmental uncertainty includes far more than the forces being unleashed by global warming and the pressures of climate change. The bounds of the market environment will change as companies seemingly remote can suddenly expand into other marketspaces. Watch how the likes of Apple have become players in the music industry, or the ambitions of ebay and Google in the telecoms industry.

As services marketers become 'gateways' to solutions so the infrastructure needs to connect a number of enterprises at once. The notion of a singular enterprise disappears, but for the services marketer the problem lies in stitching together these sometimes disparate threads. How do you ensure that the third-party call centres support your brand as required? What happens if the company that provides your in-flight meal experiences industrial action?

Services delivery

In the past, services were delivered by commercial organizations to passive receiving customers. Internet behaviour has changed this workflow. Customers are now active seekers of services; they choose the time and place, and as we said, engage in service interaction with any other human presence. In this scenario, the enterprise still has control of the interaction in some fashion. There are even more remote interactions taking place where, for example, other customers provide support services to your customers. Increasingly, software companies rely on the expertise of customer forums to ensure that customers with problems can get to resolution.

The enterprise in this scenario provides the platform for action. Many of the most exciting services businesses at this moment – Google, ebay, Paypal – provide platforms for third-party interaction in which they themselves are not principals. Utilizing the ubiquitous Internet that threads together buyer and sellers, or searcher and advertisers, creating both a commercial ecology in which they are at the top of the food chain as well as a plethora of commercial services for other inhabitants of this space. Notice the broad range of services that Google provides around the core (free) search service.

As companies look for growth, they will need to choose how they can foster an ecology around their services. In that sense how they can become a large part of customers lives.

Relationships

Building a relationship with customers has long been the goal of services marketers. Professional services practitioners have long shown how profitable such an approach can be. However, the consumer services market rarely offers opportunities for such engagement. One thing that was stable in both scenarios was that this was a conversation between the enterprise and the customer.

In our Internet future, the enterprise can often find itself remote from such conversations as consumers commune together to discuss products and services. Whilst there are many communities specializing in individual services, very few are controlled by the enterprise. With blogging and tagging consumers are creating conversations in which businesses can be subjects but are rarely welcomed as participants. It is not enough to employ evangelists to spout the party line, senior staff must engage with conversation and respond actively to consumer needs.

Whilst this scenario reduces the control, it opens exciting avenues for invoking customers in the innovation process and feedback processes. For a long time software companies have engaged senior customers in beta testing processes.

Performance

As the delivery of services become decentred and complex, so the ability to measure its performance becomes equally hard. What should be the metrics, who takes responsibility for delivery? Where does one service start and another stop?

Users of the Internet auction site ebay can have a number of relationships to the company and other users. They can be customers of ebay itself, they will also be customers or suppliers to other customers and they may be using a payment system called Paypal, which coincidentally is now owned by ebay. Within this ecology, different players enjoy different responsibility for delivering services that cannot be disentangled from each other. Ebay's solution is to coopt customers as guardians of quality and performance through the use of published feedback systems such as ratings.

In the last year or so, we have heard the phrase 'the market is a conversation' used with greater frequency. The idea of interaction and communication between equals is increasingly a feature of Internet markets and therefore all services markets. Customers talk with customers, customers talk to suppliers. As with all other elements of emerging services, the system is no longer controlled by suppliers. Indeed the measurement of service quality is often being undertaken on third-party sites where customers and prospective customers freely discuss the quality and appeal of different service providers. Hoteliers around the world know that websites like Trip Advisor are playing an ever-larger role in shaping customer decisions. As customers grow ever-more cynical of media relationships with advertisers, the old critical channels are losing their importance in comparison to customer judgements. The increasing importance of search engines demonstrates how customers are seeking out information about services before they purchase and are relying on the word of other customers.

This method of performance measurement is clearly customer-centric but may be insufficient as services become more complex or technical. Furthermore, as service delivery becomes increasingly globalized, customers may find themselves buying from suppliers that are operating outside of the customer's domestic legal framework. How many customers check terms and conditions to see under which legal system a supplier is operating; if they do, they may find that they need to sue them in Asia to gain redress.

In summary, new technologies and the falling cost of technology will allow service suppliers to enter new markets and will change the requirements for scale which is exciting for SMEs and companies from emerging economies. For consumers, this opens up new opportunities and increasing competition, whilst creating new risks for the unwary. The global market will be like all previous markets: comprised of the honest, the opportunists and the same gang of charlatans.

Sholto Ramsay
Director, HelpMeGo.To Ltd

References

1   Johns, N (1999) 'What is this thing called service?', *European Journal of Marketing*, **33** (9/10), 958–973.

2   Bowen, J and Ford, R C (2002) 'Managing service organizations: does having a "thing" make a difference?', *Journal of Management*, **28** (3), 447–469.

3   Rathmell, J M (1966) 'What is meant by services?', *Journal of Marketing*, **30** (October), 32–36.

4   Shostack, G L (1982) 'How to design a service', *European Journal of Marketing*, **16** (1), 49–64.

5   Rushton, A M and Carson, D J (1985) 'The marketing of services: managing the intangibles', *European Journal of Marketing*, **19** (3), 19–40.

6   Peters, T J and Waterman, Jr, R H (1982) *In Search of Excellence: Lessons from America's Best Run Companies*. New York: Harper and Row.

7   Wostenholme, S M (1988) The Consultant Consumer – A New Use for the Customer in Service Operations, in Proceedings of the Operations Management Association Annual International Conference, University of Warwick, pp. 192–203.

8   Teboul, J (1988) De-industrialise Service for Quality, in Proceedings of the Operations Management Association Annual International Conference, University of Warwick, pp. 131–138.

9   Bowen, D E and Jones, G R (1986) 'Transaction cost analysis of service organization – customer exchange', *Academy of Management Review*, **11** (2), 428–441.

10 Danet, B (1981) 'Client–organization relationships', *Handbook of Organization*, **2**, 382–428.

11 Bowen and Jones, 'Transaction cost analysis'.

12 Maister, D H (1985) 'The psychology of waiting lines', in Czepiel, J A, Solomon, M R and Suprenant, C F (eds), *The Service Encounter*. Lexington, MA: Lexington Books, D C Heath and Company.

13 Brown, S W and Swartz, T A (1989) 'A gap analysis of professional service quality', *Journal of Marketing*, **53** (April), 92–98.

14   Freemantle, D (1993) *Incredible Customer Service: The Final Test*. New York: McGraw-Hill, p. 3.

15   Sheth, J N and Mittal, B (1996) 'A framework for managing expectations', *Journal of Marketing Focused Management*, **1**, 137–158.

16   Kotler, P, Wong, V, Saunders, J and Armstrong, G (2005) *Principles of Marketing*. London: Pearson Education, p. 638.

17   Tansik, D A and Smith, W L (2000) Scripting the service encounter, in Fitzsimmons, J A and Fitzsimmons, M J (eds), *New Service Development*. London: Sage, pp. 239–264.

18   Levitt, T (1972) 'Production-line approach to service', *Harvard Business Review*, Sep.–Oct., 41–52.

19   Levitt, T (1976) 'The industrialization of service', *Harvard Business Review*, Sep.–Oct., 63–74.

20   Ibid.

21   Goodwin, C (1996) 'Moving the drama into the factory: the contribution of metaphors to services research', *European Journal of Marketing*, **30** (9), 13–36.

22   See the current edition, Ritzer, G (2004) *The McDonaldization of Society*, Revised New Century Edition. Thousand Oaks, CA: Sage.

23   Ibid, p. 1.

24   Boyle, D (2001) *The Tyranny of Numbers: Why Counting Can't Make Us Happy*. London: Collins.

25   Brady, D (2000) 'Why service stinks', *Business Week*, 23 October.

26   Quoted in Brady, ibid.

27   Barnes, J G, Dunne, P A, and Glynn, W J (2000) 'Self-service and technology: unanticipated and unintended effects on customer relationships', in Swartz, T A and Iacobucci, D (eds), *Handbook of Services Marketing and Management*. Thousand Oaks, CA: Sage, pp. 89–102.

28   Bitner, M T, Brown, S W and Meuter, M L (2005) 'Technology infusion in service encounters', *Journal of the Academy of Marketing Science*, **28** (1), 138–149.

29   Dabholkar, P (1996) 'Consumer evaluations of new technology based self service options', *International Journal of Research in Marketing*, **13** (1), 29–51.

30   Howard, M and Worboys, C (2003) 'Self-service – a contradiction in terms or customer-led choice?', *Journal of Consumer Behaviour*, **2** (4), 382–392.

31   Curry, A and Penman, S (2004) 'The relative importance of technology in enhancing customer relationships in banking – a Scottish perspective', *Managing Service Quality*, **14** (4), 331–341.

32   Hazlett, S A and Hill, F (2003) 'E-government: the realities of using IT to transform the public sector', *Managing Service Quality*, **13** (6), 445–452.

33   Parasuraman, A (2005) 'Technology Readiness Index (TRI): a multiple-item scale to measure readiness to embrace new technologies', *Journal of Service Research*, **2** (4), 307–320.

34   Blakemore, M (2005) Electronic Tagging of Workers 'Battery Farm' Workplaces, Report Commissioned by the General and Municipal Boilermakers Union.

35   Timmons, S (2003) 'A failed panopticon: surveillance of nursing practice via new technology', *New Technology, Work and Employment*, **18** (2), 143–153.

36   Moore, Wendy, see www.channel4.com/health/microsites/0-9/4health/stress/saw_call-center.html

37   Chatha, J, Decon, S, Edwards, S, Marks, S and Vale, D (2004) Hanging on the Telephone: CAB evidence on the effectiveness of call centres, Citizens Advice Bureau, September.

38   Bain, P, Watson, A, Mulvey, G, Taylor, P and Gall, G (2002) 'Taylorism, targets and the pursuit of quantity and quality by call centre management', *New Technology, Work and Employment*, **17** (3), 170–185.

39   Taylor, F W (1911) *Scientific Management*. New York: Harper and Brothers.

40   Taylor, P and Bain, P (1999) ' "An assembly line in the head": work and employee relations in the call centre', *Industrial Relations Journal*, **30** (2), 101–117.

41   Bain, P and Taylor, P (2000) 'Entrapped by the "electronic panopticon"? Worker resistance in the call centre', *New Technology, Working and Employment*, **15** (1), 2–18.

42   Best Practice in Call Centres (2004) Communication Workers Union Research.

43   Marr, B and Neely, A (2004) *Managing and Measuring for Value: The Case of Call Centre Performance*. Cranfield University School of Management, UK.

44   Bain *et al.*, op. cit.

45   Gilmore, A (2001) 'Call centre management: is service quality a priority?', *Managing Service Quality*, **11** (3), 153–159.

46   Beirne, M, Riach, K and Wilson, F (2004) 'Controlling business? Agency and constraint in call centre working', *New Technology, Work and Employment*, **19** (2), 96–117.

47   Lankshear, G D, Mason, P, Cook, G and Coates, S (2001) 'Call centre employees responses to electronic monitoring: some research findings', *Work, Employment and Society*, **15** (3), 595–605.

48   Mintzberg, H (1982) A note on that dirty word "efficiency", *Interface* (Institute of Management Sciences), **12** (5), 101–105.

49   Hallberg, G (1995) *All Customers Are Not Created Equal*. New York: John Wiley and Sons.

50   *Observer*, 21 February 1999, p. 10.

51   Zeithaml, V A, Rust, T R and Lemon, K (2001) 'The customer pyramid: creating and serving profitable customers', *California Management Review*, **43** (4), 118–142.

2

Organization for service

☐ Introduction

How and why services are organized is important. Consequently we need to analyse the structure and unearth the dominant and prevailing values and beliefs with a view to arriving at some explanation for the character and performance of the service. In all of this, there must be a determination to ascertain whether, and if so which, organizational factors lead to success or failure in providing a good service.

Management may well lay down the organizational parameters. However, employees will be active in whether these parameters are adhered to or subverted. Equally, it will be the organization that customers will judge when it comes to providing quality service. Ultimately, the organization will be seen as worthy or undeserving of praise.

■ 2.1 'Organization realities'

Services and products are not created in a vacuum. They are produced by organizations that vary in size, structure and culture. Knowledge of how organizations operate, and why, assists our understanding of behaviour in organizations. This is particularly important for services, as customers are involved in varying degrees in the production and delivery process. According to one leading authority in services marketing, *'how to organize to implement the services strategy is among the most crucial of decisions'*.[1] Unfortunately, the literature on organizational behaviour (as expressed in standard textbooks) is contested by some as not adequately reflecting organizational realities – realities that may obstruct any move toward determining the 'optimum organization for service'.

Images of organizations as solid, permanent, orderly entities run through many textbooks. But, in our view, these books tell only half the story. They obscure the other half: the life and activity that buzzes behind the apparent order. Sometimes this bursts into view, revealing chaos even – such as when computer systems break down, when there is delay or an accident on an airline, when products are sent to the wrong destinations or when bookings are made for the wrong dates. They also obscure the immense human efforts and energies that go into keeping organizations more or less orderly.[2]

Initially we thought of our task as writing an alternative organizational book, one which redressed the inaccurate account of organizational behaviour contained in many texts in our field. Standard textbooks in this area say surprisingly little about the character of the phenomena with which they are centrally concerned – the behaviour routinely exhibited by people in organizations. What they do say suggests, as much by implication as direct assertion, that behaviour in organizations is, almost conforming and dutiful.[3]

Besides shedding light on what managers really do, observational studies also provide insights on why managers often find contemporary models of management and organizational behaviour discrepant with the real world and why they frequently do not follow the resulting prescriptions.[4]

The above quotes should compel us to consider, in a much more forthright manner, the nature of reality inside organizations and the effect that can have not only on service performance but equally on those responsible for delivering it. In the process, views of employees at or near the front line (in services) merit as much attention as those in managerial positions further up the organization. One method of addressing the various views is to draw up, either independently or with the assistance of respondents, a list of concepts or terms that might constitute a language for business (Box 2.1).

The list in Box 2.1 is simply illustrative but serves to remind us of the need to define or determine the territory for investigation. The format for a study in this area may be a list of statements in which respondents indicate their degree of agreement, or how true each statement is, for their own work situation (see Figure 2.1 for an example).

From a study of this nature two main conclusions can be drawn:

1 How much agreement there is over the language used for organizations.
2 Once a list of terms has been determined, how much of a discrepancy or gap there is in the views of particular categories: management and employees, males and females, long serving employees and relatively new recruits, and different departments. Any one of these categories or others may serve as a sample for this study.

Box 2.1 A language for business

Alienation	Empathy	Respect
Authority	Empowerment	Responsibility
Commitment	Expectations	Rules
Communication	Fairness	Sincerity
Competence	Hierarchy	Status
Conflict	Morale	Stress
Control	Power	Targets
Effectiveness	Productivity	Teamwork
Efficiency	Quality	Trust
Emotion	Resources	Workload

This area falls under what is commonly referred to as organizational culture/climate (discussed later in the chapter). However, at this point, it is worthwhile considering one study[5] (see Box 2.2) that demonstrates the challenges involved. The focus of the research was two nearly identical warehousing/distribution operations located in the

	Strongly agree	Agree	Disagree	Strongly disagree
People are treated fairly in this organization				

	Very true	Somewhat true	Somewhat untrue	Very untrue
I feel respected as a person				

Figure 2.1 Question format

Box 2.2 Organizational climate and service quality

	Location		
Quality improvement factors	A (%)	B (%)	Difference (%)
1 Management personnel demonstrate teamwork/cooperation with each other	66	33	33
2 We practise effective two-way communication	74	43	31
3 People receive effective feedback on their performance	68	39	29
4 We have effective corrective-action procedures in place	72	44	28
5 Our organization follows up on quality problems	69	42	27
6 Improving quality is an organizational priority	81	56	25
7 We can effectively measure quality	78	54	24
8 Our operation has effective supervision	68	48	20
9 Workers demonstrate teamwork/cooperation with each other	75	55	20
10 Standard operating procedures/policies are effective	70	53	17
11 Managers are properly trained to perform their jobs	66	51	15
12 We have clearly defined quality standards	79	67	12
13 Workers are properly trained to perform their jobs	69	59	10
14 Our operating system/technology is effective	73	64	9
15 We have adequate resources/equipment to do our work	71	65	6

Midwest area of the USA. Both operations were part of the same large organization that implemented a Total Quality Management (TQM, see Chapter 5 for discussion) process and were similar in several respects: computer systems, technology, measurement systems, equipment, order processing, product mix, number of personnel and human resource management systems. Employees from both operations were surveyed. The questionnaire asked respondents a series of agree/disagree statements that assessed the degree to which the organization had implemented 15 key factors that have been found necessary to support ongoing quality performance and improvement. Box 2.2 contains the agreement percentages for those factors at the two different locations.

The results show location A as being more effective than location B. In offering an explanation for the difference, the authors cite the importance of management commitment and support when attempting to implement and sustain a TQM initiative. It is important to remember that in studies similar to the above, employee perceptions are being measured. Unlike the physical climate, analysis of the organizational climate is unable to draw upon objective measures. Climate logistics, for example, are able to measure objectively a variable known as the wind-chill factor made up of temperature and wind velocity. People's perception of feeling cold may not always agree with the wind-chill score but at least there is an objective measure against which perceptions may be compared. Whether standards are 'clearly defined', workers 'properly trained', resources/equipment 'adequate' (from Box 2.2) is solely a matter of perception. Furthermore, analysis of why employees across locations responded in the way they did is necessary before concluding that one location is more effective. Equally, how well did each location perform in terms of timely delivery, proper documentation and a complete, damage-free order? Tools of service quality are available (see Chapter 5 on service quality) for answering this question.

Much of what passes for organizational reality does not appear to be reflected or accommodated in the standard portrayal of organizational structure. It is to this we now turn.

2.2 Structure of organizations

The structure of any organization is normally conveyed by means of a chart. It is essentially 'a pictorial record, which shows the formal relations which the company intends should prevail within it'.[6] Figure 2.2 illustrates a typical organization structure of a business and conference hotel in the 1990s.[7] Charts will vary depending on type and size of organization. However, it will largely remain a hierarchical structure of control and domination.

What the organizational chart does not reveal is:

- The informal organization structure
- The effectiveness of the prevailing communication channels
- The source and nature of power within an organization
- The existence of cross-functional relationships (e.g. in Figure 2.2 between marketing and operations) that enables information to flow around the organization
- The importance attached to the functions
- The degree and nature of conflict within the organization
- The distribution of authority, responsibility and accountability.

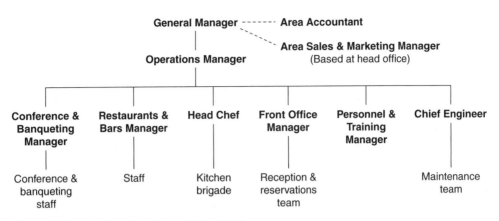

Figure 2.2 Organization chart of a hotel in the 1990s

For quality service to be delivered, communication and coordination should flow both across and up and down the organization. Unfortunately, for reasons already cited (e.g. power, politics, vested interests etc.) such a goal for many organizations remains elusive. It has been suggested,[8] as a way of reducing the gap between customer expectations and management perception of customer expectations, that the number of levels in an organization be reduced, thereby flattening the structure. By doing so:

- Barriers, in the form of multiple levels, that inhibit communication and understanding between senior management and front-line employees, are reduced.
- Upward communication becomes more effective. Not only in terms of the message reaching management but also in its original form.

However, communication effectiveness is not simply a function of the number of levels in an organization. It is also a matter of management willingness to listen and act upon, where appropriate, employee concerns. Whether that is achievable may depend on whether management perceives its position as being undermined and that of the employee overstated by soliciting views from the front-line. There is some evidence that the 'command and control' hierarchical form of organization is giving way to fewer layers and more horizontal coordination.[9] On the other hand, fewer levels has not resulted in fewer managers and those middle managers have frequently been depicted as the source of inertia and rigidity.[10] Moreover, the search for flexibility through teamwork and delayering has not led to power and authority becoming less concentrated.[11] Functional entities (marketing, operations etc.) as depicted in the organization are not about to disappear in the drive for more flexibility and working together. They have continued, nevertheless, to come in for some criticism in the drive to deliver the level and nature of service the customer desires. The following observations are illustrative:

Arguing that the functional structure is not really the best model for great service delivery, '*For many services, the functional structure obscures the focus on satisfying the end customer and constrains the customer-service talent and energy potentially available within the organization. By limiting customer contact to employees at the end of the service chain, functionalism discourages internal servers from claiming end customers of their own. The system of functional "handoffs" from one department to another diminishes internal commitment to the end customer'.*[12]

Weighing the benefits of functional specialization, greater efficiency and quality within a given function, against the costs, poorer teamwork, slower service, more errors between functions, *'… managers of individual departments tend to perceive other functions as enemies rather than as partners in the battle against the competition. "Silos" are built around departments: tall, thick, windowless structures that keep each department's affairs inside and everyone else's affairs out'.*[13]

It is arguably not so much a question of the existence of functions rather agreement over what is expected of them. Emphasis continues to be placed on the behaviour and performance of employees within work units whether they are in the form of departments, teams, functional groupings. Interest is also being shown in functioning between groups. Achieving internal organizational effectiveness lays the foundation, it is contended, for delivering quality service externally. The role set is a framework that allows for an examination of inter-group functioning. For one role set illustrated in Figure 2.3 a research study sought to determine whether differences

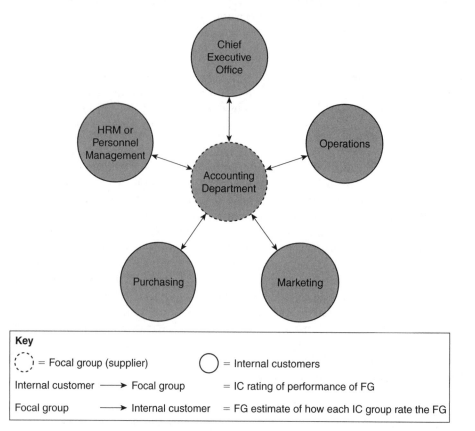

Figure 2.3 The role set
Source: Adapted from Gilbert (2000)[14]

existed between how employees in the focal group (the accounting department) estimate how their internal customers rate them and how their internal customers actually rate them.

The main finding was that the focal group's estimate of how their internal customers would rate it on a number of variables, e.g. courtesy, competence, prompt service, was significantly higher than the actual ratings attributed to the focal group by its internal customers.

Although the hierarchical form is giving way to more horizontal communication and coordination, it remains a defining characteristic of organizations. Relationships between top and bottom of the organization offer up as much, if not greater, potential for influencing the quality of service as do relationships across the organization. Unlike the horizontal, however, the vertical displays much greater disparities of power, status, authority and general working conditions. Some advocate inverting the levels of the traditional pyramid as a way of generating and delivering service excellence (Figure 2.4).

Some questions arise from Figure 2.4:

- Is (a) characteristic of a structure unable and/or unwilling to deliver excellent service?
- Why cannot the management of (a) be similarly supportive as the management in (b)?
- Assuming that power, status and authority remain similar in (a) and (b) what, other than support, differentiates (a) from (b)?
- It appears that the front-line in (a) is devoid of support. Is this a realistic proposition?
- Does the role of the front-line in (b) differ from that in (a) and if so in what respect(s)?

There may be other concerns, notably the reaction or perception of employees and customers.

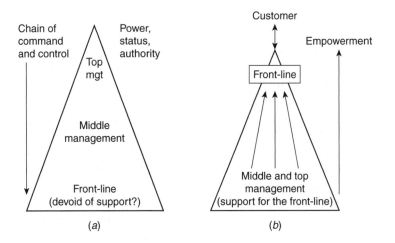

Figure 2.4 (a) The traditional organization pyramid; (b) the inverted pyramid with a customer and front-line focus
Source: Adapted from Lovelock and Wirtz (2004)[15]

▮ 2.3   Culture of organizations

Trying to understand and explain what happens in organizations can be a frustrating experience. The concept of corporate culture is viewed as offering some hope for unravelling the mystique of organizational life. The essence of culture is reserved for the deep level of basic assumptions and beliefs shared by members of an organization that operate unconsciously and define (in a basic taken-for-granted fashion) an organization's view of itself and its environment.

In brief, the corporate culture framework stresses:

- Values and assumptions prescribing what is important
- Beliefs on how things work
- Norms defining appropriate and inappropriate behaviour.

The concept of corporate culture has been summed up rather memorably in the phrase *'the way we do things around here'*.[16]

▮ 2.4   Types of organization culture

Based on the work of Harrison[17] and Handy,[18] the following cultural typologies are significant for service organizations:

Culture	Characteristics and examples
Role	<ul><li>Large pyramid organizations</li><li>Authority based on place in hierarchy</li><li>Emphasis on roles and job titles</li><li>Fast, efficient systems designed to produce uniform and predictable outcomes</li><li>Rules and procedures predominate</li><li>Customers feel depersonalized</li><li>Uncaring, rigid, unresponsive, e.g. private and public utilities, government departments, banks</li></ul>
Club or power	<ul><li>Small organizations where the owner exerts a strong influence</li><li>Emphasis on personal interaction rather than memos and meetings</li><li>Personality and speed of response often critical</li><li>Service delivery can be erratic and range from excellent to poor</li><li>Demand can outstrip organization's capacity to cope, e.g. plumber, garage, hairdresser, guest house</li></ul>
Task	<ul><li>Organization is active and creative</li><li>Dedicated to excellence, innovation, professional integrity</li><li>Warm and friendly with little emphasis on hierarchy and procedure</li><li>Challenging and questioning environment</li><li>Staffed, usually, by young, clever, energetic people, e.g. advertising agency, consulting firm</li></ul>

Person
- Puts the individual rather than the organization first. Individual talent is all important
- Do not think in terms of 'organization and management'
- Employees can have considerable autonomy
- Can be chaotic, e.g. solicitor, accountant, university professor

Support
- Compassionate, caring, responsive, receptive
- Listening to customers/clients, empathizing, responding to their concerns
- The essence of the support culture is 'what can we do for you?', e.g. the caring services like social work

The nature of the service operation can therefore pigeonhole an organization. The UK National Health Service, however, is an interesting example of the clash of two cultures – the caring professionals and the business efficiency of the administrators.

The personal culture of the professionals like lawyers is giving way to more organizational disciplines. The support culture has historically been associated with the social services but any service organization or individuals within it can adopt the values of caring, responsiveness, receptivity and a sense of belonging.

Overall, what is clear is that regardless of the type of service there is a growing emphasis on areas such as organization, management, efficiency, budgets and performance measurement. In other words, 'progress' toward a 'business culture'.

A major feature of the literature on corporate culture in general, and for service excellence in particular, is that perceptions and beliefs about what is important and why those things are important should be shared by employees throughout the organization. This is necessary if an organization is to be effective in its basic processes – communication, cooperation, commitment, decision making and implementation. Through recruitment and selection policies and socialization processes (training and development) organizations seek to shape employee beliefs and behaviour in accordance with the prevailing values and norms of the organization. However, organizational culture can be a 'contested reality'.[19] Not everyone or every group always shares the established view.

> The 'organization' in 'organizational commitment' typically is viewed as a monolithic, undifferentiated entity that elicits an identification and attachment on the part of individuals. Yet there is a substantial body of literature that depicts organizations not as undifferentiated wholes, but as composites of coalitions and constituencies, each of which espouse a unique set of goals and values that may be in conflict with the goals and values of other organizational groups.[20]

Nowhere is this more pressing an issue for services than the potential for deviant behaviour (see later in this chapter) on the part of employees in the front-line. Commenting on culture at the bottom of organizations, one observer noted that, 'a common formative element of culture at the lower organizational levels is the sharing of a common antagonism against the dominant managerial culture or against other sub-groups internal or external to (e.g. customers) the organization.[21] The difficulty for the management prescribed service culture is that it runs the risk of being trivialized or debased. Counter-cultures emerge opposing the dominant value system or the values of those who dominate.[22]

2.5 Organizational climate

Organizations routinely communicate statements, internally and externally, about service philosophy and standards. Surveys of customers are invariably conducted to obtain feedback on service. However, a fuller understanding of service performance requires that we undertake a survey of employees' views of how well their organizations are functioning. Research on organizational climate has been primarily focused on obtaining the employee perspective. Climate has been defined as 'the relatively enduring quality of the total (organizational) environment that (a) is experienced by the occupants, (b) influences their behaviour and (c) can be described in terms of the values of a particular set of characteristics (or attributes) of the environment'.[23] In similar vein, climate is referred to as 'employees' perceptions of the events, practice and procedures as well as their perceptions of the behaviours that are rewarded, supported, and expected'.[24]

Debate has arisen over the difference between culture and climate. Broadly speaking, climate is seen to be rooted in or a manifestation of culture and is subject to quantitative research. Culture, on the other hand, refers to the deep structure of organizations[25] and is more amenable to qualitative research methods. In short, assumptions refer to culture and perceptions to climate.

Undertaking a survey of climate perceptions involves the identification of appropriate climate variables, e.g. training, and determining a series of statements for each variable. A typical example is illustrated in Box 2.3.

What the above study and others seek to examine is the relationship between certain organizational variables and employees' perceptions of the customer service climate. Such variables can act as impediments as well as aids in the quest for excellent service. They have been characterized as obstacles, either social or technical in nature.[27] If employees perceive management failure in the provision of proper support, encouragement and rewards, it is hardly surprising if customers perceive the service as unsatisfactory.

2.6 Defensive behaviour

Earlier, reference was made to organizational misbehaviour and how many texts fail to acknowledge its existence. This apparent oversight means that our understanding of service level and service quality is less than complete. The underlying assumption on the part of organizational management appears to be that employees will be malleable, compliant and committed, with consequential effects for motivation and productivity. Amongst some writers there is a belief that management policy is moving away from the hierarchical command and control style and toward a softer, more inclusive approach based around empowerment, trust, involvement and flatter organizational structures.[28] Misbehaviour would be rendered inappropriate or incompatible in the new organizational climate. Employees would be heralded as having positive attitudes and behaviours, a position that the service management literature has held for some period of time.[29] Misbehaviour has been defined as 'anything you do at work you are not supposed to do'.[30,31]

It will not occur when there is a precise correspondence between what is expected of people and what people are willing to do.[32] Deviant behaviour is a more general

Box 2.3 A selection of scale items from a climate survey

Reward/Recognition

- How satisfied are you with the recognition you receive for doing a good job?
- My work gives me a feeling of personal accomplishment.

Employee voice

- As a result of this employee opinion survey, I think senior management will address employees' concerns.
- I am free to discuss work-related problems with my immediate manager/ supervisor.

Training

- How satisfied are you with the training you received for your present job?
- The training made available to me helps me do a better job.

Information and technology

- I have the right equipment to do my job well.
- I have enough information to do my job well.

Work environment

- How satisfied are you with the space to work in your working environment?
- How satisfied are you with the noise level in your work environment?

Work design

- I have enough time to get the job done well.
- My job makes good use of my skills and abilities.
- I have been given the appropriate authority needed to do my job.
- There is sufficient staff to handle the normal workload in my work unit at the required level of service.

Organizational commitment

- I feel a sense of commitment to our company.
- I am treated with respect and dignity in my job.
- I feel too much pressure in my job.
- There is good employee morale in my work unit.

Customer service climate

- How do you rate your work unit in meeting the needs of its customers?
- How do you rate our company in terms of integrity and fairness in dealing with customers?

Depending on item content response options ranged from strongly agree to strongly disagree, one of the best to one of the worst, very good to very poor, very satisfied to very dissatisfied.

Source: Lux, D (1996)[26]

term associating itself with desirable and undesirable behaviour where a norm (what should or ought to happen) in the form of a rule or procedure is not adhered to. In terms of undesirable behaviour, sabotage materializes as a practice 'intentionally designed negatively to affect services'[33] (see Chapter 6 on The Service Encounter).

Whereas misbehaviour signifies negative actions and consequences there remains a general defensive form of behaviour in organizations. It has been defined as 'reactive and protective actions intended to reduce a perceived threat to or avoid an unwanted demand of an individual or groups'.[34] The motivation is protection of self interest. For service organizations characterized by a great deal of human involvement and interaction, defensive behaviour represents an obstacle in the drive for quality service performance. Behaviours are cited below that customers and employees of service organizations should recognize.[35]

2.6.1   Avoiding action

- **Over-conforming:** Action is often avoided by resorting to a strict interpretation of one's responsibility, e.g. 'The rules clearly say …' and citing supportive precedents, e.g. 'It's always been done this way'. Rigid adherence to rules can be potentially explosive in a service like social security. The situation may be defused by distancing oneself from the rules, e.g. 'I don't make the rules', or 'Listen, if it were up to me …'.
- **Passing the buck:** Responsibility for doing something is passed to someone else, e.g. 'I'm too busy' or 'That's not my job'.
- **Playing dumb:** An unwanted task is avoided by falsely pleading ignorance or inability, e.g. 'I don't know anything about that …' or 'X is better able to handle that …'.
- **Depersonalizing:** Unwanted demands from clients or subordinates are avoided by treating them as objects or numbers rather than people, e.g. a doctor may refer to hospital patients not by name but by their illness, talking about them in the third person, using medical terminology incomprehensible to patients, avoiding eye contact, and providing curt and patronizing answers to patients' questions.

2.6.2   Avoiding blame

- **Buffing:** This term was coined to describe the practice of rigorously documenting activity or fabricating documents to project an image of competence and thoroughness. It is widely referred to as 'covering your ass'.
- **Playing safe:** Situations that may reflect unfavourably on a person are avoided.
- **Justifying:** Responsibility for a certain event is minimized by acknowledging partial responsibility and including some expression of remorse.
- **Scapegoating:** Blame is deflected to others.

2.7   Explanation for defensive behaviour

There may be organizational and individual factors causing defensive behaviour.[36] Of particular relevance for service organizations are the following:

- **Individual factors:** Factors which may be of interest to service organizations are insecurity and anxiety, emotional exhaustion and work alienation. Employment in service organizations can be stressful due to the nature and amount of personal contact with customers. The full range of emotions must be held in check at least for front-line employees. Smiling and generally being nice is the rule. Work alienation stems from a lack of job involvement and identification with the organization. Many service occupations are simply 'dead-end jobs'. Service organizations, characterized by uncertainty and intensity of demand, are more of a pressure chamber than their manufacturing counterparts where a more orderly and less hectic routine is in evidence.

- **Organizational factors:**
  - The specialization of tasks and formalization of rules and procedures in a bureaucracy encourage defensive-type behaviour. For example, specialization means people feel responsible for a specific, not the whole task, creating a tendency to pass the buck, play dumb, over-conform and depersonalize. Formalization of rules and procedures tells people what they can and cannot do, which again may promote over-conforming, passing the buck, playing dumb.
  - Defensive behaviour may also be a means of coping with a work environment in which there is uncertainty felt over areas of responsibility and the interpretation and application of rules and procedures. People may feel that the demands of the work environment are just too great and a feeling of powerlessness only makes the incapacity to cope even worse.

2.8 Organizing for service

From the discussion so far it is evident that organizational life is not exempt from problems. Delivering a service that satisfies customers remains a challenge. In terms of both organization structure and process for service delivery two (contrasting?) schools of thought continue to be debated. They can be summarized as follows:

- **The control model:** This is a hierarchical structure with standardized or routinized procedures. It is characteristic of bureaucratic-type organizations and equates the organization of service as akin to the production line in manufacturing. Based around the writings of Weber,[37] Taylor,[38] Levitt,[39] and Ritzer,[40] the emphasis is on control, efficiency, rationality and predictability. There is a clear division of labour, tasks are simplified and roles clearly defined. Where possible, technology replaces labour and employees are afforded little in the way of discretion. When working well, customers are in receipt of a fast, efficient service. On the other hand, employees and customers can feel dehumanized and alienated. For customers in particular, anger and frustration is the outcome when the system fails to deliver as promised or expected. As the process of McDonaldization gathers momentum across a range of service organizations further tensions may arise between the service provider's need for reliability and efficiency and the service consumer's right to feel satisfied.
- **The 'new' service management school:** Newness in this context does not simply mean recency. Rather, it is viewed as a departure from the traditional way of thinking expressed in the control model. Developed in the USA in the 1980s, it prescribes a new set of management practices toward service employees in particular. According to supporters of this school of thought, contemporary service

work requires a new form of organization 'transcending bureaucracy and the role of the employee as a cog in the machine, or mere subject of exploitation'[41]. Human resource management is seen as being at the centre of this approach. Its key features are said to be:[42]

- Careful selection – front-line workers are hired not for their knowledge and technical skills but for possessing the right attitude and personality traits ('nice people').
- High-quality training in the organization will develop employees' technical skills and knowledge and the all-important interactive skills necessary in service encounters. The aim is to develop a strong orientation towards satisfying the customer.
- Well-designed support systems – to deliver quality service, employees will require the necessary information technology and physical facilities.

2.9   Empowerment

It has been stated that 'many organizations have discovered that to be truly responsive to customer needs, front-line providers need to be empowered to accommodate customer requests and to recover on the spot when things go wrong. Empowerment means giving employees the desire, skills, tools and authority to serve the customer'.[43] (See Box 2.4 for critical comment on the notion of empowerment.)

- Teamwork – the traditional control model operates vertically whereas teamwork emphasizes horizontal cooperation between employees from different functional areas, coming together to form a team.
- Appropriate measurements, rewards and recognition – employees should be rewarded for performance in meeting customer-based standards.
- Development of a service culture – throughout the organization there needs to be a recognition of the importance of service.

2.10   Criticism of the new service management school of thought

In the new competitive climate where demand for good quality service is paramount, it has been noted that the old, inappropriate production-line approach (or control model) must be replaced with one based on empowerment.[48] By de-industrializing the service, treating workers in a human way, hiring the right kind of people[49] and promoting a positively perceived service climate,[50] the three parties in service engagement benefit.

This, then, is the circle completed for the 'win:win:win' fairy tale: customers win because they receive qualitatively superior service, workers win because they become empowered to act on their firmly-held customer service values, and are freed from the industrial tyranny, and managers win because customers keep coming back to the firm.[51]

Box 2.4 A critical tool for front-line employees

At the centre of the new approach to organizing for service is the concept of empowerment. The controversy surrounding it merits some further attention. Those in favour of its application in services will echo the view of Zeithaml and Bitner.[43] Others take a more critical view.

> ... the concept of empowerment serves not to reduce managerial control, but facilitates and extends this control through the manipulation of norms and values ... (Collins, 1996)[44]
>
> Let us stop a moment and ask ourselves how there can be empowerment when there is neither guesswork nor challenges – when the job requirements are predetermined and the processes are controlled. For employees operating in such a world, the environment is not empowering; it is foolproof. (Argyris, 1998)[45]
>
> Strategies such as student empowerment and dialogue give the illusion of equality while in fact leaving the authoritarian nature of the student/ teacher relationship intact. (Ellsworth, 1989)[46]

It is remarkable that the prominence and positive portrayal of empowerment in the services literature is matched not only by comments similar to those cited above but also by acknowledgement of 'just how difficult it is to change from a command-and-control culture to a world of empowerment'.[47] Consequently a number of questions remain as worthy of debate:

- Does empowerment signify a new language for business?
- What does the adoption of empowerment mean for authority, responsibility, accountability and employee skills and capability?
- Should empowerment be applied universally across all service situations?
- Are employees simply the recipients of a new form of management manipulation?
- Is empowerment a demonstration of managerial confidence in its employees?
- What impact would greater research and representation of employees' view of empowerment have on the service literature and management practice?

Thinking along the lines of the new school of thought probably originated and acted as a catalyst in the much acclaimed and much publicized aphorism from J Willard Marriott (Marriott Hotels) in the 1970s that, 'you can't make happy guests with unhappy employees'. From that point on, the assumption, and subsequent claims, developed in the form of:

Satisfied employees = Improved performance = Happy customers

Research in support of this has been interpreted as inconclusive[52] and contrasted with arguments elsewhere.[53] One of the main areas of contention revolves around the definition of happy, satisfied employees (well-being) and how that should be measured. Where the supporters of the 'new school' have originally been deficient in convincing their detractors is through their failure to acknowledge or take into account the characteristics and symptoms of service work, e.g. lack of job enrichment/boredom, low pay, job insecurity, high turnover, stress. More fundamentally, the three parties to the exchange (employees, management and customers) are viewed as operating in a climate of shared interests and goals free of conflict. Harmony is the norm.

2.11   The virtual organization

Whilst traditional organizations remain the norm, a relatively new phenomenon, the virtual organization, has arisen as an additional form of doing business. It has been defined as,

> ... a new organizational form characterized by a temporary or permanent collection of geographically dispersed individuals, groups or organization departments not belonging to the same organization – or entire organizations that are dependent on electronic communication for carrying out their production process.[54]

The first part of the definition usually refers to what is commonly known as outsourcing where, for example, a small core operating company engages a network of other companies (often small) in providing services that the core requires, e.g. recruitment and selection of staff, date processing. The second part of the definition usually encompasses electronic forms such as virtual banking where all activity between customer and organization is completed online in real time. Time and distance no longer represent barriers in the delivery of service. 'Virtuality' in the form of technology and front-line employee access to the required information offers the potential for flattening the organization which in turn facilitates the delivery of a fast responsive service. Much may be made in future of the benefits and drawbacks accruing to customers engaged in virtual exchange and consumption. Will the reliability and perfection of technology raise customer expectations to an unduly high level? Furthermore, what is to be the fate of the 'real' customer in face of the onslaught of the 'virtual' affectionately known as 'the customer in the machine'.[55] For employees of the virtual office concern is being expressed now over the matter of trust and the rise of electronic monitoring.[56] Equally, where flexibility and sharing information are positive features of networking, the lack of social interaction and control over outsourced suppliers is perceived as an area requiring particular attention.[57] It has also been suggested that development and management of 'virtual employees' will require careful scrutiny by human resource management professionals.[58] For all the concerns regarding virtual organizations, however, and there are many, it would appear that virtuality offers little to organizational analysis and 'the problems that typically and persistently preoccupy managers do not simply disappear with the move towards the virtual organization or the virtual team'.[59]

Summary

The realities of organizational life are not always in accordance with those found in standard textbooks. For services in particular, the experiences of the front-line employee do not appear to figure prominently. This is important as much of the organization's effectiveness will hinge on how well they perform.

Reading about the nature of organizations, you have encountered, among other things, a language for business and an organization chart. How these language terms are interpreted will have a significant impact for success or failure. The organization chart on the other hand conceals more than it reveals. To further our understanding beyond the chart we must turn to an examination of organizational culture or climate. Put another way, we are now looking at the 'way we do things around here' and why! We may find that people do not always behave in accordance with their prescribed status and roles, specified rules and regulations. This is known as deviant behaviour or misbehaviour.

As an alternative to the traditional top-down structure, which is sometimes the cause of misbehaviour, is a new service management school. It gives more emphasis to employee considerations such as empowerment, teamwork, rewards and recognition. Although it is based on the premise of better quality service, it is not without criticism.

References

1   Berry, L L (1995) *On Great Service*. Glencoe, IL: The Free Press, p. 121.
2   Gabriel, Y, Fineman, S and Sims, D (2000) *Organizing and Organizations*. London: Sage, p. 1.
3   Ackroyd, S and Thompson, P (2003) *Organizational Misbehaviour*. London: Sage, p. 1.
4   Davis, T R V and Luthans, F (1980) 'Managers in action: a new look at their behaviour and operating modes', *Organization Dynamics*, Summer, 64–80.
5   Longenecker, C O and Scazzero, J A (2000) 'Improving service quality: a tale of two operations', *Managing Service Quality*, **10** (4), 227–232.
6   Buchanan, D and Huczynski, A (1997) *Organizational Behaviour: An Introductory Text*. Harlow: Prentice Hall, p. 304.
7   Jones, P (2002) *Introduction to Hospitality Operations: An Indispensable Guide to the Industry*. London: Continuum Books, Figure 4, p. 57.
8   Zeithaml, V A, Parasuraman, A and Berry, L L (1999) *Delivering Service Quality: Balancing Customer Perceptions and Expectations*. Glencoe, IL: The Free Press, pp. 61–66.
9   Webb, J (2004) 'Organizations, self-identities and the new economy', *Sociology*, **38** (4), 719–738.
10   Scarborough, H and Burrell, G (1996) 'The axeman cometh: the changing roles and knowledges of middle managers', in Clegg, S and Palmer, G (eds), *The Politics of Management Knowledge*. London: Sage, pp. 229–245.
11   Webb, 'Organizations'.
12   Berry, op. cit, p. 129.
13   Ibid.
14   Gilbert, G R (2000) 'Measuring internal customer satisfaction', *Managing Service Quality*, **10** (3), 178–186.
15   Lovelock, C and Wirtz, J (2004) *Service Marketing*. Englewood Cliffs, NJ: Prentice Hall, p. 334.
16   Deal, T R and Kennedy, A E (1982) *Corporate Cultures*. Reading, MA: Addison-Wesley.
17   Harrison, R (1972) 'Understanding your organization's character', *Harvard Business Review*, **50** (May–June), 119–128.
18   Handy, C B (1993) *Understanding Organizations*. Harmondsworth: Penguin.
19   Jermier, J M (1991) 'Critical epistemology and the study of organizational culture: reflections on street corner society', in Frost, P J, Moore, L F, Louis, M R, Lundberg, C C and Martin, J (eds), *Reframing Organizational Culture*. London: Sage, pp. 223–234.
20   Reichers, A E (1985) 'A review and preconceptualization of organizational commitment', *Academy of Management Review*, **19** (July), 465–476.

21   Davis, T R (1985) 'Managing culture at the bottom', in Kilmann, R H, Saxton, M J, Serpa, R and Associates, *Gaining Control of the Corporate Culture*. San Francisco: Jossey-Bass, pp. 163–184.

22   Gabriel *et al.*, op. cit, p. 200.

23   Tagiuri, R and Litwin, G (1968) *Organizational Climate: Explanations of a Concept*. Boston, MA: Harvard Business School.

24   Schneider, B, Wheeler, J K and Cox, J F (1992) 'A passion for service: using content analysis to explicate service climate theories', *Journal of Applied Psychology*, **77** (5), 705–716.

25   Denison, D R (1996) 'What is the difference between organizational culture and organizational climate? A native's point of view on a decade of paradigm', *Academy of Management Review*, **21** (3), 619–655.

26   Lux, D, Jex, S M and Hansen, C P (1996) 'Factors influencing employee perceptions of customer service climate', *Journal of Marketing-Focused Management*, **1**, 65–86.

27   Brown, K A and Mitchell, T R (1993) 'Organizational obstacles: links with financial performance, customer satisfaction, and job satisfaction in a service environment', *Human Relations*, **46** (6), 725–757.

28   Ackroyd and Thompson, *Organizational Misbehaviour*, pp. 147–148.

29   Ogbonna, E and Harris, L (2002) 'Exploring service sabotage', *Journal of Service Research*, **4** (3), 163–183.

30   Ackroyd and Thompson, *Organizational Misbehaviour*, p. 2.

31   Sprouse, M (ed.) (1992) *Sabotage in the American Workplace*. San Francisco: Pressure Drop Press.

32   Ackroyd and Thompson, *Organizational Misbehaviour*, p. 11.

33   Ogbonna and Harris, 'Exploring service sabotage'.

34   Ashforth, B E and Lee, R T (1990) 'Defensive behaviour in organizations: a preliminary model', *Human Relations*, **43** (7), 621–648.

35   Ibid.

36   Ibid.

37   Weber, M (1978) *Max Weber Economy and Society*, Vols 1 & 2, eds G Roth and C Wittich. Berkeley, CA: University of California Press.

38   Taylor, F W (1911) *Scientific Management*. New York: Harper and Brothers.

39   Levitt, T (1976) 'The industrialization of service', *Harvard Business Review*, Sep.–Oct., p. 6.

40   Ritzer, G (2004) *The McDonaldization of Society*, Revised New Century Edition. Thousand Oaks: Sage.

41   Sewell, G (1992) 'Empowerment or emasculation?', in Blyton, P and Turnbull, B (eds), *Reassessing Human Resource Management*. London: Sage, pp. 79–115.

42   Korczynski, M (2001) *Human Resource Management in Service Work*. London: Macmillan/Palgrave, pp. 19–41.

43   Zeithaml, V A and Bitner, M J (2003) *Services Marketing*. New York: McGraw-Hill, p. 333.

44   Collins, D (1996) 'Control and isolation in the management of empowerment', *Empowerment in Organizations*, **4** (2), 29–39.

45   Argyris, C (1998) 'Empowerment: the Emperor's new clothes', *Harvard Business Review*, May–June, 98–105.

46   Ellsworth, E (1989) 'Why doesn't this feel "empowering"?', *Harvard Educational Review*, **59** (3), 297–324.

47   Randolph, W A (2000) 'Re-thinking empowerment: why is it so hard to achieve?', *Organizational Dynamics*, **29** (2), 94–102.

48   Bowen, D E and Lawler, E E (1995) 'Organising for service: empowerment or production line?', in Glyn, W J and Barnes, J G (eds), *Understanding Services Management*. New York: John Wiley & Sons, pp. 269–295.

49   Heskett, J, Sasser, W and Schlessinger, L (1997) *The Service Profit Chain*. New York: The Free Press.

50 Ibid.
51 Korczynski, M (2001) 'The contradictions of service work: call centre as customer-oriented bureaucracy', in Sturdy, A, Grugulis, I and Wilmott, H (eds), *Customer Service: Empowerment and Entrapment*. London: Palgrave, pp. 79–102.
52 Ibid., pp. 28–37.
53 Mudie, P (2005) 'Internal marketing: a step too far', in Varey, R J and Lewis, B R (eds), *Internal Marketing: Directions for Management*. London: Routledge, pp. 254–281.
54 Travica (1997) in Sieber, P and Griese, J (eds) (1998), *Organizational Virtualness*. Proceedings of the Workshop, 27–28 April, available from http:virtual-organization.net/.
55 Hughes, T A, O'Brien, J, Randall, D, Rouncefield, M and Tolmie, P (2001) 'Some "real" problems of "virtual" organization', *New Technology, Work and Employment*, **16** (1), 49–64.
56 Ariss, S, Nykodym, N and Cole-Laramore, A A (2002) 'Trust and technology in the virtual organization', *S.A.M. Advanced Management Journal*, **67** (4), 22–26.
57 Franks, J (1998) 'The virtual organization', *Work Study*, **47** (4), 130–135.
58 Bierbaum, R (1999) 'Towards the virtual organization', *Human Resource Management Journal*, **9** (1), 88–90.
59 Hughes *et al.*, ' "Real" problems of "virtual" organization'.

3

Design of the service

Introduction

Services require an operating and delivery system in order to function. That system should be designed in such a way as to offer effective customer service and an efficiently operated process. As you will read, that in itself represents a difficult balancing act. The drive to achieve both efficiency and service quality can become unstuck to the detriment of provider and/or customer. As services comprise a range of elements, the achievement of a smooth running system and the delivery of customer satisfaction remains a challenge. Design formats can, of course, vary with the type of service, and even within a typical service there may be different approaches to what constitutes the best design. Whatever is decided, the design is the service.

3.1 The concept of design

The traditional understanding of the word 'design' is of 'a plan or drawing produced to show the look and function or workings of a building, garment or other object before it is built or made' (*The New Oxford Dictionary of English*, Oxford University Press, 1998). We usually associate design, of course, with manufactured products, e.g. a car, washing machine, DVD etc. It usually starts with a concept or idea followed by a design specification that will spell out how it works, how it looks and what it symbolizes. In support of this, decisions have to be made in respect of colour, styling, durability, reliability, materials, cost of manufacture and so on.

Design of a service, on the other hand, offers up a somewhat different challenge. Importantly, and in keeping with product design, there will still be tangible entities that need to be addressed, e.g. colour, furnishings, equipment, lighting etc. (see Chapter 4). However service, as you will have noted, is a process where people interact with the production and delivery of an experience. Service design, therefore, should encapsulate all aspects of that experience:

- The role of the customer
- The balance between front and back office
- The impact of technology, e.g. the involvement of equipment
- The location of service consumption (e.g. a fixed single facility, multi-site, mobile)
- Employee skills/behaviour and degree of discretion
- The nature of the service process, e.g. standardized, customized
- The significance of procedures
- The nature and channels of communication
- The contribution of the physical evidence (see Chapter 4) to service satisfaction
- How design advances operational efficiency and service quality.

The above points suggest that three important functions should work together and be actively involved in the design of a service: marketing, human resource management (HRM) and operations management. One area where the three should come together is that of the employee uniform. Sometimes overlooked, it is nevertheless a significant aspect of service. Agreement over its design may nevertheless be difficult to achieve. Consider the concerns of each function and in doing so, whether they may be in conflict.

- **Marketing:** Does the uniform create the right impression or image? Will it elicit a positive, or negative response from customers?
- **HRM:** Will the uniform make the employee feel confident, credible and professional? Will it degrade or humiliate the employee?
- **Operations:** Does the uniform feel comfortable? Is it easily cleaned? Will it interfere with performance? Does it help customers identify employees easily?

Similar exercises can be carried out for the many 'moments of truth' customers experience in the course of a service delivery.

A valuable technique that will facilitate the design of a service is called blueprinting or service mapping (see later in this chapter). From this you can identify moments of truth together with a sense of how the service operates. By bringing together all the facets of a service it should focus your mind on how a service works and why. Not everything can be spelt out in a blueprint, e.g. organization climate, employee attitudes, but it should serve as a building block for addressing these and other matters of relevance in the delivery of service quality.

3.2   Service classification: a design issue

In addition to the conceptual and analytical skills of the designer, several issues and concerns have been raised in the marketing/operations literature that are significant for the development of a service operations and delivery system. You will recall from Chapter 1 the thoughts of Levitt,[1,2] writing in the 1970s, calling for the industrialization of service in the form of a production-line approach. That, in itself, was an early indication of how services might be designed with the attendant implications for consumer involvement and operational efficiency. Since then several authors have sought to establish critical dimensions for the design and classification of services.

Thomas, in 1978,[3] proposed a classification of services as either 'equipment-based' or 'people-based'. Equipment-based services were further classified as being automated (vending machine, car wash), monitored by relatively unskilled operators (taxis, dry cleaning), or operated by skilled operators (airlines, computer time-sharing). People-based services rely on unskilled labour (janitorial services, guards), skilled labour (car repair, plumbing) or professionals (lawyers, accountants) for service production. Importantly, he regards the classification as a spectrum where services may move from people-based to equipment-based and vice versa. According to Thomas, placing a service on the spectrum necessitates answering two questions:

1 How is the service rendered?
2 What type of equipment or people render the service?

Thomas further acknowledged that 'many companies are in more than one type of business'. This portrayal of the mixture of 'high-tech' and 'high-touch' has been echoed more recently.[4] Although this classification is from an operations standpoint, it can serve to remind us of an ongoing tension between mechanization of a service and a desire for human contact on the part of the customer.

Maister and Lovelock, in 1982,[5] gave prominence to the customer in a 2 × 2 matrix for service classification:

Classifying dimension	Service operation type
Low client contact / Low customization	→ Factory
Low client contact / High customization	→ Job shop
High client contact / High customization	→ Professional service
High client contact / Low customization	→ Mass service

Unfortunately, the extent of customer contact and customization are not explained and they do not provide examples of services for each of the matrix quadrants. However, they do identify, as mentioned above, client contact as a classifying dimension but fail to address the ambiguity surrounding it. The issue of customer contact will be discussed later in the chapter.

Degree of interaction and customization

		Low	High
Degree of labour intensity	Low	**Service factory:** • Airlines • Trucking • Hotels • Resorts and recreation	**Service shop:** • Hospitals • Auto repair • Other repair services
	High	**Mass service:** • Retailing • Wholesaling • Schools • Retail aspects of commercial banking	**Professional service:** • Doctors • Lawyers • Accountants • Architects

Figure 3.1 The service process matrix
Source: Schmenner (1986)[6], reproduced by permission from Tribune Media Services

Schmenner, in 1986,[6] suggested two elements (Figure 3.1) that can be used to classify different kinds of service businesses:

- **Degree of labour intensity**, which is defined as the ratio of the labour cost incurred to the value of the plant and equipment. As it is a ratio, Schmenner observes that even a hospital employing large numbers of doctors, nurses, technicians remains comparatively low in labour intensity because of the very expensive plant and equipment it deploys.
- **Degree of interaction and customization**, which is acknowledged by Schmenner as a more confusing element as it combines two similar but distinct concepts. A high level of interaction is present where a customer can actively intervene in the service process. High customization is in evidence when a service is designed to respond to individual needs and preferences. Although customization and interaction go hand in hand for many services, Schmenner does concede instances where one may be high and the other low. The value of this classification lies in the challenges specified for service management in each quadrant. For example, where the degree of interaction and customization is low standard operating procedures can be adopted whilst at the same time seeking to make the service warm and inviting through design of the service facility.

Haywood-Farmer, in 1988,[7] pointed to the diversity of the service sector, prompting the need for classification to make the management job possible. Using dimensions from earlier authors, he sought to remove any existing confusion (over previous classifications) by advocating a three-dimensional model (Figure 3.2). The degree of contact asks whether the customer has to be present, as is the case with a haircut; degree of labour-intensity raises the issue of whether it is possible to automate the service, as with automatic teller machines; and the degree of service customization examines how much standardization is possible, e.g. can a standard programme be devised for all customers of a health club? Haywood-Farmer illustrates the significance of his classification for service management. For example, where a service is low in all three dimensions (cell 1) it is in reality like a factory, with emphasis on quality control and focusing on physical facilities and procedures. The back office of

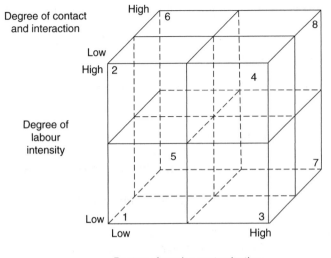

Degree of contact and interaction

Degree of labour intensity

Degree of service customization

Some examples of services in each octant:

1 Utilities, transportation of goods
2 Lecture teaching, postal services
3 Stockbroking, courier services
4 Repair services, wholesaling, retailing
5 Computerized teaching, public transit
6 Fast food, live entertainment
7 Charter services, hospitals
8 Design services, advisory services, healing services

Figure 3.2 A three-dimensional classification scheme
Source: Haywood-Farmer (1988), reproduced by permission from Emerald Group Publishing Ltd

a bank is an example. As one moves towards cells 5–8, two factors become prominent. Where the service is low in labour intensity, the customer's impression of the physical facilities, processes and procedures is important. Additionally, care must be taken to make sure equipment is reliable, easy to use and user proof. Secondly, as high contact and interaction services increase in labour intensity, more attention must be paid to making sure staff behave appropriately.

As customization increases (moving towards cells 3, 4, 7 and 8) the service process and product must be designed to fit the customer. In services high on all three dimensions, physical facilities, procedures, processes, personal behaviour and professional judgement all become important.

Wemmerlöv, in 1989,[8] identified three variables that can aid the design of service systems: type of customer contact (discussed later in chapter), degree of routinization and objects of the service process.

The degree of routinization is characterized as having the following attributes:

- Low level of task variety and technical skills
- Low level of information exchange between the service system and customer
- Both service employee and customer make few judgemental decisions
- The volume of goods, people, or information per unit of time is usually high

- The arrival rate of customers or jobs is often fairly predictable or controlled by the service system
- The process can involve several customers or objects simultaneously
- The response time to a customer-initiated service request is often short.

On the other hand, a fluid service process is characterized by:

- Higher levels of technical skills
- Larger amounts of information to be exchanged between the service system and customer
- The service employee going through unprogrammed search processes and making several judgemental decisions
- A usually low unit of time for handling the volume of goods, people or information
- High uncertainty of the workflow
- One customer (or object) at a time
- A fairly long response time to a customer-initiated service.

3.3   Objects of the service processes

Design issues will be affected by what is being processed. Where people are to be processed the question of whether or not they need to be physically present for the service to be rendered will require to be answered. If physical presence is necessary, the design of the service facility, the skills of the employees and the management of the customers need to be addressed. Where customer possessions is the object of service processing, employee technical skills, quality of equipment and capacity planning are of particular significance. The final category is that of information processing. For particular services, e.g. banks, building societies, insurance companies, much if not all of the service activity can occur in a back office, factory-type setting where efficiency is the crucial operating feature.

Wemmerlöv[9] argued that his classification scheme can, amongst other things, 'help management to better understand design and operational aspects of service systems by relating classified service processes to critical management tasks'. Amongst his 'uses of the taxonomy', he noted that 'the combination "no customer contact", "rigid processes" and "goods" creates a category that normally is thought of as manufacturing. In the same view, the combination of "direct customer contact", "interaction with service workers", "fluid processes" and "people" or "information" might be considered pure service.'

3.4   Customer contact

A central and recurring theme in the classification and design of service systems is the extent and nature of customer contact. As you are already aware from Chapter 1, Levitt[10,11] had encouraged service managers to think of their operations as manufacturing processes. In an article entitled 'Where does the customer fit in a service operation' Chase[12] took up the mantle of Levitt, urging companies to reduce their contact with the customer in the name of increased control. Customers were regarded as interfering with the smooth running of service operations (see Danet, B, reference 10 in Chapter 1). To address the issue of customer contact and service operational efficiency, Chase proposed that service systems should be viewed as falling along a continuum from high customer contact to low customer contact. Specifically, he asserted that 'the potential efficiency of a service system is a function of the degree of customer contact entailed in the creation of the service product'. In effect, the more physical contact the service had with the customer, the less efficient it would be, and vice versa. He proposed a formula[13] which stated that:

$$\text{Potential Operating Efficiency} = f\left(1 - \frac{\text{customer contact time}}{\text{service creation time}}\right)$$

where, **customer contact time** refers to the physical presence of the customer in the system and **service creation time** refers to the work process entailed in providing the service.

Extent of contact is the percentage of time the customer must be in the system relative to the total time it takes to serve him/her.

If we apply the formula hypothetically in two contrasting situations, hotels (high customer contact) and the bank branch office (low customer contact), the efficiency measure might be:

$$\text{For hotels:} \quad 1 - \frac{2 \text{ hours}}{4 \text{ hours}} = 50\% \text{ efficiency}$$

$$\text{For bank branch:} \quad 1 - \frac{0.25 \text{ hours}}{2 \text{ hours}} = 87.5\% \text{ efficiency}$$

The ratio of customer contact time related to service creation time is obviously much greater in the case of hotels but does that mean that they are that much less efficient? Furthermore, if the hotel was to take an 'inefficient 8 hours' to create the service, the resulting efficiency index would be 75%! Clearly, the nature, as well as the amount of customer contact merits attention. Customer input to the hotel facility would be defined as rather passive, whereas a relatively low contact organization like a bank branch office may experience a degree of uncertainty in terms of customer requests.

Chase subsequently reviewed his original position of shifting service activities to a remote back office in order to maximize efficiency.

This, after all, seemed to work well for manufacturers because it kept outside influences, that is, customers, from disturbing the production process. If a technician is assembling a widget, you don't want the customer asking him what he's doing. Or if a clerk is processing forms, talking to the customer on the phone takes her [sic] away from her job. In retrospect, this closed system philosophy overlooked the fact that there are positive benefits to both the customer and the organization by having the customer closely linked to the server, even though the job is traditionally performed in the customer's absence. From an information exchange perspective, the greater the links between consumer and producer, the easier it is to understand and respond to the customer's needs.[14]

In addition, Chase[15] expanded the notion of contact from the original of 'physical presence in the system' to a range of 'contact technologies' (mail, telephone, face-to-face). Contact remained unclear with further reformulation of the original model defining distance contact as direct, indirect and none. Unfortunately this approach simply reaffirms the method of contact over the nature of the contact.

Chase's model, however, remains of value even today. The physical contact he professed to be so concerned about is still for many services a matter of significant importance. For certain services the physical presence of the customer is necessary, for example hairdressing, a train journey, a health spa, etc. For others physical presence is not a prerequisite, for example electronic banking. Physical presence will also vary within a service as well as across services, for example a visit to your local bank branch to finalize a loan application. The remainder of the processing of that loan application occurs independently of your physical presence. With the development of call (or contact) centres and information technology, services are looking to minimize physical contact with customers in line with organization goals for efficiency. But the pursuit of greater and greater efficiency may come with a cost in the form of poorer service quality. Increases in customer complaints, system failures, being cut off etc. – are these evidence of an efficient system?

Where the method of contact appears important is in determining the division of a service between front and back office:

The front office is that part of the system directly experienced and visible to the customer. This is where the service is performed and is thereby open to customer scrutiny, e.g. the hotel dining room.

The back office is that part of the system from which the customer is (physically) excluded, e.g. the hotel kitchens. It is often referred to as the manufacturing side of the service, not seen by the customer. This means that the technical core of an organization (commonly referred to as the production process) is sealed off from any uncertainties that may occur in other parts of the organization. The back office becomes decoupled,[16] separated from the front office and is allowed to work without hindrance or interference. The main objective is to enable efficiency to be maximized in the 'production processes'.

A framework has been suggested as to how the front and back office should be organized and coordinated.[17] The following concepts were viewed as significant for determining the design options and conduct of service work between the customer, front and back office.

- **Input uncertainty** – refers to the service organization's incomplete knowledge of what the customer is going to bring to the service and how he or she is likely to behave. Input uncertainty will vary with the two environmental variables: customer willingness to participate and diversity of demand.
- **Customer willingness to participate** – refers to how far customers wish to play an active part in the service. Customers' capacity to become involved can be limited by lack of knowledge, skills and understanding of their role.
- **Diversity of demands** – refers to the uniqueness of customer demands. Are they to be met in a customized or standardized way?

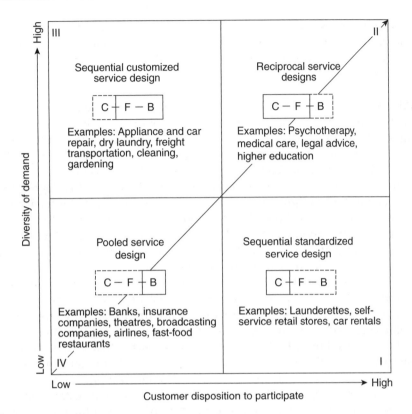

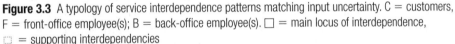

Figure 3.3 A typology of service interdependence patterns matching input uncertainty. C = customers, F = front-office employee(s); B = back-office employee(s). ☐ = main locus of interdependence, ⬚ = supporting interdependencies
Source: Larsson and Bowen (1989)[17]

- **Interdependencies** – refers to different patterns with respect to division of service work (between front and back office and customer) and customization versus standardization of standard actions and interdependencies.

The four service design options can be seen in Figure 3.3. A brief explanation of each follows.

- **Sequential standardized service design:** a customer-dominated design in which they serve themselves after service employees have provided the goods and facilities needed for self-service. It is a standardized service in which the front and back office can be decoupled to allow for efficient delivery of service.
- **Reciprocal service design:** joint participation of the parties 'in which the output of each becomes the input for the others'.[18] The service is produced largely on the basis of significant interactions between front-office employees and customers.
- **Sequential customized service design:** the bulk of the work here is performed by the service employees in a system of strong interdependence between back and front offices.

- **Pooled service design:** most of the work done by an efficient back office, largely decoupled from front-office disturbances. Customers do not interact extensively with service employees but engage in the sharing of resources that makes mass service possible.

Striking the right balance between front and back-office activities and responsibilities can be a difficult exercise. As Wostenholme[19] observed, 'There is a "back office" mentality currently permeating service operations thinking. The front office is seen as a complex interactive process where the customer is variable and unpredictable. The back office, on the other hand, is controllable and affords labour cost savings by restricting the number of customer contact personnel. Further, the degree and type of customer contact is progressively moving towards the "hard" forms of contact as witnessed by the introduction of ATMs and ticketing machines.' The precarious future for the front office (as a physical entity accessible by the customer) is reflected in his[20] comment that, 'There is undoubtedly a clearly definable trend towards the distancing of the service organization from the source of its wealth – the customer.' What all this means is that in the drive for operational efficiency and control (back office supremacy), service organizations run the risk of neglecting customer expectations of what constitutes a satisfactory experience (front-office impoverishment).

The thinking behind Figure 3.3 represented a significant advance for service design. It recognized the interdependence of three parties to a service exchange, the customer, the front-office employees and the back office. Depending on the extent of customer uncertainties the degree of service standardization/customization, division of work and relationship between the three parties can be established. Of particular interest in this model is the specification of a front-office facility wherein (physical) contact is made with the customer. This is reminiscent of the original position held by Chase. Additionally, physical contact occurs where the service provider must perform the service at the customer's location (cleaning and gardening in quadrant III).

Three questions arise out of the discussion so far:

1 How much contact with the customer is necessary? (This could be measured in time as a percentage of the total service creation time, the original Chase model, and evaluated in terms of activity-based costing of resources deployed in customer contact).
2 What should be the nature of that contact (standardized/customized, passive/active)?
3 Does the customer need to be physically present to receive the service?

In an ongoing process of addressing these questions, services will be subject to classification and reclassification. Some, by their very nature, will remain dominated by a front-office operation, e.g. hairdressing, dentistry. Others will forge ahead in terms of back-office concentration, e.g. telecommunications, utilities. The rest will be characterized by an unending tension between back and front office. The health service is an example of this category. Formerly patients were treated mainly in hospitals. Now only the most major surgery or specialist operations will occur in hospital. With the advent of new technology in the delivery of medical care patients will be diagnosed and monitored from afar by using telemedicine facilities, e.g. NHS24 and the Internet. For many situations the front office and direct physical contact with highly skilled medical staff will disappear to be replaced with self-management and lower qualified medical assistance. A further impact on the definition and deployment of front and back office has been the rise of the call centre. The front office is now only accessible from a distance and often through fully automated phone systems where there is no option to speak to a human being. It is as if the front office is displaying back-office characteristics, namely efficiency, rationality, manufacturing oriented systems. In place of the traditional role of exclusive engagement with customers, front-line service work now 'acts as a buffer between the relatively rationalized sphere of back office service production and the relatively, unrationalized sphere of consumption'.[21]

3.5   Service blueprint

A service blueprint is basically a flowchart of the service process. It is a map in which all the elements or activities, their sequencing and interaction, can be visualized. There are a number of essential steps in blueprinting a service.[22]

1 Draw, in diagrammatic form, all the components and processes (Figure 3.4). The service in this case is simple and clear-cut and the map is straightforward. More complex services may require large, complicated diagrams.
2 Identify the fail points – where things might go wrong. In Figure 3.4 the shoeshiner may pick up the wrong wax.
3 Set executional standards – these are tolerances (band or range) set around each function and regarded as acceptable from a customer and cost viewpoint. Time is a good example. In Figure 3.4 the standard execution time is 2 minutes, and

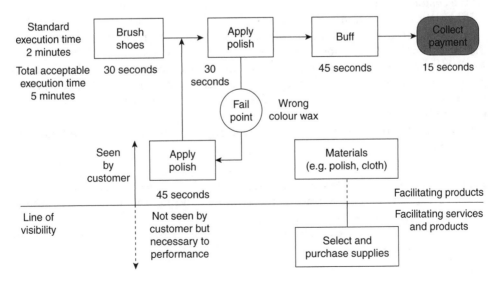

Figure 3.4 Blueprint for a corner shoeshine
Source: Shostack (1984)[22]. Reproduced by permission of *Harvard Business Review*, © 1984 by the President and Fellows of Harvard Colleges. All rights reserved

research showed that the customer would tolerate up to 5 minutes before lowering his or her assessment of quality.

4 Identify all the evidence (see Chapter 4) that is available to the customer. Each item represents an encounter point.

5 Analyse profitability – delays in service execution through errors or working too slowly affects profit. The shoeshiner estimates the cost of delay; anything greater than 4 minutes execution time and he loses money.

Consider the application and value of blueprinting for a car repair service. The perspective is that of a customer using it for the first time (Figure 3.5).[23] Prior to making the initial contact with the garage (phoning for appointment and arrival at the garage), the customer will have formed some expectations from, for example, word of mouth and advertising. The telephone call and particularly arrival at the garage will go some way towards confirming or contradicting the customer's expectations, and are in fact more powerful tools once he has made contact. The customer will use various pieces of evidence (telephone response time and manner, attitudes and appearance of proprietor/employees, equipment and layout etc.) as clues to the likely quality of service. Making assumptions about service quality from the type of evidence mentioned above is understandable but has the potential to mislead. The seemingly chaotic, untidy garage manned by employees covered in oil and possessing little by way of modern equipment may be perceived as likely to render a poor service. Yet the opposite may be nearer the truth.

The diagnosis represents an encounter point where the customer may, for example, describe symptoms to assist in determining the problem. It is critical in the sense that promises made to the customer and the resource implications of the job are determined on the basis of the diagnosis. If the diagnosis is subsequently found to be incorrect, relationships with the customer may be impaired. After the initial diagnosis the customer will depart, without ever seeing the repair section.

Where the organization draws the line of visibility, distinguishing the front office from the back office, is of some significance for service organizations. The nature of the service and how it is delivered offers guidance on where to draw the line, e.g. a hairdresser's operation will be predominantly front office, while a credit card company operates a very large percentage of its service in the back office. Other services, like a restaurant, may feel ambivalent about where to draw the line separating the front and back office.

In making the distinction a service organization needs to address the following questions:

- How much of the service does the customer need to witness/experience?
- Will greater involvement lead to more understanding and favourable impressions, i.e. improved effectiveness?
- What effect will there be on efficiency if the customer is allowed greater access to the service process?

As already mentioned earlier in the chapter, a delicate balance may have to be struck between the need for efficiency and the desirability of customer involvement. In the case of the car repair business, allowing the customer to experience the service may

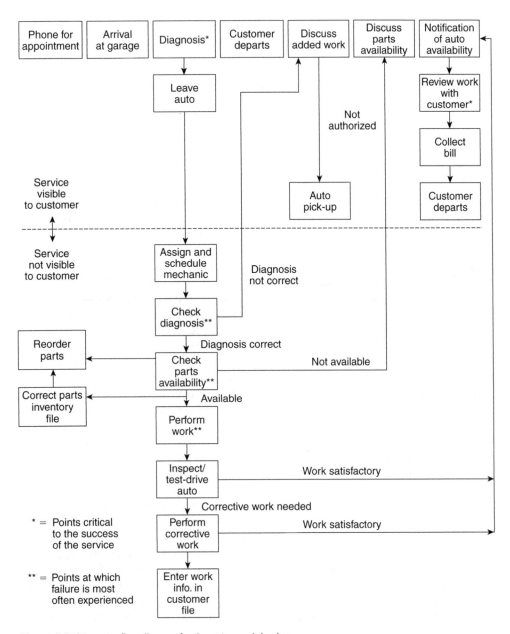

Figure 3.5 A process flow diagram for the auto repair business
Source: Heskett *et al.* (1990)[23]

create minimum disruption in terms of efficiency but maximum reward in terms of customer education and understanding.

The repair process in Figure 3.5 is sealed off from the customer but the objective must be to schedule work, deploy the necessary skills and arrange the timely availability of parts in order that promises made to the customer can be achieved.

On paper this is a good example of the construction of a service blueprint. Undertaking such an exercise provides an opportunity for the service provider to take a fresh look at the service and how it works. Stephen H. Baum, Vice-President of Booz, Allen and Hamilton Inc, New York, believes three factors are critical to making a pay-off:[24]

(a) The value delivered: what customers perceive they have actually received.
(b) The service mix: the features and levels of service the customers really care about. (c) Plans and budgets: signals they send employees that are consistent or inconsistent with what management is trying to do.

He cites the example of a fast-food business intent on cost savings in the kitchen which was convinced that automation would result in cost reduction. 'But they were wrong,' Baum said. The issue, according to Baum, was not automation, but labour and time management. His analysis led him to the conclusion that 'Employees spend a lot of time waiting, walking, and doing other things that customers did not perceive as adding value. Much of the problem was caused by equipment choices, process sequences, and layout – not by employee performance.' Baum was able to show, through blueprinting, that automation would actually increase idle time and that by focusing on value-added time major reductions of in-store labour could be effected.

Blueprinting, then, can be regarded as a valuable and versatile tool in systems design. Its deployment can range from the simple design of a hotel bathroom through to monitoring the process flow of an important and confidential company document.[25] In developing a service blueprint it is worthwhile considering 'Who does what, to/with whom, how often, and under what conditions'.[26] Whatever the process under scrutiny, the aim must always be improvements in service operation that will both deliver customer satisfaction and utilize organizations' resources efficiently. Improving the capacity, ability and willingness to serve must always be the expressed goal of any service organization. It will not be an easy task as the process moves away from the standardized design of a fast-food restaurant where time is the major design element. Clearly, performance standards, in terms of response time, are easier to set than, for example, degree of care and attention required by employees in other service situations. Of equal importance is the establishment of critical or pressure points and fail points. In many cases these are the 'moments of truth' for the customer and any vulnerability to breakdown must of necessity be minimized.

From an organizational culture perspective the blueprint allows all the employees to see their role in the process. Such an approach may bring to the surface previously unspoken tensions, but at the same time it can give, particularly to the front-line employees, a voice in how the service should be delivered. Far too often the customer contact employees are simply left to 'carry out orders'. It may well be, as a result of a blueprinting exercise, that the way these orders are carried out requires drastic overhauling. Management can be criticized, sometimes, for thinking they know best. Mapping out the process is as much a test of the validity and endorsement of management's belief as to how things do or should work.

A process cannot be improved until there is a clear understanding of how it works. There may well be different viewpoints as to how a process should be performed and monitored. It is advisable, therefore, that the views of management, employees and even customers should be solicited. Several types of information must be gathered and in so doing a distinction drawn between peoples' perceptions of the existing processes and their suggestions for improvement.

The areas for investigation should be:

- Process activities
- Information required to perform the process
- Products generated by the process, e.g. documents, services, etc.
- People and equipment required to perform the process
- Documents that direct how the process is to be accomplished.

3.6 The 3 logics

To fully appreciate the workings of any service system reference must be made to what is known as 'the 3 logics'. Logic is defined here as 'a way of reasoning' or a 'perspective'. Underlining the significance of the 3 logics, Kingmann-Brundage[27] stresses that they are 'crucial to accurate diagnosis of any service situation'. The attractiveness of this approach lies in its quest for a seamless (without failure/breakdown) and unified (cross-functional cooperation) service system. Through the determination of organizing principles, the service logical model proposes how and why a unified service system should work.[28] The 3 logics are defined as follows:

- **Customer logic** is the underlying rationale that drives customers' behaviour, based on their needs and wants. It will be evident in what customers expect of the service and how it might compare with other services.
- **Technical logic** is seen as the 'engine' of the service operation. It is essentially concerned with the way things are done dictated largely by organization policy, rules and regulations.
- **Employee logic** is the underlying rationale that drives employee behaviour. It will be evident in employees' perception of working conditions, working methods, organization of work and role clarity.

The service blueprint (Figure 3.5) is an ideal framework for illustrating the 3 logics. The initial contact with the garage represents the first step in framing the customer logic. How is the customer received in relation to how she/he expects to be received? Thereafter additional work and availability of parts will need to be discussed with the customer. The extra cost and further delay will be evaluated by the customer in terms of whether it is reasonable and acceptable. Finally the garage will review with the customer the work that has been done and the customer will depart reflecting on whether the service has offered value for money.

Technical logic reflects on how well the service has worked in terms of resolving the problem(s) to the customer's satisfaction. The correctness of the diagnosis, the availability of parts and the quality of work performed on the car will indicate how well the service system is working from a technical logic perspective. The final logic, that of the employee examines how working conditions and the related matters of morale and motivation impact on job performance.

Ideally, for the service logic model to operate a unified system and provide a seamless service, the 3 logics must share a common interest. This is not inevitably so. To take just one example in practice, management efforts to contain costs and be more efficient/profitable (technical logic) may come at the expense of customer satisfaction and employee support. In the view of Leidner,[29] referring to the three parties to service work as customers, management and employees, 'it is not uncommon for the aims of the three parties to diverge and in the case of employees and management, be diametrically opposed'. So, although service logic appears attractive in principle, it has some way to go to overcome the hurdles in practice.

Summary

However a service is portrayed, it is a function of design. A range of decisions have to be made from seemingly straightforward issues such as employee uniform design through to the degree and nature of customer contact. Various classifications and options have been suggested, incorporating major variables.

One feature that remains contentious is the balance between front and back office. For many services the front office appears under threat, not only in terms of its retention but also the nature of its operation. Specifically, the front office may adopt the characteristics of the back office.

One tool that is valuable for specifying the precise details of a service is the blueprint. It enables the provider to determine critical/fail points the existence of which can be attributed to a design issue. But no matter how attractive the design is on paper, the tensions exhibited by 'the 3 logics' illustrate the design challenge in practice.

Appendix 3.1   A procedure for blueprinting a service

Select a relatively simple service, ideally one you have experience of (are familiar with) as employee and/or customer. To facilitate understanding of the process, you will probably need to draw upon the knowledge/experiences of management, employees and customers.

Part I: Drawing a service blueprint

You will develop a blueprint of the process steps involved in creating and delivering the service you have selected. Keep your blueprint as simple as possible.

- Show the process for delivering the intended service outcome; e.g. answer the questions 'What happens first, second, third, etc.?' and 'Who performs each step or makes each decision?'
- Which parts of the service process work well, and why?
- Where do things 'go wrong' (break down) in the service delivery, and why?
- How well does the service process deliver the key dimensions of service quality, i.e. tangibles, reliability, responsiveness, assurance, empathy?
- What measures or indicators are used/should be used to evaluate overall performance, e.g. levels of customer and employee satisfaction, revenue/profit/usage, etc.?

Part II: Interpreting the service map

After you have drawn the map, the next step is interpreting the service process. The following issues are simply illustrative of those you may wish to address.

- **Customer expectations:** What can be said, in general, about the level of service customers *desire* and the level of service customers find *acceptable*? How is management planning to address this gap?
- **Customer role:** How involved is the customer in the production and delivery of the service? How would you characterize the nature of that involvement?
- **Employee role** (particularly front-line): What skills/competencies are needed (required) versus what skills/competencies do employees actually have? How is management planning to address the gap – e.g. with training, better employee selection practices, improve/simplify the service process (perhaps through technology)? How would you characterize the quality of the work environment? Consider such issues as training, pay, supervision, physical environment, etc. as explanatory variables.
- **Procedures:** Are they standardized or customized? Technology: How significant a role does it play in the process? What impact does it have on customers? On employees?
- **Organizational culture:** Consider the phrase 'This is the way we do things around here' by asking 'Is there a better way to deliver the service?' Where are the areas of organizational resistance to innovative service delivery ideas?

References

1 Levitt, T (1972) 'Production-line approach to service', *Harvard Business Review*, Sep.–Oct., 41–52.
2 Levitt, T (1976) 'The industrialization of service', *Harvard Business Review*, Sep.–Oct., 63–74.
3 Thomas, D R E (1978) 'Strategy is different in service businesses', *Harvard Business Review*, July–Aug., 158–165.
4 Turner, A (2002) *Just Capital: The Liberal Economy*. London: Pan Books, p. 52.
5 Maister, D H and Lovelock, C H (1982) 'Managing facilitator services', *Sloan Management Review*, Summer, 19–31.
6 Schmenner, R W (1986) 'How can service businesses survive and prosper?', *Sloan Management Review*, Spring, 21–32.
7 Haywood-Farmer, J (1988) 'A conceptual model of service quality', *International Journal of Operations and Production Management*, **8** (6), 19–29.
8 Wemmerlöv, U (1989) 'A taxonomy for service processes and its implications for system design', *International Journal of Service Industries Management*, **1** (3), 20–40.
9 Ibid.
10 Levitt, (1972), op. cit.
11 Levitt, (1976), op. cit.
12 Chase, R B (1978) 'Where does the customer fit in a service operation?', Nov.–Dec., 137–142.
13 Chase, R B and Tansik, D A (1983) 'The customer contact model for organization design', *Management Design*, **29** (9), 1037–1050.
14 Chase, R B and Hayes, R H (1991) 'Beefing up operations in service firms', *Sloan Management Review*, **33** (1), 15–26.

15 Chase, R B and Aquilano, N J (1992) *Production and Operations Management.* Holmwood, IL: Richard D Irwin, pp. 122–124.
16 Thompson, J D (1976) *Organizations in Action.* New York: McGraw-Hill.
17 Larsson, R and Bowen, D E (1989) 'Organizations and customer managing design and coordination of services', *Academy of Management Review,* **14** (2), 213–233.
18 Thompson, op. cit.
19 Wolstenholme, S M (1988) The Consultant Consumer: a new use for the customer in service operations, Proceedings of the Operations Management Association Annual International Conference, University of Warwick, pp. 192–203.
20 Ibid.
21 Kerst, C and Holtegrewe, U (2001) Flexibility and Customer Orientation: Where Does the Slack Come From? Paper presented at Work, Employment and Society Conference, University of Nottingham, September.
22 Shostack, G L (1984) 'Designing services that deliver', *Harvard Business Review,* Jan.–Feb., 133–139.
23 Heskett, J L, Sasser, W and Hart, C W L (1990) *Service Breakthroughs.* New York: The Free Press, p. 107.
24 Quoted in Coleman, L G (1989) 'Blueprint gets foundation for better service and customer satisfaction', *Marketing News,* **23** (26), 18 December, p. 24.
25 Heskett *et al., Service Breakthroughs.*
26 Kingmann-Brundage, J (1989) Blueprinting for the Bottom-line. Proceedings of AMA Annual Services Marketing Conference.
27 Kingmann-Brundage, J (1995) 'Service mapping: back to basics', in Glynn, W J and Barnes, J G (eds), *Understanding Services Management.* New York: John Wiley & Sons, pp. 119–143.
28 Ibid.
29 Leidner, R (1993) *Fast Food, Fast Talk: Service Work and the Routinization of Everyday Life.* Berkeley, CA: University of California, pp. 173–174.

4

The service setting

Introduction

The setting and surroundings in which many services are delivered is often a critical component of a consumer's service experience.[1,2] Since it is often the first tangible clue that the consumer is given about potential service delivery, it shapes expectations.

These clues shape consumers' rational, emotional and behavioural responses, and for this reason the service provider would be wise to consider all elements of both the physical and ambient setting in which the service is consumed.

The control by the designer of corporate elements that form interior spaces can impact on the success of that delivery in a variety of ways. It can influence the client's or customer's perception of the particular service sector and can enhance the function, appropriateness and ambience of the activity.

4.1   The service setting framework

The term 'service setting' is used to describe the tangible physical environment in which a service is experienced. This environment gives vital tangible and intangible clues that help potential clients, customers, employees, stakeholders and opinion-formers understand a service's character and ideology. Who and what an organization is and what it believes in ultimately determines whether or not people will believe in it, work for it and buy from it.

Another term used to describe the tangible physical environment is *servicescape*. This descriptor was first used by Bitner[3,4] as a means of differentiating those aspects of the physical environment, e.g. signage, equipment, furniture, that provide tangible clues about the service offering, from other physical evidence, e.g. uniforms and business cards, that do this too. This chapter is concerned with the former (see Chapter 9 for a discussion of the latter).

The environment can portray a strong and consistent character. It ensures employees know when they are 'on-message' and true to the character of the organization as expressed through its corporate identity or brand as well as its services. This in turn helps make the organization coherent to its constituency – its customers, clients, partners, stakeholders and opinion-formers. In short, design of the service environment is an essential process through which the distinctive character of an organization is distilled, 'packaged' and consistently expressed. In this way the service setting is an essential component of success because it can communicate distinctive and desirable qualities that give the organization a clear positioning and differentiation in today's competitive marketplace.

We are all unconsciously but acutely aware of our surroundings. Like sleepwalkers we make automatic decisions about the objects and environments around us that effect how and where we live, what we buy, where we go and how and on what we spend our money.

One way to understand the effect service design has on our lives is to slow down and unpick our everyday decisions. We're all unconscious experts and know much more about the world than we give ourselves time to discover. Think about why you chose to go to the last pub or restaurant you visited and what you like, or dislike, about the environment. Think about your choice of holiday resort or cinema – what do you like or dislike about them and what triggered you to buy them in the first place. Consider why you prefer one brand over another and their respective meanings.

When we step through the vast door of a grand cathedral we automatically feel small and introverted because we are dwarfed by the interior space. We can hear our own footsteps, feel the drop in temperature and smell the stale air. Together these elements make us aware of our mortality and our solitary existence in a much bigger world. None of these phenomena are accidental, but are techniques honed by designers over thousands of years.

In terms of service strategy it is only relatively recently that serious consideration has been given to how the design of the service setting may affect consumer feelings and responses. There are no Ten Commandments that determine how a service setting should or should not be designed. From the customers' viewpoint it is still very much a matter of taste coupled with perceptions of what is appropriate. Nevertheless, just as companies want to know how and why customers respond to packaging, price, product, advertising, service organizations need to develop an understanding of customer responses to layout, furnishings, colour, light etc. Research should focus on overall impressions and feelings (Table 4.1), followed by an investigation of specific environmental ones.

Drawing on developments in decision-making theory in which customers respond to more than simply the tangible product or service, Kotler[5] proposed that atmospherics be regarded as an important marketing tool. He suggests that, 'In many areas of marketing in the future, marketing planners will use spatial aesthetics as consciously and skilfully as they now use price, advertising, personal selling, public relations and other tools of marketing.' He maintains the atmosphere of a place affects purchase behaviour in three ways:

1 As an attention-creating medium – use of colours, noise etc. to make it stand out.
2 As a message-creating medium – communicating with the intended audience, level of concern for customers etc.
3 As an affect-creating medium – use of colours, sounds etc. to create or heighten an appetite for certain goods, services or experiences.

Table 4.1 Atmosphere and feelings

Environmental atmosphere generated	Reaction in terms of customer feelings
Elegance	Status
Professionalism	Trust, security
Welcoming	Happiness, enjoyment
Sombre	Depressed, gloomy
Forbidding	Anxious
Warmth	Comfort
Lively	Inviting

Kotler concludes with an example of antique retailing. Many antique dealers also make use of 'organizational chaos' as an atmospheric principle for selling their wares. The buyer enters the store and sees a few nice pieces and a considerable amount of junk. The nice pieces are randomly scattered in different parts of the store. The dealer gives the impression, through his prices and his talk, that he doesn't really know values. The buyer therefore browses quite systematically, hoping to spot an undiscovered Old Master hidden among the dusty canvasses of third rate artists. He ends up buying something that he regards as having a value. Little does he know that the whole atmosphere has been arranged to create a sense of hidden treasures.

4.2   Types of service setting

It is often useful in determining the role/function of a particular service setting to consider the nature of the anticipated consumer relationship with the organization. In this context, services can be classified in terms of two dimensions (see Figure 4.1): the extent to which customers/employees are present during service delivery and the degree of complexity associated with service consumption.

In terms of the first dimension, there are some services where the customer is self-serving, e.g. ATMs, voice messaging services, online shopping services. In these services, the organization should be more concerned with planning the service experience to maximize satisfaction, than with any considerations for the physical environment, since the setting is not seen by the consumer.

Then there are some services where both customer and service employee are present – restaurants, hotels, air travel. Here the designer has to consider the needs of both. There is little point concentrating solely on one, even customers, since this may reduce staff morale and consequently motivation. How many of us have experienced a pleasant service setting ruined by disenfranchised staff? The current outbreaks of the MRSA superbug in hospitals have been largely attributed to poor standards of cleaning by hospital staff. Who knows, they might clean more effectively if some consideration had been given to their needs in the design of the service setting.

At the other end of the spectrum are services where only employees are present, e.g. telephone mail ordering. Consequently the focus of those designing the setting should be on such matters as staff motivation and productivity.

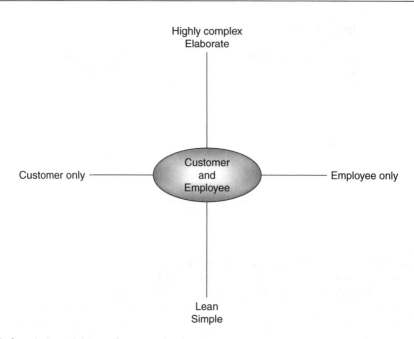

Figure 4.1 Complexity and degree of customer involvement

In terms of the second dimension – the extent of complexity associated with the service consumption – Bitner[6] suggests that services can be classified as either *lean* or *elaborate*. Lean environments are those that are simple, with few elements. In such environments design decisions tend to be relatively straightforward. Elaborate environments, on the other hand, tend to be complicated, containing many elements and forms. Hospitals, hotels and schools are some examples of elaborate environments. These are the most complex service settings to design.

4.3   The role of the service setting

We have previously mentioned the role that the service setting plays in helping position and differentiate a service provider. Given the intangible nature of many services, the setting gives important clues about the organization. Consider the imposing portals of a bank's corporate headquarters compared to the 'shop window' of the local plumber. Each is different, but then the user groups and services provided are so very different also. One would expect the setting to reflect this. Note that the setting can often lead consumers to infer a higher quality (and therefore higher expectations of price) on an item found in an exclusive setting, than where the identical item appears in a lower quality setting.[7]

Even within an industry, service providers often use their settings to differentiate from competitors. Think of the difference between the setting of the Royal Opera House in Covent Garden from that of a fringe venue at the Edinburgh Festival. Research has shown that there are various cues that customers use to differentiate services within the same industry.[8]

A key role of the setting may be to facilitate the roles and performances of those taking part – customers and employees. In doing so, a key objective is often to improve productivity or reduce costs. So banks and airlines in their increasing use of self-serve have to design their service environments in a different way to that of ten years ago. Many hotel chains too are asking customers to become more involved in the production of the service. So breakfast is from a buffet, tea-making and clothes-ironing is in the room. These factors impact on the design of the setting.

Finally in some organizations the primary objective in the design of the service setting may be to encourage socialization between staff and/or between staff and customers. So in many advertising agencies, board members have large, well-furnished imposing offices, whilst the new graduate trainee is lucky to get a corner of a desk. The same agencies will often have bars, games rooms or soft play areas where staff can unwind and socialize with one another. In health clubs and other leisure industries staff are often expected to socialize with customers and some area of the service setting is designed to facilitate this.

4.4   The service setting and consumer behaviour

Like any other stimulus, service environments work on consumers at cognitive, affective and connative levels – in other words, they work rationally, emotionally and behaviourally/physiologically. We will not enter the debate about the order in which cognitive or affective states are experienced. Nor will we discuss whether these states are antecedents to the behavioural outcome, or consequences of them. There is substantial debate about both these matters in the consumer behaviour literature.

4.4.1   Cognitive response

In terms of cognition, the perceived service setting can play an important part in belief formation. The setting can provide vital cues and clues that convey meaning through what is referred to as object language.[9] The fixtures and furniture in a hotel will often influence a consumer's beliefs about the level of service to expect (and the price to pay). It's not difficult to think of others.

In some cases industries can be categorized into different types of setting. The belief is that the clues and clues offered shape participating consumers' rational response. They help inform them of what is expected: so, on the low-cost airline there are none of the segregated seating or executive lounges of the traditional carrier. These differences affect consumers' cognitive responses.

In truth the majority of service experiences are fairly routine with little high-order level cognitive processing. We tend to be on 'auto pilot' and follow simple service scripts. However, should higher level processing be triggered, it is the interpretation of this surprise that determines a consumer's affective response.[10]

4.4.2   Affective response

In general, greater emphasis nowadays is placed on the affective or emotional response to the physical evidence of the service environment: how a consumer feels becomes an important consideration in the design of the setting. The designer will employ many elements (colour lighting etc.) to elicit the desired emotional response. On a ghost train ride, the desired affective response might be one of fear, excitement and terror, whereas in the funeral parlour, the service provider will be looking for an environment to elicit/empathize with other emotions.

Research conducted by environmental psychologists in this area has shown that any environment will elicit emotions that can be captured on two basic dimensions: the extent of arousal and the extent of pleasure/displeasure.[11,12] The simplicity of this model allows service providers to assess how customers feel while they are in the service setting. It can also assist those tasked with designing the service environment. If a service is in the pleasure/non-arousal quadrant (see Figure 4.2), the designer might want to build in elements that heighten arousal. Conversely, those services operating in the unpleasant/non-arousal quadrant would not want to build in arousal – this would take them into the distressing category. Instead, they should attempt to incorporate elements to shift the horizontal positioning.

4.4.3   Physiological/behavioural response

In environmental psychology there are two possible behavioural outcomes to the affective response – *approach* or *avoid* – pleasant emotional responses leading to the former and unpleasant ones the latter. Those charged with designing settings for service providers will most probably be tasked with eliciting behavioural responses beyond that of *approach*.

The setting may be designed to encourage the consumer to linger or browse on the basis that this is likely to increase the value of their shopping basket. The bookseller Waterstones does this to good effect. It has seating areas, and coffee shops. Or it may be designed to take customers speedily through the service experience on the basis that revenue can be maximized by encouraging speedy customer throughput. Many

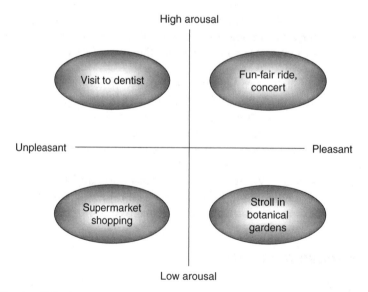

Figure 4.2 Emotional/affective responses

fast-food restaurants do this. The chairs are a little uncomfortable, the tables close together and the lighting is bright.

Remember that in many service operations, the environment should be designed to elicit desired behavioural responses not only from the customer, but also from staff. Hospital staff are expected to work in an efficient, hygienic and calm way. Their environment gives all sorts of clues about this. Soft furnishings are kept to a minimum, and the space is designed to be uncluttered and germ-free. Designer retail outlets have no seats for their sales advisers. Instead they have to stand, making them ever-ready to assist the customer.

4.5   Environmental dimensions of the service setting

In Bitner's[13] model of the servicescape, the key dimensions of the service setting that condition the consumer response are highlighted. These are the ambient conditions, space and functionality, and the use of signs, symbols and artefacts (see Figure 4.3).

4.5.1   Ambient conditions

These are elements of the service setting that affect our senses. Elements such as lighting, music, noise, colour, temperature and scent. The service provider should consider these factors in the design of the environment. They can play a significant role in achieving desired behavioural responses. For example, a number of studies have demonstrated the effect of 'musak' in supermarkets on consumers' buying patterns.[14,15] It appears that 'musak' lulls the shopper into a semi trance-like state where they are more easily persuaded to part with their money and spend time waiting in queues.

Lighting
This is often a key element in the design of the service setting. The design and specification of lighting schemes is a specialized activity.

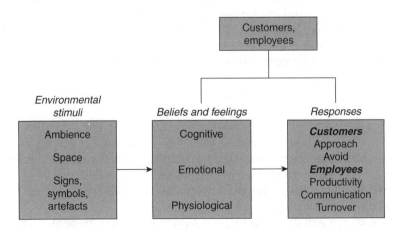

Figure 4.3 A service-setting framework for understanding behaviour and relationships
Source: Adapted from Bitner (1992)[3]

When considering lighting design for a service setting the following factors must be taken into account: daylighting, colour, the nature of the activity to be performed in the space(s), the service provider's perception of the task, levels of vision, and finally ambience, the desired mood:

- Daylighting and the way in which it is controlled influence heat, glare, penetration, visibility and the perception of colour – most schemes take account of the orientation of the building to the sun, its changes daily and seasonally, as well as poor daylighting conditions and darkness.
- The direction and strength of daylight affect the perception of colour.
- The particular activities to be undertaken in the space under consideration must be clearly defined: accuracy, speed, safety, recognition etc.
- What does the organization really want from the space? Is it to sell visual satisfaction or is it to sell hamburgers? Is it to indicate the conservative solidity of the world of financial services or is it to reassure people about to board an aeroplane?
- The level of vision required can depend upon the nature of the task. It can also depend upon the age of the client or customer. If the task requires detailed work from the customer or service provider then strong light is required. If the background setting is well lit then even greater intensity of light will be required for the detailed work as the eyes become accustomed to the relative lessening of the contrast.
- In many situations the achievement of the desired mood or ambience of the space is paramount. A church or library would generally exude a peaceful calm whereas a fast-food diner or modern music store would wish to create a youthful, exciting, gregarious atmosphere.

On a scientific level, the perception of colour and lighting is governed by a vast array of data such as the depth of penetration of daylight, glare, or the reflectance value of the surface that light is falling on and the psychology of colour contrasts. Other constraints on the design of lighting systems have to do with variables such as energy conservation, heat gain and ease of maintenance programmes.

For the designer there is the additional burden of wanting to create magic. The creative use of light can bring an interior to life – the interaction of light and shadow can sculpt, expand, scale, highlight, silhouette, sparkle and most importantly can move merchandise.

Colour

Colour has a language of its own. Much like music, it can evoke moods and emotions – excitement, happiness, serenity, sadness. We daily refer to 'feeling blue', 'seeing red', 'being green with envy', 'in the pink' etc. The symbolic nature of colour has for centuries fulfilled a role in religion, magic, heraldry, communication, and ritual, as well as being a major player in creative processes.

The 'fashion' element of colour use is a subject in its own right but suffice to say that as with most fashions, its use can be traced in cycles. Ancient classical architecture of the Greek and Italian empires used brilliant, bold colours.

Colour is composed of three elements:

- Hue – the name of the colour, e.g. red, blue, yellow.
- Value – the lightness or darkness of a colour.
- Chroma – the intensity of strength or purity of colour.

There are numerous theories about the way in which colour works. It is not sufficient, however, to consider colour without an understanding of the effects of light, the discrimination of relative colours – that is, the different appearance of one colour or hue which is in the proximity of another hue – and also the spatial and the emotional effects of colour.

It is always dangerous to pragmatize when discussing a variable such as colour, and any statements that might appear as 'rules' should only be read as examples in the context of suggestions for the particular service settings discussed.

Colour can only be measured *in relation to other colours*, and while an adult with normal vision can distinguish probably two thousand colours, this experience is, at best, highly subjective. Colour can never be isolated and the resultant experience modifies the perception. Look at a strong red sample for about a minute and then focus on a white surface – the resultant green vision is the after-image of a colour's opposite or complement. A colour always has to be considered in relation to its neighbour in any successful lighting design. In simplistic terms one can say that colour schemes that are largely monochromatic (different values of the same hue) are the safest solution. Next best in terms of little risk are schemes that rely on using colours that are adjacent in the spectrum and therefore have one hue in common. The riskiest and therefore sometimes the most rewarding or interesting schemes are those based on complementary colours or those of high contrast. This almost elementary appeal perhaps stems from experiences and memories we had as children. Nature, of course, employs exotic schemes in the plant world and colours of courtship or warning in animals, fish, birds and insects.

A further consideration in managing colour in the service setting is to plan a scheme such that adjacent rooms share some relationship or harmony. Generally speaking, large spaces are better balanced by using a scheme of soft, low-intensity colour with strong, vibrant hues reserved for accent or highlight value. Again as a general rule, background colours are selected and developed first for the large planar areas (floor/ceiling/walls) with 'accessories' (equipment, furniture, curtains, pictures) figuring as stress or accent points.

Also important is an understanding that colours have *optical and emotional values*. Warmth and coolness are easily distinguished by colour choice so that red, orange, yellow and their family are warm while green, blue, violet and their family are cool. A finer division can occur at junctions in the spectrum so that red-violet and yellow-green can occupy both camps or form a bridge between warm-cool.

Red indicates danger, excitement, stop etc. – the pulse rate and blood pressure of a viewer increase when shown the colour. Conversely, green indicates peacefulness, safety, go etc., likewise for blue. Perceived sizes of areas of colour vary with the selection of hue – warm colours appear to advance towards the viewer, cool colours to retract or recede. Colour choice can therefore be used to modify the perceived size and shape of areas.

It will come as no surprise to the reader to learn that these colour theories can be, and are, used as a functional tool in the design of interiors. Colour is utilized to improve efficiency in the workplace; colour can help people to relax, it can help lower accident rates, aid convalescence, help market merchandise or create an appetite where food is served. Specifics will be discussed below under the five colours selected.

In their book based on the television series *The Colour Eye*, Cumming and Porter[16] give some valuable insights into colour psychology. For example:

- **Red** – the colour of fire and passion, suggesting activity, energy, joy. It is used by interior designers to increase comfort levels in unheated spaces and is also regarded (along with pink) as good for restaurants, especially the fast-food variety. One study showed that red stimulated diners to eat more quickly and move on for the next person.
- **Orange** – although researchers have claimed that an orange environment improves social behaviour, cheers the spirit and lessens hostility and irritability, it is seldom used by professional designers.
- **Yellow** – conflicting evidence here which, on the one hand, suggests its ideal stimulative effect where concentration is required. However, if used too strongly those in its environment are likely to get 'stressed up'.
- **Green** – symbolizes the natural world and is widely believed to be a calming hue. Ideal for areas where relaxation is required and along with blue is found to enhance our appetite; thus good for dining areas.
- **Blue** – symbolizes authority and implies truth, prudence and wisdom; ideal for banks and building societies. It is considered as having a calming effect which makes it ideally suited for hospital cardiac units.
- **Purple** – regarded as disturbing and psychologically 'difficult'. In a Swedish study it was the most disliked colour in terms of environmental settings.

4.5.2   Spacial considerations/planning

Most design training is based on historical precedent and takes its ideas from either nature and/or mathematics. Precedent has meant that the most common source of creativity has come from a vast visual dictionary that has evolved from concepts that have been tested and re-tested until principles are established. Symmetry, proportion, rhythm, texture, colour and other fundamentals are combined and developed to present the viewer or user with a rational and emotional response.

Space planning

In an ideal world, the interior designer works alongside the architect from the initial planning concept stage – by doing so, coordination of the arrangement of all of the interior elements with the architectural features is assured. A large proportion of the sites interior designers encounter, however, do not offer this luxury – most jobs are concerned with refurbishment of spaces and buildings originally designed for other purposes. Certain 'rules' do make up the fundamental approach to the planning process.

Generally speaking, the planning exercise with most interiors falls into five categories:

1 The identification of the issue (the brief)
2 The synthesis of the solution
3 The design development
4 The solution
5 The testing of the efficiency of the solution.

The identification of the space planning issue will fall into several subsections. For example:

- What are the functional requirements?
- How will the users circulate?
- What does the client wish to feel like?
- What does he or she wish to see?
- What does he or she want others to see?
- What is going on in adjoining spaces?
- What are the safety and legislative requirements?
- Are exterior spaces involved?
- What kind of lighting, heating and other services are required?
- What is the desired 'mood' or character of the space(s)?
- What is the likely budget?
- How long must the scheme last before refurbishment?
- Are future developments, growth or flexibility prerequisites?

The synthesis or sketch designs of the planning process can take several forms. The most common is to formulate a graphic or schematic model which enables the designer to rank the requirements. Usually this process begins without regard to the physical constraints of the particular site and designers can indicate space relationships and traffic throughput on a purely functional level and can test their ideas against the model formed in the brief.

The development phase occurs when the designer transcribes findings from this schematic visual into the constraints of the actual space: the fitting of furniture and equipment into the space, establishing correct circulation routes, working out all the complex requirements to enable the drafting of a floor plan and associated working drawings and details.

The solution begins to take shape when all of the other phases are in place. It lasts from the time of client approval to the opening ceremony of the successfully completed building.

The final phase is the testing and modifying of the solution when the user or client can be interrogated and suggestions for improvement taken on board. This is as important a phase as any of the other four described. A list of priorities can be formulated without being dogmatic in terms of 'generalized rules'.

Circulation is of primary importance – not only traffic levels and direction of the user but also allowing sufficient space around objects, equipment and furniture to enable them to be used efficiently and safely. Unobstructed approaches to doorways, corridors and escape routes are obvious considerations. The designer above all hopes to create interest and a particular ambience to the space which is appropriate to its function. A sense of scale, balance of proportion and interaction between adjoining space is important. Simplicity in planning is invariably successful and can lay the foundation for all of the other elements which make up the service setting.

Furniture/equipment/furnishings

Furniture can host people, or it can form a barrier between people. It can host equipment such as computers, cables and cash registers. It can protect precious or delicate objects. It can project or display. Furniture can be welcoming or austere and can have a great deal to say about the status of the owner or user.

Places, tools, furniture and decoration are interdependent elements of our lives. They contribute to our quality of life by dint of functionality and aesthetic enrichment. They can be designed, controlled, and become tools to further the designer's intentions.

Furniture and equipment can take on architectural proportions when one considers the cost of subdividing rented space. Often modern refurbishments have a 'designed-in' longevity – two years, five years, ten years. The cost of partitioning and its accompanying rigidity soon provides good reasons for considering the functions of walls and doors being replaced with free-standing furniture elements. Most of the established thinking to do with the subdivision of space is fast becoming outdated with the proliferation of office and business automation. Wide, open spaces are no longer required. The need to keep people in proximity is redundant as office information now flows down cables. In a modern building with a life expectancy of, say, thirty to forty years, the initial capital cost is only 10% of the complete cost. Ninety per cent will be devoted to staff costs associated with maintaining a working environment and the machines and technology necessary for the purpose.

In general terms there is incredible freedom of choice available to the occupier of a commercial interior – artificial environmental qualities (light, ventilation, heating etc.) are controllable. Heights and inclinations of chairs and worktops are variable, furniture and equipment can be 'high tech' or soft and domestic in nature.

Technological development has brought overwhelming change to the service setting; the office-based service industry means that the office can now be a club, it can be a factory, a series of cosy meeting places, a streetscape or a marketplace. This choice will, hopefully, reflect some of the functions of the particular service. Another social change – the shrinking of class differentials – has impacted on the construction of the service setting in that in many environments designers no longer have to consider the status of its users.

Perceptions of equipment are also changing. The typewriter keyboard was invented in the 1860s – this meant the standardization of the layout of the letters (obvious but nonetheless staggering). The mechanical keyboard is now electronic and pressure requirements are infinitesimal in comparison to the earlier typewriters but operator posture and ergonomics have changed to accommodate the new requirements. Operators rarely view paper, displays are on VDUs. Five or ten years ago an operator in the service sector would probably search for documents in a filing system, make notes, write letters and memos, use the telephone, exchange words with colleagues and be constantly on the move. Now as a link in the technology-based environment, eye contact might only be between customer/client or VDU and the service operator. The office today is still a 'shelter' to its occupants but is also a 'display window' to the clients and customers of that particular service sector. The demonstration of the efficiency of the now visible 'working parts' of the organization is a tangible sales promotion tool. The idea of 'front office' as the only area visible to the client is long gone. The customer has also experienced the impact of technological change. Most people have drawn money from an ATM (automatic teller machine), spoken to an answerphone or received a computer printout on some occasion.

4.5.3   Signs, symbols and artefacts

Service providers use signs, symbols and artefacts to guide customers through the service delivery process. They signal to the customer how to behave, and where to go. New customers, and probably seasoned users of a service, would become disorientated causing anxiety and distress if there were none of these artefacts.

Signage

Graphically transmitted messages or signage are fundamental to communication in all areas of the service sector. The visual appearance, the placing, the physical construction, the colour, lighting and choice of typeface are all important and interdependent.

'Letters are signs for sounds'. This is a well-known quote and serves as an apt definition of what signs are about. A good sign is one that imparts information as simply and directly as possible. As with colour and spatial considerations, letter forms can evoke emotional responses.

Signs, unlike print, are read quickly and therefore the choice of weight of the letter form is paramount. It should seek to provide maximum clarity and contrast from the sign's surroundings.

Signs can be of some importance in many service settings. The 'you are here' map (YAH) is designed to answer the questions 'Where am I?' and 'How do I get from here to there?'. The trouble with many of these maps, apart from not being particularly well designed, is that they are not always aligned with the territory. The difficulty seems to be that YAH maps are usually placed vertically on a wall. 'If', as stated by Levine, Marchon and Hanley[17] 'the direction which is in front of you is up, on the vertical map, the map and the terrain are aligned and the map will be relatively easy to use. If, on the other hand, the direction in front of you is down on the map, they are contraligned, the map will be relatively difficult to use'. Counter-alignment and alignment can be demonstrated quite simply (see Figure 4.4).

4.6   Three service settings

4.6.1   Financial services

The public interface with financial services, especially in banking and other high street institutions, has undergone radical change in the last generation. We have witnessed

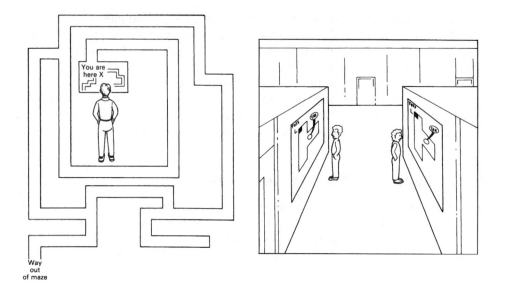

Figure 4.4 Alignment and counter–alignment of YAH maps
Source: Levine *et al.*

the metamorphosis from elegant, dark, expensive and foreboding interiors to the 'fun money shop' era of the past decade to the current trend of serious design, professional service and interaction between people.

During the 1980s, the yuppie mentality was all. High street banks and building societies resembled retail establishments and nightclubs in contrast to the Victorian approach of previous decades. Neon light, distressed surface finishes and dreamy uplighting housed high-tech machines that obviated the need for personal contact. Banks and the like became 'take-away' or 'fast money' outlets resembling the franchised fast-food chains that proliferate in every shopping mall or provincial high street. There is no doubt that the money business itself has undergone radical change. Building societies initiated the change by offering attractive interiors. The banks followed to continue to compete successfully.

In general terms, layouts tend not to vary and follow a common design. Entrances have become lobbies that house self-service cash dispensers (and other routine transactions – deposits, statement provision etc.). These are often fitted in fairly sturdy surroundings that recognize the out-of-banking-hours activities and the need for anti-theft, anti-vandal and in some cases anti-weather protection. The reception area is found behind this area and this first point of customer–staff interface is afforded adventurous front-line reception desking that is generally modern and colourful. The transition for the customer is marked by a change in floor covering from marble or tile or hard surface to soft surface such as carpeting of a warm hue. Wall surfaces likewise will blend from a stone cladding or laminate surface to a textile base or wallpaper and lighting will change from security conscious task lighting to uplit pools that are warmer and more 'domestic' in context. Beyond the reception point is the area designed for financial consultations where bandit-proof glass screening and counter tops are being replaced with informal, low-level, comfortable and discrete consulting areas. The customer will feel that he or she is being afforded status and personal attention. Much of the brutality of design approach has disappeared to be superseded by a thoughtful more gentle approach where the customer is allowed to feel less threatened.

Behind the area designated for personal consultations, the working area of the institution often remains as open-plan and clearly visible personnel movements reflect the exposed working kitchen seen in McDonald's and Burger King establishments.

The financial service sector is also responding to the rapidity of change by generally reviewing interior design policy every five years or thereabouts and recognizes that the 'service setting' is an increasingly important asset in its marketing armoury.

4.6.2   Fast-food restaurants

Born in the USA out of the hot-dog stand or lunch-wagon genre, the fast-food chains and franchises have spread throughout the world. Previously the menu revolved around 'burgers and fries'. The quick-service/short-order restaurant industry has changed out of all recognition since the early part of the 1980s. The 'yuppy youth' culture demanded healthy food, salads, baked potatoes, pulses and pastas, fresh fruit and vegetables. The menu says it all. The interior design reflects the menu and what it says is 'quick turnover'.

A successful design is the one that attracts customers into the restaurant, organizes their traffic flow, creates just enough (and no more) comfort, arranges seating configurations that are economic and then hustles the customer out.

Fast-food outlets have produced a lot of innovative designs. Successful schemes (financially rewarding *and* aesthetically pleasing) invariably combine slick and lively ambience with often whimsical, youthful, colourful surroundings enhanced with a good portion of pop music or musak.

Wall and floor surfaces are invariably hard – usually tile or laminate for durability, ease of maintenance and cleaning. Soft base colours always serve to contrast with a dramatic splash of colour, red or green. All interior materials are simple and appear inexpensive. Seats are just too short and just too close to the next table to encourage customers to linger. The emphasis is often on serve yourself and dispose of the debris yourself in self-consciously signposted receptacles. The kitchen is the focal point, always busy, clean in appearance and in some instances forming a stage or 'altar' in the case of pizza ovens.

Lighting is brutally harsh and no attempt is made to pool light over individual tables as this would create an intimate ambience and invite diners to dally. Graphics are over-sized, unmistakable and again centre around blown-up versions of the menu. In this industry, success or failure may depend on the ability of the service setting to stimulate a speedy throughput of customers.

4.6.3   Hotels

Hotel design and creative manipulation is a complicated and lucid combination of sensitivity and imagination that is woven seamlessly within architectural and economic parameters. These in turn are set by social and cultural demands past and present.

There are several questions to consider when tackling a hotel project:

- Who is the clientele? What does the clientele want? What does the clientele need?
- What does the building want to be? Is the project a 'new build' or has it history to tell?
- Should this influence our design solutions?
- Who built the building originally and for what use?
- What does a hotel need to be? How does this relate to the building?
- How can you address this hotel design in ingenious and unexpected ways?
- How does the context influence your decisions?
- Do hotels and other social spaces provide a respite from public life?
- Do hotel spaces represent a cross-section of our society of recent years?

Although local notions of luxury in London are not necessarily the same as those in New York, now that international travel has homogenized our expectations of comfort and service, it is often left to design, in the broadest sense of the word, to add the distinction that local manners would once have imposed.

Design helps to identify, divide or individualize each hotel or chain of hotels. The way that the designer creates an experience whilst practically facilitating all the needs of a varied and demanding clientele is key to a successful hotel design. Be it traditional, mainstream, original, designer or a new build hotel of architectural significance it is essential to create space and environments that remove the guest from their everyday life and provide an experience, which can manipulate feeling through well refined methods. These include: the design philosophy of the threshold or transitional spaces, the creation of views internally and externally, spatial manipulation structurally and aesthetically, circulation and the detailed use of light, colour and materials.

The threshold or transitional spaces are extremely important in that they link environments rather like a film editor links scenes within a movie or television program. The editor's choices are to seamlessly blend the scenes together, create a contrast to punctuate individual characteristics of both scenes, or to create a common visual language so that each scene complements one another. Moving through the space within a hotel is relatively similar in that the user moves from one space (or scene) to another. The entrance or foyer is a transition between the exterior and interior. The entrance is the first and the last element that is experienced and therefore the image most likely to be remembered. It is therefore essential to get the design of these threshold areas just right in regards to the hotel and its position within the marketplace. Does the hotel come out to meet you on the street in the form of its flooring, leading you off the street and up into an experience of luxury and hospitality? Does the caring start from the street by providing a protective canopy to shelter you from the elements, which also doubles as a sign or beacon as to the hotel's presence? Is the entrance set back, allowing privacy and a quiet transition between street and hotel? Are the steps up to the entrance an extension of the street where hotel and street meet with a mutual respect with regard to façade materials and design or does the hotel entrance allow the street in and straight to the reception desk, delivering the guest and blending the streetscape with the interior, creating a relaxed transition?

Views play a key role in the design of a hotel space, whether by connecting the guest to the exterior, making the most of key contextual features such as Edinburgh's Castle, or by creating internal views to other parts of the hotel, such as the restaurant or bar. These views or windows of information are created to draw the guest through a space or give depth and orientation to the spatial experience. The enticing view to the bar, for instance, creates visual and emotional stimulation whilst drawing potential custom from the foyer or even from the street.

Spatial manipulation with regards to surface, light and colour are the core elements to a successful hotel design. The surface planes are important, in that they often separate and highlight boundaries within the hotel, the horizontal plane (usually ceilings and floors) and vertical planes (normally, walls and partitions) dictate the areas. The foyer, for example, could benefit from having a higher ceiling creating an airy and spacious feeling that will promote relaxation and calm. The areas that lead off and link to the foyer, such as the reception and service areas, may drop to a lower more practical level of ceiling, thus signifying a change of use. Floors are also used to separate areas whether by leading you upwards via stairs to a timber-floored restaurant or leading you to a lower level where the lounge and shops can be accessed. Although these elements are not dividing the spaces as walls and partitions do, they have the same effect visually and psychologically.

Walls and partitions have a more obvious role in dividing space; however, it is important to understand the effects on circulation, light and aesthetics that a wall can have on a space. Although excellent in places where, perhaps, an area needs to be secured, a high level of privacy is needed, or an acoustic separation is required, a wall could have a negative effect by impeding light, interrupting the line of sight between important spaces or generally creating a claustrophobic environment.

The design intent with regard to surface materials varies from hotel to hotel. It is the materials amongst other things such as lighting and colour that give the space texture, character and personality and therefore should reflect the individual hotel's image.

In general, the materials used to denote service are hardwearing, robust and maintainable, such as, tiles, concrete, steel or plastics. In contrast, materials that denote relaxation or leisure are often natural materials such as timber, glass, stone and natural fabrics. The use of material runs far deeper than reflecting an ambience but can be used in subtle and sometimes more important ways. The handrail of a stair, a bar top or even the door handles used to gain entrance need to be designed so that where the hand touches the material should reflect the spatial integrity.

Lighting is a critical element of design. Too much light can destroy the character of the space. Too little light can be hazardous to the user and depress the hotel's atmosphere. Whether lighting is used to create points of interest, identify individual spaces, safely illuminate circulation or pick out architectural intervention, it is important to specify the lighting accurately. Lighting is often the largest single factor dictating feeling and spatial atmosphere. A great deal of effort has been taken to hide and recess the light fittings but without losing the impact of the different light effects required. Light draws the eye to the space throughout the building and provides windows of information and interest. A more utilitarian light effect has been used to punctuate the service areas, but the design intent is the same, i.e. recess the lighting (which applies to all the services, such as the ventilation and fire detection for example).

Materials also play an important part in dictating and manipulating the use and atmosphere of a space. The stair in Figure 4.5 for instance is made from the same material as the floor that leads from the street to the reception. The stair seems then to invite the guest up to the next level, where a timber-clad welcoming pier awaits the arrival.

Spatial boundaries are defined by a change in light, materials, vertical and or horizontal planes. The timber floor (horizontal plane) denotes a place of relaxation. The

Figure 4.5 Radisson SAS Hotel, Glasgow, UK in 2002

natural materials gently reflect light and calm the senses, in contrast to the harder tiled surface that indicates service, circulation and movement.

The structural glass wall (vertical plane) divides the circulation area from the reception space, whilst linking both floors physically and visually it has a key role to play in the manipulation of the guest's feelings. With its colour and material qualities, the structure is seductively suggesting 'this way to a restful environment, a quiet and relaxing bedroom suite'. The glass wall's surface is the only surface to have a rich reflective surface, which exudes depth and integrity.

The ceilings (horizontal plane) are pale and unobtrusive, stepping back in order to give added prominence to the key design elements such as the skylight. The skylight highlights and signals the circulation routes. It also creates a light and airy atmosphere as it draws the guest up the stair.

Summary

Where a service takes place is now receiving the attention it deserves. Designers are being called upon by organizations to create an environment that will support and reflect the service being offered.

Atmospheres must be engendered that will stimulate appropriate customer feelings and reactions. To achieve this the designers apply their knowledge and skills in respect of space idealization, lighting, colour and so on.

There are no Ten Commandments which state that different service activities should be designed in particular ways. It will be for the customer, in the final analysis, to decide whether the design has any meaning and impact on what is being received.

The three 'case studies' emphasize the point that there is no exclusive design for a certain service. However, there will be clues from the selection of colours, lighting and the layout of space etc. as to the nature of the activity in operation.

References

1 Gilmore, J H and Pine, B J (2002) 'The experience is the marketing', *Strategic Horizons*. Ohio: Aurora.
2 Pine, B J and Gilmore, J H (1999) *The Experience Economy: Work is Theater and Every Business is a Stage*. Boston, MA: Harvard Business School Press.
3 Bitner, M J (1992) 'Servicescapes: the impact of physical surroundings on customers and employees', *Journal of Marketing*, **56**, April, 57–71.
4 Bitner, M J (2000) 'The Servicescape', in Swartz, T A and Iacobucci, D (eds), *Handbook of Services Marketing and Management*. Thousand Oaks, CA: Sage.
5 Kotler, P (1973) 'Atmospherics as a marketing tool', *Journal of Retailing*, **49** (4), 48–64.
6 Bitner (1992), op. cit.
7 Baker, J, Grewal, D and Parasuraman, A (1994) 'The influence of store environment on quality inferences and store image', *Journal of the Academy of Marketing Science*, **22** (4), 328–339.
8 Gardner, M P and Siomkos, G (1986) 'Towards a methodology for assessing the effects of in-store atmospherics', in Lutz, R J (ed.), *Advances in Consumer Research 13*. Ann Arbor, MI: Association for Consumer Research, pp. 27–31.
9 Rapoport, A (1982) *The Meaning of the Built Environment*. Beverly Hills, CA: Sage.
10 Lovelock, C and Wirtz, J (2003) *Services Marketing*, 5th edn. Englewood Cliffs, NJ: Prentice Hall.
11 Russell, J A and Pratt, G (1981) 'A description of the affective quality attributed to environments', *Journal of Personality and Social Psychology*, **38** (2), 311–322.
12 Russell, J A and Lanius, U F (1984) 'Adaptation level and the affective appraisal of environments', *Journal of Environmental Psychology*, **4** (2), 199–235.
13 Bitner (1992), op. cit.
14 Hui, M K, Dube, L and Chebat, J C (1997) 'The impact of music on consumers' reactions to waiting for services', *Journal of Retailing*, **73**, 87–104.
15 Chebat, J C, Gelinas-Chebat, C and Filliatrault, P (1993) 'Interactive effects of visual and musical cues on time perception: an application to waiting lines in banks', *Perceptual and Motor Skills*, **77**, 995–1020.
16 Cumming, R and Porter, T (1990) *The Colour Eye*. London: BBC Books.
17 Levine, M, Marchon, I and Hanley, G (1984) 'The placement and misplacement of you-are-here maps', *Environment and Behaviour*, **16** (2), 139–157.

5

Service quality

Introduction

It is widely acknowledged that efforts to define and measure the quality of products has proved more successful than the definition and measurement of service quality. Even the word itself has evoked a variety of views as to its meaning. For services the setting of standards represents one way of communicating quality. However, the workings of the service organization itself must come under scrutiny in the quest for delivering quality. The Gaps Model is a useful framework for understanding the impact of the organization on quality. A technique for determining what to measure, and how, has been developed for service quality. It is called SERVQUAL. Additional approaches for managing service quality are discussed in the chapter.

5.1 The quality challenge

Quality is a word that enjoys widespread usage whilst failing to capture an agreed definition. From established dictionaries quality is defined as:

- Property, attribute, characteristic, mark, distinction
- Grade, calibre, rank, status, importance, value, worth
- Old fashioned eminence, prominence, excellence, superiority, distinction, supremacy
- General excellence of standard or level
- A distinctive attribute or characteristic possessed by someone or something
- A level of superiority that is usually high
- Of superior grade.

The theme that emerges from these definitions appears to be, unlike among established writers and researchers, one of agreement that quality implies 'a condition of excellence' or 'achieving or reaching for the highest standard'. Quality then, is not only of a high level but is also universally recognizable as such. ('That's quality' is a frequently heard refrain.)

Not everyone, however, wants or can afford a high level of excellence, so there are degrees of quality and service. Consider the example of two models of car: Mercedes and Renault Clio. If each car conforms to its formally stated specifications and requirements (free from defects, and consistency in delivering a specified level of performance) both are regarded as quality cars. Although the Mercedes will perform at a higher level, both cars will in their own way meet and fulfil the needs of their respective markets. So again, each is regarded as a quality car. Therefore, to add to the confusion, quality can mean both 'better' and 'cheaper'. In line with earlier comments above this may seem a difficult concept to accept by those who view quality as emanating from the inclusion (in a product or service) of more expensive ingredients, materials, skills and equipment. One possible way of addressing this apparent conundrum is to regard quality as the difference between how things ought to be and how things are, or to put it more plainly in respect of services:

- What is the service supposed to do?
- What does the service actually do?

There will still be a degree of subjectivity in this along with disagreements between customer and service provider, senior management and service employees.

Not surprisingly then, the tension between how things ought to be in terms of quality provision versus how things are, continues to be the subject of much interest. What is arguably not in dispute is that many service organizations fall short, for a variety of reasons, in pursuit of service quality excellence. Coupled with rising expectations and increased scrutiny (from consumers and a range of organizations), closing the gap between what is received and what is desired remains a challenge. For consumers and providers alike, knowledge of how quality has been defined and framed should be an indispensable first step in addressing this issue. Thus, it is to the definitions that we now turn.

5.2 Definitions of quality (and implications for service quality)

Quality has been the subject of many and varied definitions leading to the view that 'no one definition (of quality) is "best" in every situation because each definition has both strengths and weaknesses in relation to criteria such as measurement and generalizability, managerial usefulness and consumer relevance'.[1]

David Garvin is noteworthy for analysing the range of quality definitions, classifying them into five groups.[2]

5.2.1   The transcendent approach

According to this view, quality is synonymous with innate excellence, absolute and universally recognizable: 'You will know it when you see it'. It emphasizes quality as a mark of uncompromising standards. The origin of quality as excellence dates back to the Greek philosophers who referred to it as 'the best', 'the highest form', 'the highest idea'. If, then, we are to grant the title 'quality' only to those products and services that achieve the highest standards, what is to be said of the rest? It would seem we are left with individual perceptions or judgements of a service's attributes. That, some might argue, is the current marketing approach to the identification and measurement of service quality. As the chapter develops the significance of this matter should become more apparent. Unlike the Greeks in ancient times philosophizing over the concept of quality, practitioners in the world of business seek something much more practical. For them quality should be capable of implementation, delivery and measurement.

5.2.2   The product-based approach

The emphasis here is on quality as a precise and measurable variable. Any differences (in quality) that do occur reflect differences in the quantity of some ingredient or attribute possessed by a product.[3] This approach leads to a vertical or hierarchical ordering of quality. Products are raised according to the amount of ingredients/attributes that each possesses. However, an unambiguous ranking is possible only if the ingredients/attributes in question are considered preferable by all buyers.[4] For services, on the other hand, precision and measurability represent an ongoing challenge.

5.2.3   The user-based approach

This approach starts from the premise that quality 'lies in the eyes of the beholder'. Consumers are said to have specific wants or needs and those products that best meet their preferences are those that they view as having the highest quality.[5] There are two problems with this approach. First, with so many different preferences in the marketplace it is going to be difficult arriving at an agreed definition of quality. Second, it tends to equate quality with satisfaction. As Garvin[6] perceptually notes, 'a product that maximizes satisfaction is certainly preferable to one that meets fewer needs, but is it necessarily better as well'.

Garvin's user-based approach focuses exclusively on the customer in the determination of quality. His other four approaches are rooted in manufacturing/operations and engineering and consequently have difficulty confronting the unique characteristics of services. Meeting and/or exceeding customer expectations grew out of the services marketing literature in the mid-1980s.[7] It still commands a vast amount of interest within services but it is not without criticism (see SERVQUAL later in the chapter). The undeniable strength of this approach is that it allows the customer the overriding say in defining quality. Unfortunately that strength may also be construed as a weakness. As with the issue of preference variety mentioned earlier, expectations can also be highly varied, and personal. Securing agreement over expectations is therefore problematic. Furthermore, customers may not be in a position to articulate their expectations due to a lack of knowledge and understanding. Where customers are encouraged to state their expectations, service organizations may find them to be impractical, unreasonable and unprofitable.

5.2.4   The manufacturing-based approach

Whilst the user-based approach to quality is rooted in the subjectivity of consumer preferences, the manufacturing-based approach, as the name suggests, focuses on internal matters. It has come to be known as conformance specifications. Products are designed and manufactured according to predetermined specifications. Quality control techniques (see later in chapter for examples) are used for detecting deviations from the specification. For service organizations the back office operations (the technical core) are amenable to specifications. On the other hand the front office is often not so responsive to the imposition of specifications. However, even here under a process of standardization or routinization (McDonaldization in Chapter 1) services are subject to a form of standard operating procedures or models. Specifications can be written for aspects of service that would appear, on the surface, to present difficulties. Take courtesy as an example: A courteous employee (1) reflects a 'welcome' attitude; (2) shows consideration and respect for the customer; (3) listens to the customer, takes a friendly helpful attitude; (4) talks to the customer; (5) tries to understand the feelings, needs and requests of a customer; (6) explains the situation to the customer; (7) sees the customer is satisfied; (8) offers to help the customer at any time; (9) thanks the customer.[8]

5.2.5   Quality is value

In contrast to quality as absolute (the excellence level of thought), the value approach regards quality as relative to price. Monroe[9], a leading authority on pricing, suggests that a buyer's perception of value represents a mental trade-off between the quality or benefits perceived relative to the sacrifice perceived by paying the price. Thus,

$$\text{Perceived Value} = \frac{\text{perceived benefits (gain)}}{\text{perceived sacrifice (give)}}$$

Buyers, in effect, use price as an index of quality as well as an index of the sacrifice that is made in purchasing it. According to Feigenbaum, the notion of value has to be included in any quality definition:

> Quality does not have the popular meaning of 'best' in any absolute sense. It means 'best for certain customer conditions'. These conditions are (a) the actual use and (b) the selling price of the product. Product quality cannot be thought of apart from product cost.[10]

The last sentence in the quotation above is noteworthy as it suggests that 'you get what you pay for'. Value, therefore, should be viewed as higher price/higher quality, lower price/lower quality. However the price set is, in addition, a reflection of market conditions, internal costs (material, labour, equipment) and operating efficiencies.

Depending on the impact of these factors price may not reflect quality. Customers unable to comprehend market conditions and cost behaviour are thereby exempted from making an informed judgement of value. A 'high price' for whatever service is not necessarily an indicator or reassurance of excellent quality.

5.3 Standards

Reference was made above (under a manufacturing-based approach) to what is required of a courteous employee. What that signified is a service setting some form of standard for employee behaviour. Service employee conduct, knowledge and appearance is one, albeit important, element in debates over the standard of service. In general terms the word standard (often used interchangeably with quality) implies a level of performance that customers will find at the very least acceptable. However much that level is of importance to customers, how and why a particular level is arrived at should additionally warrant scrutiny. Unfortunately, judgements (by the customer) over the level of service are not informed by knowledge of why it is at that level. Whilst the formation of customer expectations has aroused interest, the process by which standards are determined has not attracted much attention in the services literature. Not surprisingly, we must resort to the view that standards should be set in accordance with customer requirements or expectations. An illustration of the contrast in view between what customers expect and a stated standard along with the actual level of performance can be seen in Figure 5.1.

The standard in this illustration is a time period for responding to enquiries or resolving complaints. For the customer, the standard is expressed in terms of expectations. (Note that expectations can be viewed as either a normative standard in the sense of what a service should offer, or a predictive standard in the sense of what a customer feels a service will offer.) The former interpretation is used here. The standard set is an expression of the service provider's view as to how long the process of responding to enquiries or resolving complaints should take. Service performance is

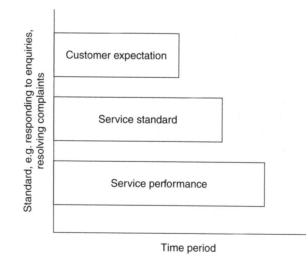

Figure 5.1 Standard: expectation and delivery

the time it actually takes. The customer loses out not only in terms of failure to meet expectations but also in terms of performance not even meeting the standard. Questions must be raised in respect of a standard that not only fails to meet what the customer desires but also falls short of what is actually delivered. (This issue will be further considered later in this chapter, under 'The Gaps Model of Service Quality'.)

5.4   Hard and soft standards

The standards experienced by customers of a service fall into two categories: hard and soft.

Hard standards often involve counts or timed actions of how many, how accurately, how quickly. Two of the five quality dimensions (see SERVQUAL later in chapter) are particularly receptive to hard measures. For reliability the ultimate standard is either 'right first time' (e.g. the correct order delivered to the customer), or 'right on time' (e.g. trains run when they are meant to run, the doctor keeps to the patient's scheduled appointment time and the dry cleaner cleans the customer's clothing by the promised date). For the second dimension, responsiveness, time or speed of response, is what's looked for in a standard. Basically it refers to the amount of time a customer has to wait between calling a service and receiving a response, e.g. waiting to get through to a service by telephone, waiting for a plumber to arrive. Even though we are dealing here with something that can be objectively measured, Figure 5.1 acts as a reminder of how far apart are the views of provider and customer as to what the standard should be.

Soft standards are areas that are more difficult to measure objectively and agree a standard. Soft standards are developed in response to customers, who invariably ask themselves:

- How was I made to feel?
- Was I involved, informed and consulted?
- Did I like how I was treated?

Service customers want to experience courtesy, trust, care and understanding. These attributes are encapsulated in a further two dimensions of service quality, namely empathy and assurance. To determine the extent to which they are present during a service encounter we need to contact the customers for their opinions and guarantees. This can be done through group discussions and/or customer surveys.

Establishing standards requires a detailed assessment of the entire service process, as in blueprinting or service mapping (Chapter 3). Questions can then be raised as to how far each step in the process requires and is amenable to specific behaviour or action to complete. The greater the degree of specificity the easier it will be to set a standard.

5.5   The Gaps Model of Service Quality

To enhance knowledge of service quality and encourage investigation of the key issues, a model has been developed – the Service Quality Gap Model[11] (Figure 5.2) – which has made a substantial contribution to our understanding of service quality. The

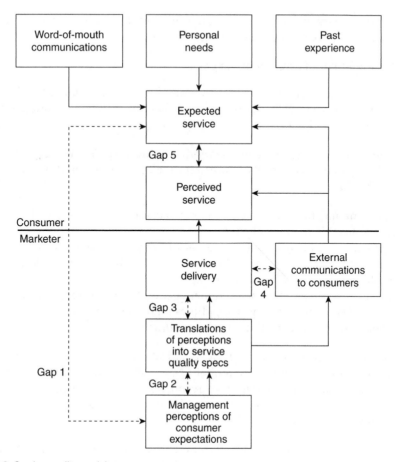

Figure 5.2 Service quality model
Source: Parasuraman *et al.* (1985)[7]

authors regard a gap as representing a significant hurdle in achieving a satisfactory level of quality. The overriding attractiveness of this model is that it should encourage us to consider service quality in more than definitional terms. Rather, it looks to the workings of a service organization for explanation of the 'how' and 'why' of service quality delivery.

The model's key features are:

- The identification of key attributes of service quality from a management and consumer perspective
- Highlighting the gaps between consumers and service providers with particular reference to perceptions and expectations
- Understanding the implications for service management of closing the gaps.

The most important insight obtained from the research on the service quality model has been:

A set of key discrepancies of gaps exist regarding executive perceptions of service quality and the tasks associated with service delivery to consumers.

These gaps can be major hurdles in attempting to deliver a service which consumers would perceive as being of high quality.

The following is a brief account of the gaps:

Gap 1 – states that many service organizations simply do not understand what customers expect and what really matters to them. This gap can only be bridged through customer research and, more particularly, knowledge from front-line employees.

Gap 2 – even where customer expectations are understood, management experiences difficulty in translating that understanding into service quality specifications. This exists because:

- Management may believe that customer expectations are unreasonable or unrealistic. A test for this remains elusive.
- Management may believe that the degree of variability inherent in service defies standardization. Ironically, reduction of variability has become a key motivator for the standardization of services (Chapter 1).
- There is an absence of wholehearted management commitment to service quality. In the face of short-term financial deadlines many service companies are reluctant to pursue customer satisfaction or quality efforts.

Gap 3 – even when formal standards or specifications for maintaining service quality are in existence, the delivery of a quality service is by no means certain. This is caused by poor, inadequately deployed resources in terms of people, systems and technology. The implications for the human resource or personnel management function should be obvious.

Gap 4 – advertising and other forms of communication by a service organization can affect consumer expectations. The danger is that promises made are not kept. Many service organizations use the brochure or prospectus (some very glossy) for communicating with potential customers. It should be a statement of what the customer will receive, not an attractive set of promises that cannot be delivered.

Gap 5 – this gap represents the key challenge. To ensure good quality the provider must meet or exceed customer expectations. Perceived service quality is the result of the consumer's comparison of expected service with perceived service delivery (see SERVQUAL).

5.6   SERVQUAL (what to measure)

Service quality is viewed as a multi-dimensional concept. Consumers assess and evaluate a number of factors or dimensions. The fifth gap in the Gaps Model of Service Quality gave rise to SERVQUAL, a self-administered questionnaire purported to be a generic measure of service quality.[12] In other words, it was designed to be applicable to a wide variety of services. The dimensions to be measured in the scale are:

Reliability – the ability to perform the promised service dependably and accurately. It is regarded as the most important determinant of perceptions of service quality.

This dimension is particularly crucial for services such as railways, buses, banks, building societies, insurance companies, delivery services and trade services, e.g. plumbers, carpet fitters, car repair.

Responsiveness – the willingness to help customers and to provide prompt service. This dimension is particularly prevalent where customers have requests, questions, complaints and problems.

Assurance – the employees' knowledge and courtesy, and the ability of the service to inspire trust and confidence. This dimension may be of particular concern for customers of health, financial and legal services.

Empathy – the caring, individualized attention the service provides its customers. Small service companies are better placed (though not necessarily better at) for treating customers as individuals than their larger, invariably standardized counterparts. However, relationship marketing is designed to offer a more individualistic approach for customers of large organizations.

Tangibles – the appearance of physical facilities, equipment, personnel and communication materials. All of these are used in varying degrees to project an image that will find favour with consumers. Tangibles will be of particular significance where the customer's physical presence at a service facility is necessary for consumption to occur, e.g. hair salon, hotel, night club.

To apply these dimensions to a particular service organization will require definition in specific action and behavioural terms. For example, what does reliability mean in service A as distinct from service B? How does an organization show responsiveness? How does assurance differ between service A and service B? What can a service do specifically to demonstrate empathy? On a more general level, it has been argued that service organizations should be subject to a quality audit as well as the legally required financial audit. Generally accepted service principles (GASP)[13] would provide service organizations with explanations of upward and downward trends in quality, just as companies explain good and bad trends in terms of sales and profits. The findings of a service quality audit may, in part, be portrayed as in Figure 5.3, and it might prove quite revealing for any service to ask of its customers, 'Of the four service arenas, which one best reflects us?'

In today's society there is now much more of an 'audit culture' particularly in the public sector with various bodies charged with overseeing and monitoring quality standards. For services in general, awards and certification are granted to companies who meet certain criteria in respect of standards. Additionally there are programmes such as Total Quality Management (TQM) which companies can adopt (see later in this chapter).

In contrast to external monitoring and the development of universal standards, SERVQUAL is a technique that purports to measure the customer's view of quality at the level of a specific service organization. A summary of how it works together with possible limitations is considered next.

Four service arenas

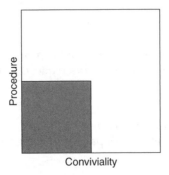

The 'freezer' service characteristics:

Procedural	Convivial
slow	insensitive
inconsistent	cold or impersonal
disorganized	apathetic
chaotic	aloof
inconvenient	uninterested

Message to customers: 'We don't care'

The 'factory' service characteristics:

Procedural	Convivial
timely	insensitive
efficient	apathetic
uniform	aloof
	uninterested

Message to customers: 'You are a number. We are here to process you'

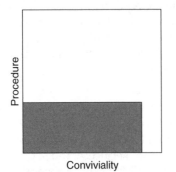

The 'friendly zoo' service characteristics:

Procedural	Convivial
slow	friendly
inconsistent	personable
disorganized	interested
chaotic	tactful
inconvenient	

Message to customers: 'We are trying hard, but we don't really know what we're doing'

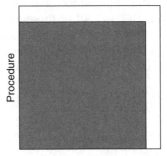

The 'full balance' service characteristics:

Procedural	Convivial
timely	friendly
efficient	personable
uniform	interested
	tactful

Message to customers: 'We care, and we deliver'

Figure 5.3 Four arenas of service quality
Source: Martin (1986)[14]

5.7   The SERVQUAL Scale

The scale was first published in 1988; improvements and revisions have been made since then. There are 21 items distributed across the five quality dimensions. One scale is devoted to perceptions, the other to expectations. Service quality is indicated by the gap between perceptions and expectations. Box 5.1 illustrates the reliability dimension.

Box 5.1 Extract from SERVQUAL: The reliability dimension – perception and expectation statements

	Strongly disagree						Strongly agree
	1	2	3	4	5	6	7

Perception Statements

1 When XYZ company [e.g. a particular bank] promises to do something by a certain time, it does so

2 When you have a problem, XYZ shows a sincere interest in solving it

3 XYZ performs the service right first time

4 XYZ provides its services at the time it promises to do so

5 XYZ insists on error-free records

Expectation Statements

1 When excellent banks promise to do something by a certain time, they will do so

2 When customers have a problem, excellent banks will show a sincere interest in solving it

3 Excellent banks will perform the service right the first time

4 Excellent banks will provide their services at the time it promises to do so

5 Excellent banks will insist on error-free records

Note in the expectations section the word 'will' substituted for the word 'should' which appeared in the original version. The criticism of 'should' was its idealistic meaning pushing respondents to the strongly agree end of the scale. What a survey, using the scale, shows is that where perceptions are lower than expectations, quality is poor. Where perception exceeds expectation quality is deemed to be good.

Whilst SERVQUAL remains a significant contributor in the literature, a number of criticisms have been made (see references 15–23 for a selection). A brief summary of the major criticisms is set out below:

- It focuses on the functional aspects of the process[15] (the 'how' of the service process), neglecting the outcome. Of course services are by their very nature experiences, making the functional aspect of key importance. However services can and do deliver a tangible outcome, e.g. plastic surgery. SERVQUAL does not allow for that.
- Its application across the service sector has been called into question.[16] Services can vary in many respects, revealing quite different and unique dimensions.
- It is not clear how the evaluation of expectations and perceptions occurs,[17] i.e. as specific points on the scale. Equally, how do expectations and perceptions change over time.[18]
- A respondent who circles 1 in response to a perception item has a potential range on the difference score (P − E) of 0 (if his/her expected level is 1) to −6 (if his/her expected level is 7). On the other hand a respondent who perceives the service to be good (and circles a 6 in response to the perception item) has a much more constrained potential range (0 to −1).
- How are gaps between P and E to be interpreted particularly where the same gap score, in this case −1 can be produced in 6 different ways (P = 1, E = 2; P = 2, E = 3; P = 3, E = 4; P = 4, E = 5; P = 5, E = 6; P = 6, E = 7). Do these tied gaps mean equal perceived service quality?[19]
- Following on from the last point, where a respondent scores perceptions at 3 marginally exceeding his/her score of 2 for expectations can it be concluded that this customer is seen as having received good quality service? It has been argued that SERVQUAL predicts that:
  - Customers will evaluate a service favourably as long as their expectations are met or exceeded, regardless of whether their prior expectations were high or low, and regardless of whether the absolute goodness of the (service) performance is high or low. This unyielding prediction according to some is illogical, arguing that 'absolute' levels (e.g. the prior standards) certainly must enter into a customer's evaluation.[20]
  - As Francis Buttle[21] perceptibly points out, '"SERVQUAL" assumes that an E-score of 6 for Joe's Greasy Spoon Diner is equivalent to an E-score of 6 for Michel Roux's Le Lapin French restaurant. In absolute terms, clearly they are not'. Consequently, some have argued for the term 'expectations' to be dropped in favour of the generic label 'standard'.[22]
- Is there a need to incorporate expectations into the measurement scale? The authors of SERVQUAL have argued in favour of its diagnostic value for management. Expectations serve as a kind of benchmark, anchor or reference point in the assessment of service performance. Others have argued for a perceptions-only measure of service quality.[23]

5.8   Tools of quality

Quality tools and techniques have been widely used in manufacturing. Their use in services is far less evident. Measurement in services was simply regarded as too difficult. However, quality tools are today being used in service industries.[24] This is not altogether surprising as service industries become increasingly subject to a process of specification and standardization. Moreover, given the pressure on costs, the need to satisfy customers and meet performance targets means the use of quality control tools may become more prevalent across the service sector. Those who do introduce quality control tools will undoubtedly emphasize the benefits. Equally they will have to acknowledge and address the difficulties and barriers surrounding effective implementation.[25]

5.8.1   Flowchart (What is done?)

Flowcharting is perhaps the simplest yet the most helpful in terms of overall service process improvement. The easiest and best way to understand a process is to draw a picture of it – that's basically what flowcharting is. It presents information that allows management to analyse the way a service is being delivered. As the format, in terms of the picture, becomes more elaborate, reference is made to a service blueprint or service map (see Chapter 3).

5.8.2   Cause and effect diagram (What causes the problem?)

'Quality begins with education and ends with education.' These words, attributed to the late Kaoru Ishikawa, sum up a principal philosophy of quality. To improve processes, one must continuously strive to obtain more information about those processes and their output. One unique and valuable tool for accomplishing this goal is the cause and effect diagram. The diagram's purpose is to relate cause and effect. It is also known as the Ishikawa diagram, or the fishbone diagram because it resembles the skeleton of a fish.

   All that is required is the identification of an effect and then to work backwards in order to attribute the cause(s). The diagram (see Figure 5.4) helps managers to focus on a specific problem faced in a quality management context, e.g. late deliveries, and to identify the factors contributing to that problem. The versatility of the cause and effect diagram means the words in each box will vary depending on the situation. Consider the case of a service/distribution business that has determined five areas as the main potential causes of dissatisfied customers (Figure 5.5).

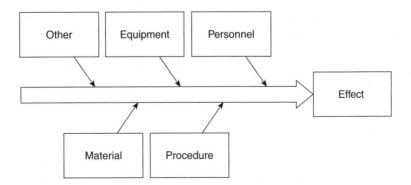

Figure 5.4 Cause and effect diagram

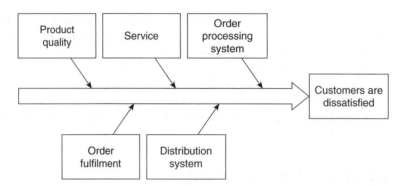

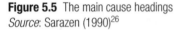

Figure 5.5 The main cause headings
Source: Sarazen (1990)[26]

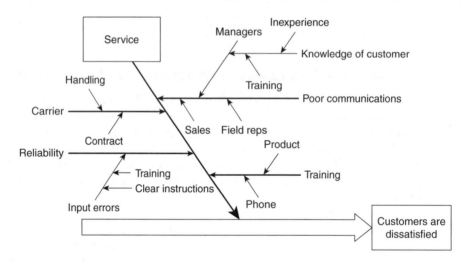

Figure 5.6 A detailed look at the main cause
Source: Sarazen (1990)[26]

After these areas were determined, the next step was to brainstorm all the possible causes of problems in each of the major cause categories. These ideas are captured and applied to the diagram as subcauses. Figure 5.6 shows the completed portion of the diagram for one of the main causes: service. The company identified reliability issues, carrier issues (e.g. a trucking company), poor communications, and lack of, or poor training.

The next level of causes was identified by asking the question 'What would cause a problem in these areas?'. In the case of the poor communications, the company focused on functions and jobs – sales people, field representatives and managers – as potential causes. It can be seen that lack of knowledge of the customer can cause managers to communicate poorly. Subsequently it can be seen that inexperience and training can be two key contributors to a manager's lack of customer knowledge. Thus, there are six levels of causes in this example.

Table 5.1 Causal factors with a Pareto distribution

Causes	% contribution to failure in meeting target response times
(a) Giving order to kitchen	3
(b) Shortage of drivers	8
(c) Slowness in preparation of pizzas	3
(d) Drivers unfamiliar with faster route	30
(e) Breakdowns in delivery vehicles	15
(f) Traffic congestion	25
(g) Weather conditions	6
(h) Slowness in boxing cooked pizzas	3
(i) Extent of catchment area	7
	100

Three points should be borne in mind in respect of a cause and effect analysis:

- Where difficulties are experienced in creating a diagram for a specific situation, use should be made of the generic diagram (Figure 5.4).
- All employees with an involvement in the problem should be party to identifying the causes and suggesting solutions.
- The objective of cause and effect analysis is to determine which of the causal factors are major influences on results. To illustrate this we need a Pareto chart.

5.8.3   Pareto chart (What are the big problems?)

The Pareto principle is named after Vilfredo Pareto, a nineteenth-century Italian economist who found that a large share of the wealth was owned by relatively few people. It came to be known as the 80/20 rule which suggests that 80% of any problem or phenomenon is often due to 20% of the possible causes. Therefore, around 80% of most companies' sales are produced by about 20% of its products. Similarly, in a service context, 80% of service failures may be accounted for by only 20% of causes.

A study done for a pizza parlour experiencing problems with its home delivery service revealed possible causes of failure and their contribution in not meeting target response times (Table 5.1). A Pareto chart (Figure 5.7) can be constructed from the survey. It shows three factors (d, f and e) which together account for 70% of the causes.

5.8.4   Histogram (What does the variation look like?)

A histogram can also be used to illustrate variations. It is a distribution showing the frequency of occurrences between the high and low range of data. Figure 5.8 shows two histograms illustrating times taken by two organizations to perform a particular service. From the histograms it is clear that the variation of company A's service process is smaller than B's. The question is why the quality of A's service performance should be much better than B's. Possible reasons are better equipment, better trained employees and more effective procedures.

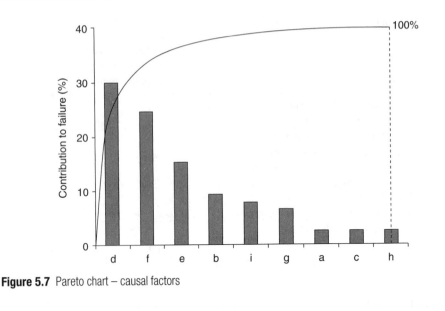

Figure 5.7 Pareto chart – causal factors

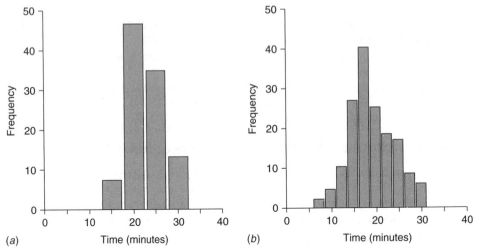

Figure 5.8 Time taken by two organizations to perform a particular service

5.8.5   Control charts (Which variations are to be controlled and how?)

Variation is a fact of life. In our personal life we are often surprised when the mail does not arrive at the same time every day, complain when the weather forecast is inaccurate and become frustrated when our train does not leave or arrive on time.

All processes vary to some extent, e.g. a machine will never give precisely the same result every time it is used: materials will vary a little, operator performance will differ marginally, the environment in which the process takes place will vary. Variations which derive from these common causes can never be entirely eliminated (although they can be reduced). Common cause variation occurs in processes that are essentially stable. A stable process such as order processing time displays a random pattern and its future behaviour is predictable.

How much common cause variation occurs will depend on the circumstances. However, the question that needs to be asked is 'Is this variation in the process performance acceptable'? The answer will lead to the determination of what is often called a tolerance or specification range. In other words, an upper and lower control limit will be set within which performance will be allowed to vary and be deemed acceptable. The control chart displays this performance over time against specific quality criteria.

Not all variation in processes is the result of common causes. Something may be wrong with the process which is assignable to a particular and 'preventable' cause. The causes of such variation are called assignable or special causes. It will appear on the control chart as a point outside the upper or lower control limits. Whereas common cause variation focuses on improving the system, special cause variation requires a problem-solving approach of finding the cause and developing solutions to prevent its recurrence.

The upper and lower limits on the control chart usually represent three types of value:

- **Measurable data**, e.g. time spent in a service or time spent waiting for service, order processing time
- **Percentages**, e.g. the percentage of orders delivered late or the percentage of customers complaining
- **Counting data**, e.g. the number of mistakes in an order, number of complaints.

Each of the above types of value is represented on the vertical Y axis and the horizontal X axis represents a period of time, e.g. a week, month, year. An example of a control chart for stability testing of customer complaints is shown in Figure 5.9.

The figure indicates that the process is out of control. First, the number of complaints for week 20 is outside the upper control limit. Second, eight observations beginning in week 17 on the top side of the central time indicate a statistically significant non-random shift in the process average. The control chart upper and lower limits are established by calculating above and below the grand mean.

Determining whether or not the process is stable is an essential step in the quality improvement process. Attempting to correct an unstable process provides no assurance that corrective action will improve the process because of the possible counter-effects of the variables causing the process to be out of control. In the control chart of Figure 5.9 it was noted that the customer complaint process was out of control. The control chart in Figure 5.10 covers the six-month period after correction of the causes of the out-of-control process.

The process is now under control, and the average number of complaints has been reduced from 11.3 (Figure 5.9) to 5.7 (Figure 5.10). Also note that the variability of the process has been reduced. This can be seen by comparing the upper and lower control limits for Figures 5.9 and 5.10. Before control of the process was accomplished the span between the upper and lower limits was 21; after control the span was reduced to 13.

It should be remembered that careful consideration needs to be given to the presentation of key performance indicators to ensure that the results are easily interpreted and not misleading. For example, look once again at Figure 5.9. Although it

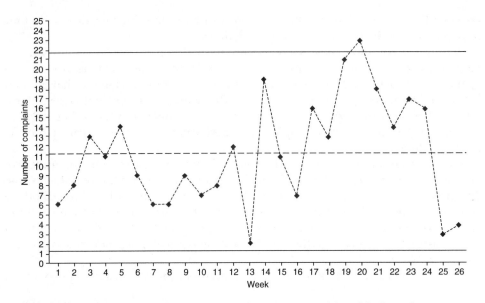

Figure 5.9 Testing for stability: statistical control chart for customer complaints, July–December
Source: Cravens (1988)[27]

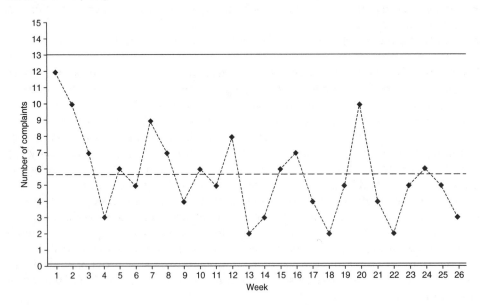

Figure 5.10 Customer complaints: process under control, January–June
Source: Cravens (1988)[27]

appears that the number of complaints has increased over the period analysed, the information must be taken in context. The graph would have been a much more useful performance indicator if the number of complaints had been presented in relation to the number of customers taken on over the period. Without an understanding of the customer numbers, we are not in a position to determine whether the rise in customer complaints, as represented in the graph, is a worrying trend or not.

Figure 5.11 Scatter diagram: strong positive relationship

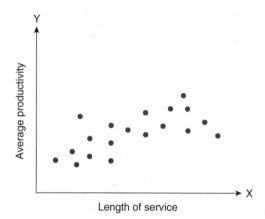

Figure 5.12 Scatter diagram: weak relationship

5.8.6   Scatter diagrams (What are the relationships between factors?)

In many situations we may come across two sets of data which seem related. These relationships can be non-mathematically evaluated by using a scatter diagram, the *Y* axis is usually reserved for the characteristic we would like to predict (the dependent variable) and the *X* axis for the variable that we are using to make the prediction (the independent variable). Figure 5.11 does seem to show a clear relationship between number of service failures and number of complaints.

It could be argued that one would reasonably expect there to be quite a strong relationship between number of service failures and number of complaints, though not always so. Figure 5.12 shows a situation where evidence of a strong relationship is not quite so clear-cut.

Factors other than length of service may be better predictors of productivity levels, e.g. willingness to work, financial incentives, competency, etc.

5.8.7   Tallies or check sheets (How often does it occur?)

A tally or check sheet is perhaps the most commonly used method for collecting and compiling data. A computer will normally do the counting.

Method

1 List the possible categories.
2 Work through the column of data systematically, putting a stroke next to the appropriate category.
3 Every fifth mark should go diagonally across the previous four, as on a gate, to make counting the marks at the end very easy.

Table 5.2 illustrates a tally or check sheet recording the incidence of complaints by subject.

Table 5.2 Tally/check sheet

Subject of complaint	Number of complaints	Total
Delivery times	卌 卌 卌 卌 II	22
Installation	卌 卌 I	11
Company personnel	卌 III	8
Product	卌 卌	10
		51

Once you have your tally, look at it to see what it tells you. Consider:

- Whether the counts are what you expected
- Which are the most frequently occurring categories
- Whether looking at percentages would be a good idea (see Table 5.3).

Table 5.3 Percentage tallies

Subject of complaint	Count	Percentage
Delivery times	22	43 (22/51 × 100)
Installation	11	21
Company personnel	8	16
Product	10	20
	51	100

5.9   Quality programmes

Any discussion of quality is incomplete without reference to some formal programmes in operation, namely Total Quality Management (TQM), ISO 9000 and the European Foundation for Quality Management (EFQM). Each of these merits attention not only for its contribution to the delivery of quality but equally for its relevance in service organization.

5.9.1   Total Quality Management (TQM)

Most versions of the TQM philosophy stress three core principles, as follows:[28]

- All employees can contribute effectively to improvement. To achieve this will require training, access to information and teamwork.
- The ultimate goal of the organization's efforts is customer satisfaction. Customer interests are expected to be put first in all situations, even (in some views, especially) where these appear to conflict with other business opportunities.
- Process is at least as important as results. In this view it is the manager's responsibility to behave as a student does; he/she cannot simply achieve the right answer (result) but must demonstrate the supporting data and 'calculations' (process). As process, under TQM, also stresses teamwork, consensus must be achieved.

Whilst there may be acceptance of these principles up to a point, resistance is grounded in three opposing principles:

- Management knows better (than for example, the front-line employees)
- The customer is not always right (unreasonable, impractical, unprofitable demands)
- Not everything is a process (subjecting all aspects of work to a process excludes and frustrates the emergence of insight, instinct, talent, creativity and gut feeling crucial for innovation and improvement).

In a case study within the financial services sector[29] it was shown that often management does not understand TQM and that by 'attempting to control costs and employees while espousing the importance of the customer and the need for a trust-based culture', demonstrates inconsistent approaches. Whilst typical pitfalls (inadequate leadership, fear and resistance to change, inadequate information and its analysis, poor communication etc.) are cited[30] for management's negative impact on TQM the study mentioned above invites us to address more fundamental issues of power and managerial behaviour. Furthermore, 'for TQM to address quality more fully, greater consideration must be attached to both customers and staff, since an approach which is concerned with cost cutting and procedures is unlikely to address these issues'.[31]

5.9.2   The European Foundation for Quality Management (EFQM)

As measurement and feedback is a key element of TQM, assessment of progress in quality improvement can be made against the criteria of the EFQM. The European Quality Award (EQA) was launched in 1991 and there are several national (including British and Irish) and regional awards. Although the original purpose (expressed in the UK Quality Award) was that of promoting the concepts and techniques of TQM, in recent times there has been a drive to change from quality and TQM to excellence, which in the view of one observer is 'just a play on words'.[32] The EFQM Excellence Model (Figure 5.13) is designed for application in any organization.

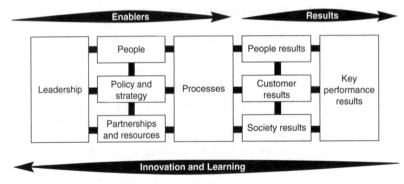

Figure 5.13 The EFQM Excellence Model

The model is structured around nine criteria that organizations can use to assess and measure performance. The criteria are split into two groups, 'enablers' and 'results'. What the organization achieves (the results) is dependent on how well the organization manages its processes and people (the enablers). The feedback arrow indicates the importance of sharing knowledge and encouraging learning and innovation.

5.9.3 ISO 9001: 2000

ISO is the International Organization for Standardization, established in 1947 to develop common international standards in many areas. Basically, the objective is to give buyers an assurance that the quality of products and/or services meets their requirements. Policies and procedures are set out in a manual, a form of quality assurance. Along with the EFQM, ISO has been viewed by critics as reducing a profound idea (quality) to a set of box-ticking exercises that fails to recognize the realities of organizational culture.

5.10 Cost of quality

The cost of quality can be defined as the total of all resources spent by an organization to assure that quality standards are met on a consistent basis.[33] Quality costs are grouped into two broad categories with two types in each:

1 **Costs of maintaining good quality**
   (a) *Prevention costs* – the costs incurred to prevent errors from occurring. These are said to include the time and effort spent in recruiting, training and reviewing performance of employees along with determining customer requirements and establishing quality standards. Of the types of quality costs, prevention costs are viewed as of central importance but they have been regarded as double counting because prevention is a normal aspect of any manager's responsibility.
   (b) *Appraisal costs* – costs incurred from inspection, testing and auditing aimed at identifying non-conforming aspects before a service or product is delivered.
   Prevention and appraisal costs are incurred because poor quality of conformance can exist.

2 **Costs of poor service quality**

   (a) *Internal failures* – these are errors and defects that are caught before they reach the customer.

   (b) *External failures* – these are problems identified by the customer and the cost may include any refunds or additional services provided at no cost to the customer.

Failure costs are incurred because poor quality of conformance does exist.

Cost of quality should be continuously monitored through making use of, amongst other things, the tools of quality. Above all organizations should perform a cost of quality audit, which is designed to identify:[34]

- The circumstances, events, activities and problems that occur within the organization that fall within the categories already mentioned.
- The frequency with which these circumstances occur.
- The resources (time, materials, money) devoted to these circumstances and events.

Of course, it has to be remembered that cost of quality was originally developed for a manufacturing context. Transferring it to the service sector is not devoid of problems. However, there are still many aspects of service that can be subjected to a cost of quality analysis. This is particularly true the more standardized the service is as the operating conditions are similar to a manufacturing facility.

As to what can be done, the following example illustrates cost of quality in a service environment. A large hotel where the average rate is £80 and length of stay is two days undertook a cost and performance review of its front desk operation. Specifically, the focus was on transactions at the front desk, primarily registration and checking-out procedures. The information was obtained from employee observations. A range of errors was considered in terms of their occurrence and cost (Table 5.4).

Table 5.4 Cost of quality calculation

Error type	Hourly wage	Time spent fixing error (hours)	Error occurrence per day	Cost over the year (£) (365 days)
1 When guests check out extra charges on the bill are incorrect	£6	0.085	70	13 030
2 Specific information about a reservation has not been entered into the computer	£6	0.15	25	8 212
3 The reservation for an arriving guest cannot be found in the computer	£6	0.12	15	3 942
4 Guest registers and is not given the requested room type	£6	0.2	3	1 314
5 The guest is checking out and the receptionist cannot find the registration card	£6	0.165	3	1 084

Source: Adapted from Luchars and Hinkin (1966)[35]

The table reveals that errors 4 and 5 individually are relatively minor. Errors 1 and 2 together comprise nearly 80% of the year's cost and therefore merit close attention. A Pareto chart (Figure 5.14) can be constructed from the data. These errors are largely external failures as they have not been caught before they reach the customer. External failures can be reworked, as is the case in manufacturing industry. For example, a customer can demand warranty repairs on a faulty car. Services are not so amenable to rework as evidenced by a faulty ATM or a bad haircut. Where rework is not possible, some form of compensation may be given.

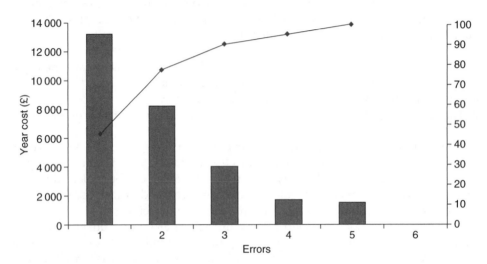

Figure 5.14 Pareto chart: error/cost analysis

The appraisal costs of inspection and testing are of fundamental importance in manufacturing. Services can equally be inspected and tested prior to consumption. However, the service as experienced by the customer cannot obviously be pre-tested or inspected. Customers, themselves, may actually share responsibility for the quality and hence the cost of service. Where a service is one of high contact, customer involvement and uncertainty can impact on cost of quality.

Summary

Customers desire a quality service but few can agree on a definition. A number of approaches have been developed based around the manufacture of products. How far do these address the particular characteristics of services? Arguably, increasing use of the word 'standard' has come to signify quality or levels of performance. Unfortunately some aspects of service as expressed in SERVQUAL are more easily measured than others. The Gaps Model of Service Quality raises further concerns. Disagreement exists over who is to define quality and how it is to be implemented.

Given the discrepancies or differences of opinion between management, employees and customers, it is ironic that monitoring the delivery and acceptability of service quality is now regarded as very important and a range of tools is available for that purpose. Furthermore, organizations are increasingly concerned about the cost of delivery service quality. Finally, the importance attached to the delivery of quality in all kinds of organizations and activities has given rise to a number of awards for quality assurance. These remain controversial as they are deemed to be only an indication of quality on paper (the systems are in place) and not of the reality of quality in practice.

References

1 Reeves, C A and Bednar, D A (1994) 'Defining quality: alternatives and implications', *Academy of Management Review*, **19** (3), 419–445.
2 Garvin, D A (1984) 'What does "product quality" really mean?', *Sloan Management Review*, Fall, 25–43.
3 Abbott, L (1955) *Quality and Competition*. New York: Columbia University Press, pp. 126–127.
4 Ibid, p. 129.
5 Edwards, C D (1968) 'The meaning of quality', *Quality Progress*, October, pp. 36–39.
6 Garvin, 'What does product quality really mean?'
7 Parasuraman, A, Zeithaml, V A and Berry, L L (1985) 'A conceptual model of service quality and its implications for future research', *Journal of Marketing*, **49** (4), 41–50.
8 Rosander, A C (1989) *The Quest for Quality in Services*. Quality Press, American Society for Quality Control, Milwaukee, Wisconsin, p. 69.
9 Monroe, K B (2003) *Pricing: Making Profitable Decisions*. New York: McGraw-Hill, ch.7.
10 Feigenbaum, A V (1951) *Quality Control: Principles, Practice and Administration*. New York: McGraw-Hill, p. 1.
11 Parasuraman *et al.*, 'Conceptual model of service quality.'
12 Parasuraman, A, Zeithaml, V A and Berry, L L (1988) 'SERVQUAL: a multiple item scale for measuring customer perceptions of service quality', *Journal of Retailing*, **64** (1), 12–37.
13 Liswood, L (1989) *Serving Them Right*. New York: Harper and Row.
14 Martin, W B (1986) 'Defining what quality service is for you', *Cornell HRA Quarterly*, February, 32–38.
15 Smith, A (1995) 'Measuring service quality: is SERVQUAL now redundant!', *Journal of Marketing Management*, **11**, 257–276.
16 Philip, G and Hazlett, S-A (1997) 'The measurement of service quality: a new P-C-P attributes model', *International Journal of Quality and Reliability Management*, **14** (3), 260–286.
17 Ibid.
18 Buttle, F (1996) 'SERVQUAL: review, critique, research agenda', *European Journal of Marketing*, **30** (1), 8–32.
19 Teas, K R (1993) 'Consumer expectations and the measurement of perceived service quality', *Journal of Professional Services Marketing*, **8** (2), 33–53.
20 Iacobucci, D, Grayson, K A and Omstrom, A L (1994) 'The calculus of service quality and customer satisfaction: theoretical and empirical differentiation and integration', in Swartz, T A, Bowen, D E and Brown, S W (eds), *Advances in Services Marketing and Management*, Vol. 3. Greenwich, CT: JAI Press, pp. 1–68.
21 Buttle, op. cit.
22 Iacobucci *et al.*, 'Calculus of service quality.'
23 Cronin, J J and Taylor, S A (1992) 'Measuring service quality: a re-examination and extension', *Journal of Marketing*, **56** (July), 55–68.
24 Herbert, D, Curry, A and Angel, L (2003) 'Use of quality tools and techniques in services', *Service Industries Journal*, **23** (4), 61–80.
25 Ibid.

26   Sarazen, T S (1990) *Quality Progress*, July.
27   Cravens, D W (1988) 'Marketing's role in product and service quality', *Industrial Marketing Management*, p. 17.
28   Feinberg, S (1998) 'Why managers oppose TQM', *The TQM Magazine*, **10** (1), 16–19.
29   Knights, D and McCabe, D (1997) ' "How would you measure something like that?" Quality in a retail bank', *Journal of Management Studies*, **34** (3), 371–388.
30   Dale, B G (2003) *Managing Quality*. Oxford: Blackwell, p. 128.
31   Knights and McCabe, op. cit.
32   Dale, op. cit, p. 476.
33   Bohan, G P and Horney, W F (1991) 'Pinpointing the real cost of quality in a service company', *National Productivity Review*, Summer.
34   Ibid.
35   Luchars, J Y and Hinkin, T R (1996) 'The service-quality audit', *Cornell HRA Quarterly*, February, 34–41.

6

The service encounter

Introduction

Whether at arm's length or face to face, interaction between customer and organization lies at the heart of service delivery. The interaction may take many forms, from a brief encounter with a directions sign to a protracted encounter with a service employee. Whatever the nature and type of contact, each represents a moment of truth for the customer. This chapter will focus on customers engaging with organizations through the medium of service personnel. How we should portray that encounter and how it should be understood will underline the discussion. Both customer and employee perspectives will be addressed together with how service organizations seek to manage the process. Several concepts/ techniques are introduced that are of fundamental importance for understanding the service encounter.

6.1   The essence of an encounter

The concept of an encounter means coming into contact with someone or something. Such contact may occur by chance or unexpectedly, e.g. running into an old friend. That will invariably be an amicable encounter. Equally more routine encounters, say with a car mechanic or a hotel receptionist, may be particularly pleasant. On the other hand, encounters in general with a work colleague, an organization or simply a 'friend' may be much less enjoyable. Additionally, an encounter can be had with an inanimate object in the form of a sign, vending machine, website, car wash. That also can be pleasing or frustrating. Clearly providers of services seek to make any encounter with a customer pleasurable. To achieve this, service organizations will resort to using a variety of tools/techniques. Although there is a growing tendency for encounters to be with 'things' most services still retain, in part or in total, face-to-face contact with the customer. For this reason, the tools and techniques cited earlier become ever-more important, and for some, the subject of controversy. Just how well or how badly customers feel they were treated comes to particular prominence in the face-to-face encounter. In particular it is a type of contact where behaviour, attitudes, emotions and body language are visible from both sides (service provider and customer). That, in itself, represents a challenge for service organizations to manage.

6.2   Service encounter as theatre

For addressing or managing that challenge, some[1] have drawn on the writings of Erving Goffman, particularly his book *The Presentation of Self in Everyday Life*,[2] and portrayed the service encounter as equivalent to a performance in the theatre. In both cases, service encounter and theatre, the aim quite simply is to create a favourable impression before an audience. On the surface the service encounter bears all the hallmarks of a theatrical production:

- **Front stage** – the setting comprising scenery, props, atmosphere. More specifically, décor, lighting, use of space, seating comfort, furnishings, equipment, noise level. (the physical evidence)
- **Front line** – service employees in the role of actors dressed accordingly and with the help of a script deploy the necessary skills and attributes to impress an audience.
- **Audience** – customers with expectations for and perceptions of the performance.
- **Process** – the manner in which the service is delivered and the actions that shape the customers' experience (the performance).

The main problems with the theatre as a framework for discussing and understanding the service encounter is that the customer (in the audience) does not interact or engage directly with those providing the performance. It is essentially a passive encounter with customer response coming at the end of the performance, coupled sometimes with laughter or applause in between. Furthermore, there is little likelihood of other members of the audience affecting the enjoyment or otherwise of the service. Such conditions are not normally characteristic of service encounters. So in considering the following elements of a theatrical nature it is important to bear in mind the impact of customer involvement.[3]

Two particular tools/techniques that emanate from a theatre perspective are however deployed by organizations in the service encounter. They are scripts and emotional labour and each is inextricably bound up with the other.

6.3   Scripts

Just as in the theatre, scripts are widely in evidence in service encounters. A script is regarded as 'a predetermined, stereotyped sequence of actions that defines a well-known situation'.[4] People experience hundreds of scripts as part of everyday life, e.g. travelling by air, visiting a dentist, eating in a restaurant, attending a tutorial, telephoning a call centre. In these and many other service situations knowledge of the script helps us understand and become involved in the sequence of events as well as how we and others are expected to behave. Basically, we are acquiring knowledge of what is supposed to happen or the rules of engagement. One of the best-known examples and one to which most people can relate is the restaurant script (see Table 6.1), developed by Schank and Abelson (1977).[5] As with other scripts, it has standard roles to be played, standard props or objects, ordinary conditions for entering upon the activity, a standard sequence of scenes or actions and some normal results from performing the activity successfully.

It appears that the script is a highly structured sequence of actions and events and in many cases that will be so. However, any script will be subject to deviations or violations. Consider the case of a restaurant where the following might occur:[6]

- An **error** – the wrongful completion of a given event (you've been served scallops instead of shrimp).
- An **obstacle** – something that removes a precondition for a given event (the waiter can't give you a menu because there aren't any or you can't read the menu as it is in French).
- A **distraction** – an event of sufficient importance to intercept script action (the arrival of a long-lost friend, a fire in the restaurant, waiter spilling soup over the customer).
- **Free behaviours** – those activities that may plausibly and commonly intermix with the ongoing script (but not e.g. throwing Frisbees in a restaurant).

How several of these events or incidents are handled will determine whether the script can get back on track and thus proceed. The impact on customer satisfaction with the service encounter is a further consideration.

6.3.1   Script generation

As already intimated, the importance of customer scripts is that they represent customer's knowledge of what to do for effective participation in the service delivery process. With this in mind, people can be asked to describe what goes on in detail during a variety of service situations. From these descriptions an understanding can be obtained of the level of agreement there is between consumer and organizations on the nature of the characters, props, actions and the order in which they occur. One study[7] of particular interest asked a group of undergraduates to write scripts about common activities. They were given the following instructions (the lecture script will serve as an example):

> Write a list of actions describing what people generally do when they go to a lecture in a course. We are interested in the common actions of a routine lecture stereotype. Start the list with arriving at the lecture and end it with leaving after the lecture. Include about 20 actions or events and put them in order in which they would occur.

Results from the study can be seen in Table 6.2. Not surprisingly, given the routine nature of the activities, a considerable measure of agreement was found over the way subjects described events. Nevertheless, for the proper conduct and management of the service encounter both customers and service provider need to agree on the essentials of the script. What is intriguing, given the year of the study and nature of respondents, is whether such agreement would be reached today.

Table 6.1 Theoretical restaurant script

Name:	Restaurant		
Props:	Tables	Roles:	Customer
	Menu		Waitress
	Food		Cook
	Bill		Cashier
	Money		Owner
	Tip		
Entry Conditions:	Customer has money	Results:	Customer has less money
			Owner has more money
			Customer is not hungry
			Customer is satisfied/ dissatisfied

Scene 1:	Entering
	Customer enters restaurant
	Customer looks for table
	Customer decides where to sit
	Customer goes to table
	Customer sits down

Scene 2:	Ordering
	Customer picks up menu
	Customer looks at menu
	Customer decides on food
	Customer signals waitress
	Waitress comes to table
	Customer orders food
	Waitress goes to cook
	Waitress gives food order to cook
	Cook prepares food

Scene 3:	Eating
	Cook gives food to waitress
	Waitress brings food to customer
	Customer eats food

Scene 4:	Exiting
	Waitress writes bill
	Waitress goes over to customer
	Waitress gives bill to customer
	Customer gives tip to waitress
	Customer goes to cashier
	Customer gives money to cashier
	Customer leaves restaurant

Source: Adapted from Schank and Abelson (1977)[4]

Table 6.2 Empirical script norms at three agreement levels

Going to a restaurant	Attending a lecture	Getting up	Grocery shopping	Visiting a doctor
Open door	ENTER ROOM	*Wake up*	ENTER STORE	*Enter office*
Enter	*Look for friends*	Turn off alarm	GET CART	CHECK IN WITH RECEPTIONIST
Give reservation name	FIND SEAT	Lie in bed	Take out list	SIT DOWN
Wait to be seated	SIT DOWN	Stretch	Look at list	Wait
Go to table	Settle belongings	GET UP	Go to first aisle	Look at other people
BE SEATED	TAKE OUT NOTEBOOK	Make bed	*Go up and down aisles*	READ MAGAZINE
Order drinks	*Look at other students*	*Go to bathroom*	PICK OUT ITEMS	*Name called*
Put napkins on lap	*Talk*	Use toilet	Compare prices	Follow nurse
LOOK AT MENU	Look at professor	*Take shower*	Put items in cart	*Enter exam room*
Discuss menu	LISTEN TO PROFESSOR	*Wash face*	Get meat	Undress
ORDER MEAL	TAKE NOTES	Shave	Look for items forgotten	*Sit on table*
Talk	CHECK TIME	DRESS	Talk to other shoppers	Talk to nurse
Drink water	Ask questions	Go to kitchen	Go to checkout counters	NURSE TESTS
Eat salad or soup	Change position in seat	Fix breakfast	*Find fastest line*	Wait
Meal arrives	Daydream	EAT BREAKFAST	WAIT IN LINE	Doctor enters
EAT FOOD	Look at other students	BRUSH TEETH	*Put food on belt*	Doctor greets
Finish meal	Take more notes	Read paper	Read magazines	Talk to doctor about problem
Order dessert	*Close notebook*	*Comb hair*	WATCH CASHIER RING UP	Doctor asks questions
Eat dessert	*Gather belongings*	*Get books*	PAY CASHIER	DOCTOR EXAMINES
Ask for bill	Stand up	Look in mirror	*Watch bag boy*	Get dressed
Bill arrives	Talk	Get coat	Cart bags out	Get medicine
PAY BILL	LEAVE	LEAVE HOUSE	Load bags into car	Make another appointment
Leave tip			LEAVE STORE	LEAVE OFFICE
Get coats				
LEAVE				

Items in all capital letters were mentioned by the most subjects, items in italics by fewer subjects, and items in text type by the fewest subjects
Source: Bower, Black and Turner (1979)[7]

6.3.2 The 'value' of the script

The following advantages and problems with regard to the use of a script are worthy of consideration.

1 **Advantages**
   - By standardizing the behaviour and actions of service employees (and customers) scripting could be said to reduce any anxieties that could arise during the service encounter.
   - The script could act as a shield against the insults and indignities employees are asked to accept from the public[8] ('Don't take it personally').
   - Job definition and responsibilities are clearly specified, lessening the prospect of role ambiguity and role conflict ('I'm sorry but our rules clearly say ...').
   - Management is able to exert a degree of control over the service encounter and this can be achieved with a minimum of direct supervision.
2 **Problems**
   - The script can be perceived as mechanical, phoney, contrived, manufactured. It simply is not real. Having to be nice at all times has been portrayed as 'a synthetic, feigned, and ultimately insincere form of friendliness'[9].
   - It can stifle flexibility.
   - Customers, consequently, can become frustrated as they seek solutions for their particular circumstances.
   - Similarly, employees may feel thwarted by a script in addressing customers' problems.
   - While seemingly protecting their dignity, employees may also feel the script undermines their sense of self worth and identity.

6.4 Emotional labour

The concept (and reality) of emotional labour gained prominence with a book by Hochschild (1983) entitled *The Managed Heart: Commercialization of Human Feeling*. It was defined thus: 'This labor requires one to induce or suppress feeling in order to sustain the outward countenance that produces the proper state of mind in others – in this case, the sense of being cared for in a convivial place.'[10] In effect, emotions of service personnel in contact with customers are encouraged and controlled by the organization. Any feelings (an employee may have) that the organization finds unhelpful are to be suppressed, disregarded or reinterpreted.[11]

Emotional labour has three potential components, of which at least one of the first two must exist along with the third for it to be performed.[12]

- It involves the faking of emotion that is not really felt.
- And/or the hiding of emotion that is felt.
- This emotion management is performed in order to meet social expectation – usually as part of the job role.

Just what constitutes an emotion has been the subject of much discussion. Summaries of primary or fundamental emotions have been identified[13,14] (fear, anger, enjoyment, sadness, acceptance, disgust, expectancy, surprise, interest, contempt, shame, shyness and guilt). Drawing on a much longer list of emotions,[15] one study sought to examine consumers' emotional experiences across four quite distinct services.[16] Findings from this study suggest that consumers feel and express a range of emotions both positive and negative. Although not part of the study, employees in those services (theatres, dry-cleaning, garages, health/sports centres) would not be free, in accordance with emotional labour, to express any negative emotions regardless of how they feel within.

6.4.1   Which jobs involve substantial amounts of emotional labour and how?

Hochschild asserts early in her book *The Managed Heart* that most of us have jobs that involve some way or another the requirements of emotional labour:[17]

- The waitress or waiter who creates an 'atmosphere of pleasant dining'.
- The tour guide or hotel receptionist who makes us feel welcome.
- The social worker whose look of solicitous concern makes the client feel cared for.
- The debt collector who inspires fear.
- The funeral director who makes the bereaved feel understood.

Near the end of her book she appears to review the position cited above by suggesting that 'among those in the professions, service work and clerical work, only selected jobs seem to involve substantial amounts of emotional labour'. (See Table 6.3 for Hochschild's original listings of jobs that involve substantial amounts of emotional labour.) Whilst an update of Hochschild's listings does not appear to have been compiled, the practice of emotional labour through the medium of 'fast-food server' script remains very much in evidence. Practised by, among others, fast-food servers, shop assistants, waiters/waitresses, receptionists and cabin crew, it is characterized by wide smiles, phrases learned by rote, clichéd greetings, long-winded introductions and an inability to cope with unusual requests.[18]

Table 6.3 Occupations that involve substantial amounts of emotional labour

• Lawyers and judges	• College and university teachers
• Librarians	• Teachers, except college and universities
• Personnel and labour relations	• Vocational and educational counsellors
• Dental hygienists	• Public relations and publicity writers
• Therapy assistants	• Radio and television announcers
• Clergymen and social workers	• Physicians, dentists and related personnel
• Social and recreation workers	

Source: Hochschild (1983)[19]

Whereas the 'fast-food server' approach is regarded as common in service industries, two other approaches are worthy of note in relation to emotional labour. The 'lawyer' script,[20] as the name implies, is reserved for professional service jobs. Here, warm and friendly emotional displays are not appropriate. By masking their emotions (hiding what may be felt) the professional asserts his/her professionalism. Health service employees (doctors, nurses, physiotherapists, administrators) manage their emotions with a view to remaining cool and objective. Medical students learn the art of 'detached concern',[21] where they convey concern but remain sufficiently aloof to retain their impartiality. Lawyers learn to act aggressively in court on behalf of their clients without having or showing confused and inconsistent feelings about the actual guilt of their client.[22]

Where followers of the 'lawyer' script need only hide their feelings, those operating under the 'fast-food server' are invariably required to hide what they feel (anger, irritation) and fake what they do not feel (enthusiasm, polite demeanour).

Furthermore, the professionals in the 'lawyer' script usually supervise their own emotional labour. Contrast that with the fast-food server whose emotions are dictated from above by management. The third script has been termed the 'debt collector'[23] and depicted as 'Have a rotten day'. It is stated as being characteristic of particular services (debt collectors, bouncers, security personnel) where the aim is one of discouraging certain attitudes and behaviours, e.g. unruly conduct, non-compliance with demands. Through the display of emotions such as anger, irritation or disapproval (by the service organizations) the consequent anxiety experienced (by the targets of these displays) will result in compliance. That, in theory, is how such rarely mentioned service encounters are deemed to work. Whereas, the 'Have a rotten day' is limited to a select number of services it may gather momentum and spread to other services. The following anecdote could be an experience that an unknown number of customers over a range of service situations may have felt or will feel in future:

> I needed a tax disc for my car and whenever I have to renew my disc, I have to travel twenty minutes in the car during the working day to my nearest main post office. Why I can't get the disc at my local post office, I don't know. Anyway, I went and queued for twenty minutes and finally reached the front desk. I produced all the documentation, only to be told, somewhat gleefully, that I had brought my insurance schedule instead of the certificate. I was pretty upset and fed up – I was late for work and would not be able to return. The counter staff's attitude was 'tough'. She just didn't even pretend to care. If I had any choice, I would not have returned to that post office.[24]

Unlike the fast-food server approach, the attitude/behaviour in the above anecdote is not liable to be enshrined in company policy or endorsed by management. As for why it occurs, two observations are worth making and they are interrelated. First, as you will read in Chapter 10 under 'Consumer Participation and Productivity', consumers of services vary in the extent to which they prepare properly for a forthcoming service encounter. In the renewal of a tax disc story the customer, for whatever reason, had failed to bring the correct documentation even though clear notification of what to bring is provided in advance. As is the case in this example, the customer is a direct contributor to the efficiency and the effectiveness of the service. Secondly, many services set rules and often deliver 'subject to certain conditions'.

Where rules and conditions must be enforced, failure to comply on the part of customers gives front-line employees a sense of control in the service encounter greater than usual. Such control might then give rise to the expression 'tough'. Whilst 'tough' implied an uncaring attitude in the post office story, it also conveys a sarcastic, if not triumphal swipe at the consumer by way of Too bad! Tough luck! Hard cheese! It may also serve to redress employee feelings of subordination in the service encounter. Whether or not this type of script ('debt collector') will become more prominent, it has been acknowledged that there are many workers whose jobs require them to flit from one script to another,[25] e.g. a team of nurses who were expected to present an emotionally flat demeanour ('lawyer' script) in the operating room, to be caring and friendly ('fast-food server' script) when talking to patients and their families and to let their real feelings of rage or disgust ('debt collector') out during breaks or informal meetings.[26]

The other party in the service encounter is, of course, the customer. How do they perceive emotional labour?[27] The key word in all of this is *sincerity*, which means honesty, trustfulness, straightforwardness, openness. In a service where things can go wrong, being honest and open about the reasons may not be in the interests of the organization. Even in the marketing of a service truth may be a casualty. Being sincere could be damaging and hurtful for the parties involved. Sincerity it would appear must be 'tempered by tact, courtesy and convention'.[28] By 'sugar-coating' relationships emotional labour is designed to appear sincere but perceived as insincere by customers, e.g. the fake smile. As one critic noted, 'human interactions that are mass-produced may strike consumers as dehumanising if the routinization is obvious, or manipulative if it is not'.[29] Emotional labour as we know is largely an expression of niceness, symbolized by the ' "Have a nice day" (Hand)'.

When confronted with the stark choice between fake niceness and downright rudeness, the niceties apparently have been found to invariably win.[30] Even when consumers are aware of it being faked, niceness is still preferred. However, the challenge for service organizations is whether that view can be sustained over a desire by consumers for feelings to be authentically felt and communicated.

6.5   The critical incident technique

Organizations need to know what customers expect from the service experience. In particular they need to study what goes on during the service encounter to see if it lives up to expectations. A method suited to achieving that objective is known as the critical incident technique. Critical incidents are events and behaviours that have been observed to lead to success or failure in accomplishing a specific task. It was developed by Flanagan (1954)[31] for identifying requirements for effective job performance. He described it as a procedure for gathering certain important facts concerning behaviour in defined situations. In his view critical incidents were defined as extreme behaviour, either outstandingly effective or ineffective with respect to attaining the general aims of an activity. In his 1954 paper he cites many studies and makes reference to situations that are clearly significant for services, particularly service employees, e.g. what are the critical requirements for dentists,[32] what does successful work as a nurse include and what do sales clerks do that makes them especially effective or ineffective?

Critical incidents in a service context have been widely studied (e.g. Bitner *et al.*, 1990;[33] Stauss, 1993;[34] Gilbert and Morris, 1995;[35] Hoffman *et al.*, 1995;[36] Chell and Pittaway, 1998;[37] Chung and Hoffman, 1998,[38] Chung-Herrera *et al.*, 2004;[39] Gremler,

2004[40]). A major attraction of this technique is that it allows the customer to identify and recall specific events and behaviours during the service encounter that were particularly satisfying or dissatisfying. Contrast this with the customer question-naire, where the organization specifies the areas on which it wants feedback. Whilst the critical incident method usually concentrates on customer/employee interactions it is important to remember that the technique has a wider reference. Customers can be given an opportunity to express their feelings towards any contacts they may have with a service, e.g. clarity of signage, accuracy and intelligibility of bills, com-fort of waiting areas, cleanliness of toilets etc. These and many others are known as 'moments of truth', giving rise to positive or negative evaluations.

Several methods can be used to collect critical incidents:

1 **Interview:** this may be conducted either face to face or by telephone. Two ques-tions may suffice:
   - Think of a time when you gained a particularly satisfying or dissatisfying impres-sion of the service at hotel X.
   - Please describe in detail the circumstances of the incident.
   Further questions may need to be asked:
   - Exactly what happened?
   - Where and when did the incident occur?
   - What exactly made you feel the incident was satisfying or dissatisfying?
   - How did you respond to the incident?
2 **Self-completion:** the above or similar points could be put together in a printed form for customers to complete and return (see Figure 6.1).
3 **Group interviews:** a group of people is brought together and then split into pairs. One person in the pair acts as the interviewer and elicits and records a service incident from the other person. The roles are then reversed. Participants continue until they run out of incidents or time. As for the number of incidents to be col-lected there are no strict rules. Around 100 incidents allows you to have confi-dence in moving to the next stage, categorization.

Critical Incident Report Form	
Where and when did the incident occur?	
Who and/or what was involved?	
Description of the incident?	
Critical points	
Was it satisfying or dissatisfying?	

Figure 6.1 Example of a Critical Incident Report Form

Once the incidents have been collected, the analysis begins. All the incidents will be grouped into categories. The naming of the categories will probably arise from the content of the incidents. Alternatively categories may be developed in advance with the danger that they may not reflect the data. An example of a category could be employee competence. In the study of dentists cited earlier the incidents were classified into four main aspects of the job: demonstrating technical proficiency, handling patient relationships, accepting professional responsibility and accepting personal responsibility. A major piece of research in the restaurant, hotel and airline industries identified categories of events and behaviours that underline critical service encounters from the customer's point of view. In all, 700 incidents were collected and analysed.[41] An update examined the employee's perspective of what underlies customer satisfaction.[42] This was a significant development in services as hitherto the main focus had been the customer. If the reasons for poor quality are to be understood, all the relevant parties to the encounter should be considered. Not only might they report different incidents but also incidents mentioned by more than one party might be interpreted differently. This could be particularly insightful when it comes to apportioning blame for dissatisfying encounters.

Bitner *et al.* in their 1994 research drew on a number of theories that might further our understanding. In the case of role and script theory there is likely to be greater agreement between the parties where these are clearly defined and the parties concerned know what to expect. For attribution theory dissimilarities in viewpoint may arise when service encounter participants have conflicting views of the underlying causes, that is when their attributions differ. Most clearly for the perceptions of service providers and customers is the self-serving attribution bias. This is the tendency for people to take credit for success (i.e. to give internal attribution for their successes, a self-enhancing bias) and deny responsibility for failure (i.e. to blame failure on external circumstances, a self-protecting bias). Given these biases employees are expected to blame the system or the customer for service failures, whereas the customer would be more likely to blame the system or the employee. The result would be different views of the causes of service dissatisfaction. In the opinion of Bitner, it is less clear that this bias would operate in the case of a service encounter success. Responses in a critical incident study however can shed enormous light on the performance of the entire service delivery system.

The use of the critical incident technique in services suggests further the inappropriateness of the theatre analogy. Negative, dissatisfactory experiences are as much a product of the service encounter as positive, satisfactory ones. Consumers expect only enjoyment from a theatrical performance. Further points are worthy of consideration:

- Much use of the argument favouring service as theatre rests on the assertion that the service a customer receives is essentially a performance. However, theatrical performances are carefully choreographed and managed, seamlessly delivered. Although services may set out to operate in like manner, they are subject to interruption when things go wrong. If the theatrical metaphor is to be retained, customers may describe some service performances as more akin to pantomime.
- Once the curtain is raised in the theatre, silence falls over the audience. The consumers in that audience are there to observe and appreciate the skills of the actors. In a typical service encounter customers may express appreciation but also, among

other things, cynicism and angst at what is on offer. What is missing in the theatrical metaphor is the potential for conflict between service provider and service recipient.

- Some advocates of the 'service is theatre' proposition observe that:

> To many people, the drama metaphor may carry the dangerous connotation of superficial 'just acting' behaviours. The 'have a nice day' phrase so dutifully mouthed by the employees of many service businesses is woefully insincere. It is imperative that the customer believe in the performance. If the public believes that a service business is presenting a 'false front' they may quickly take their patronage elsewhere. Service marketers should recognize the importance of honest actors and authentic performances.[43]

It is not clear whether in calling for more honesty and authenticity, the authors are arguing for services to be more or less like the theatre. Moreover, 'honest actors and authentic performances' appear to be contradictions. Acting is behaving in a way that is not genuine and performances, in a theatrical context, equally so. Acting is an illusion. Whereas the professional actor may only fool others (customers), the front-line service employee also fools him/herself. And that, according to Hochschild, can be particularly 'unsettling'.[44] Furthermore, the reference to customers taking their business elsewhere as a consequence of 'false fronts' is not borne out by the evidence, however limited.

- Finally, as Hochschild perceptively notes, 'acting (emotional labour) in a commercial setting, unlike acting in a dramatic context, makes one's face and one's feelings take on the properties of a resource. But it is not a resource to be used for the purposes of art, as in drama. It is a resource to be used to make money'.[45] It is thus a monetary exploitation of, in many cases, a low paid, low status employee. Contrast this with the skill and craft of the professional actor for whom personal fulfilment outweighs commercial exploitation.

6.6   Dysfunctional customers, deviant employees – an everyday occurrence in the service encounter?

The service encounter has been portrayed as a harmonious experience in which the service provider strives to meet customers' needs and expectations and they, in turn, depart largely satisfied. It is a portrayal that is still evident in practice, guided by the principle, 'The Customer is King'. But there is another reality emerging. It is one of customers 'acting in a thoughtless or abusive way, causing problems for the firm, its employees and other customers'.[46] Customers who act in this way have variously been described as jay customers,[47] problem customers,[48] deviant,[49] and aberrant.[50] Collectively, they are deemed to be dysfunctional customers who do not abide by the rules and regulations of an organization and generally accepted standards of behaviour. Worryingly there is evidence that the majority (and not the minority) of customers exhibit this type of behaviour.[51,52] Not surprisingly, those who engage in it have been branded 'Customers From Hell.'[53]

All of this appears to undermine the concept of customer sovereignty. The customer is not always right and frequently is seen to be wrong. However, we must exercise care. Whilst acknowledging the rise in verbal and physical abuse of employees across a range of service industries, we must also attend to the causes. Reporting in the media suggests a general erosion of civility in society. According to a survey by advertising agency Publicis,[54] people are less afraid of asserting themselves, with 92% agreeing we are more willing to say what we think. As Paul Edwards of Publicis notes, 'We are rejecting the British stiff upper lip in favour of more European behaviour – verbally and emotionally demonstrative, but most of all petulant. The report, entitled 'Petulance: "If you can't get even, get mad"' cites the roots of petulance:

- We don't seem to be told the truth anymore.
- We get 'spin' from politicians and companies, which enrages us.
- We work the longest hours in Europe so we are tired.
- We are faced with increasing rules and regulations (the 'nanny state').
- We interact more with machines.
- We have more money which gives us more confidence to speak out.

Echoing the findings from Publicis, Mintel's 2005 British lifestyles report[55] shows Britain harbouring a new breed of Briton – the rebellious consumer. Across both reports, banks, shopping and commuting by train come in for particular criticism.

Although there are people (who knows how many) who are predisposed (in terms of personality) to behaving aggressively, the growing trend of customer misbehaviour merits further explanation, not least for addressing the effects on service employees, namely feelings of degradation, worthlessness and humiliation.[56] We must look to the conduct of the service. Research carried out into the growing incidence of customer violence in the airline and railway industries considered that:

> the main reasons identified by respondents as the triggers and causes of passenger violence were alcohol, delays, a lack of information provided to passengers during delays, the quality of environmental surroundings, disputes over baggage and the failure to meet customer expectations. All of these causes are controlled and exacerbated by management policy, with the most notable case being the sale of alcohol on aircraft and trains. Profit maximization and cost minimization appear to take priority over the safety and health of employees.[57]

In a scene from a recent advertisement for Nambarrie tea, customers are portrayed as turning the tables by recording their own mind-numbing tunes to play back to the service companies after asking phone operators to hold for just a moment! Some time then elapses for the making of the tea at which point the customer returns to thank the service for holding and acknowledging its 'valued customer status'! The customer now becomes the tormentor. One group of customer service advisers has surveyed clients to discover ingenious ways of getting revenge (Box 6.1).

Employees are not exempt from criticism, invariably cited for being rude, discourteous and unknowledgeable. Service research, according to one view,[58] has ignored the potential for intentional, front-line anti-service behaviour and has assumed that customer contact service employees have a positive orientation to their work. Others

Box 6.1 Customer revenge

Sick of piped music and being told 'Your call is important to us,' before you're ignored again? Tired of having to go right back to the beginning when a voice automated system can't understand what you have to say? Or perhaps next time you go on holiday delays will see you camped out in departures and not on the beach as planned? Maybe you are left starving on the plane when the crew runs out of Pringles?

Research conducted by us in association with the Marketing Forum has shown that more than half of a customer experience is based on emotion. Therefore organizations such as Call Centres and airline companies are leaving their customers frustrated and annoyed.

Whilst customer revenge can leave you feeling triumphant, we would recommend only using companies who have real people to answer the phone or at the check-in desk – this is indicative of the customer-focus of the company. Bad service in the early stages of a customer relationship is often just a taster of what is yet to come.

We have observed that through reality TV, consumers are wising up to the hard line methods of the airlines and are now starting to get their own back on the operators who can turn holidays to hell before they've even started.

For example, we have now identified 'coping strategies' used by passengers to deal with frustrations and inadequacies of everyday airport life. These include **'Fast-Track'**, where passengers deliberately turn up late – but just in time – to be whisked through at the last moment, avoiding all the chaos of check-in and the departure lounge. **'Check-in Cheating'**, when members of a large group of holidaymakers split up and move to different queues, then move en masse, like locusts towards the 'best' queue. Finally, with unallocated seats becoming a common policy, **'Deterrent Techniques'** such as passengers feigning coughing fits to ensure that they end up with an empty seat (or two) next to them, are also being used by desperate holidaymakers!

I have recently unveiled Naïve to Natural®, a new model which maps out the four stages of Customer Experience orientation: Naïve, Transactional, Enlightened and Natural. In my book, *Revolutionise Your Customer Experience*, I use the N2N model to enable any customer-facing body to complete the journey by achieving best practice Customer Experience for all managers and organizations.

Companies need to stop cutting corners if they are going to keep their customers happy – because they will only respond by trying to do the same thing.

Colin Shaw
Customer Experience Guru and
CEO of Customer Experience Consultancy,
Beyond Philosophy

see such anti-service behaviour as a product of working conditions (work overload, role conflict, role ambiguity) that lead to frustration.

Whilst it is important to single out the factors in a service that cause dissatisfaction, it is doubly important to acknowledge how failure in these factors makes

Table 6.4 Categories of primary appraisal and associated examples

Primary appraisal (What is at stake)	Examples from service incidents causing dissatisfaction
Physical well-being	'I was worried about the results [of the X-ray] … I wanted to know what was going on.' 'I was getting hungry and really tired.'
Self-esteem	'… they couldn't be bothered with me.' 'I didn't feel like they were really interested in me.'
Security	'I felt really exposed.' 'I felt really vulnerable.'
Justice	'I felt we had been cheated …' 'I had paid for a room with a shower and I wanted the shower working.' 'It was the dishonesty of the whole thing …'
Belonging	'I felt like I didn't belong here … I felt really uncomfortable.' 'We were completely ignored …'
Well-being of a significant other	'… they gave alcoholic drinks to my ten year old step son and his two friends.'

customers feel (apart from being simply dissatisfied). One study[59] points us in an interesting direction for understanding why customers behave aggressively. The authors advise service providers of the need to understand the psycho-social benefits of the exchange (service encounter) as well as the functional aspects. To achieve this, service providers need to appreciate exactly what is at stake for the consumer during the encounter, such as self-esteem, a need to belong and/or a need for security or justice. Table 6.4 illustrates some of their findings.

Feelings of injustice, feelings of being wronged, can drive customers to take what many might regard as extreme action. In one case in the recent past a farmer was so enraged by his treatment at his bank that he sprayed muck over his local branch. Frustration and annoyance are now prompting customers to retaliate, or take revenge, as it is now more widely known.

Employees, also, are not averse to their own acts of revenge, or sabotage[60] as it is known, in response to difficult encounters with customers. Sabotage has been the subject of study recently in the hotel and catering industry. Just as customers might behave aggressively (as you will read below), employees equally will act antisocially as a demonstration against perceived subjugation by both management and customers. In the hotel and catering research the writers identify the causes and consequences of sabotage behaviour together with numerous accounts from front-line staff of sabotage in action. Two examples from this research illustrate acts of employee revenge towards customers:

> Many customers are rude or difficult, not polite like you or I. Getting your own back evens the score. There are lots of things that you do that no one but you will ever know – smaller portions, dodgy wine, a bad beer – all that and you serve it with a smile! Sweet revenge!

The trick is to get them and then straight away launch into the apologies. I've seen it done thousands of times – burning hot plates into someone's hands, gravy dripped on sleeves, drinks spilt on backs, wigs knocked off – that was funny – soups spilt in laps, you get the idea!

At times, from within the prison of subjugation and subordination, service employees are able to reclaim a sense of dignity and self-respect.[61] The following example is simply illustrative:

The perfect way to deal with unpleasant 'Do you know who I am?' type of customers. An award should go to the United Airlines gate agent in Denver for being smart and funny, and making her point, when confronted with a passenger who probably deserved to fly as cargo. During the final days at Denver's old Stapleton airport, a crowded United flight was cancelled. A single agent was rebooking a long line of inconvenienced travellers. Suddenly an angry passenger pushed his way to the desk. He slapped his ticket down on the counter and said, 'I HAVE to be on this flight, it has to be FIRST CLASS'. The agent replied, 'I'm sorry sir. I'll be happy to try to help you, but I've got to help these folks first, and I'm sure we'll be able to work something out.' The passenger was unimpressed. He asked loudly, so that the passengers behind him could hear, 'Do you have any idea who I am?' Without hesitating, the gate agent smiled and grabbed her public address microphone. 'May I have your attention please?' she began, her voice bellowing throughout the terminal. 'We have a passenger here at the gate WHO DOES NOT KNOW WHO HE IS. If anyone can help him find his identity, please come to gate 17.' With the folks behind him in line laughing hysterically, the man glared at the United agent, gritted his teeth and swore '[Expletive] you.' Without flinching, she smiled and said, 'I'm sorry sir, but you'll have to stand in line for that, too.' The man retreated as the people in the terminal applauded loudly. Although the flight was cancelled and people were late, they were no longer angry at United. (Jill Colonna@OECD.org at internet-gateway)

Acts of revenge and sabotage are receiving more attention in the services literature, the media and from various consultancy organizations. Whether it gathers further momentum remains to be seen. The service encounter is evidently not as smooth running as we have traditionally been led to believe. Will it become even more fractious?

Summary

In this chapter we have addressed what can turn out to be a thorny issue, namely the service encounter. This is the point at which customers come into contact, in one form or another, with the service organization. To assist our understanding of this encounter some have likened it to a theatrical performance. Although there are lessons to be learnt from the theatre, the unpredictability and variability of customer behaviour and attitudes suggests that this analogy is not completely accurate.

From the service organization point of view the use of scripts and emotional labour are important components for delivery and performance. Customers, on the other hand, can find being on the receiving end of these techniques frustrating and humiliating. Service employees are also not exempt from such feelings.

Given the importance of the service encounter, one technique gathering interest is the critical incident. Use of this technique enables services to determine what customers, in particular, found satisfying or dissatisfying in the service encounter.

Finally, we draw attention to a growing trend of service encounters as a sector for disagreeable behaviour. This trend represents a real challenge for service organizations.

References

1 Grove, S J, Fisk, R P and John, J (2000) 'Service as theatre: guidelines and implications', in Swartz, T A and Iacobucci, D (eds), *Handbook of Services Marketing and Management*. London: Sage, pp. 21–35.

2 Goffman, E (1959) *The Presentation of Self in Everyday Life*. New York: Doubleday and Co.

3 Grove, S J and Risk, R P (1997) 'The impact of other customers on service experiences: a critical incident examination of "getting along" ', *Journal of Retailing*, **73** (1), 63–85.

4 Schank, R C and Abelson, R P (1977) *Scripts, Plans, Goals and Understanding*. Hillside, NJ: Erlbaum.

5 Ibid.

6 Abelson, R P (1981) 'Psychological status of the script concept', *American Psychologist*, **36** (7).

7 Bower, G H, Black, J B and Turner, T J (1979) 'Scripts in memory for text', *Cognitive Psychology*, **11**, 177–220.

8 Leidner, R (1993) *Fast Food, Fast Talk: Service Work and the Routinization of Everyday Life*. Berkeley, CA: University of California Press.

9 Mestrovic, S G (1997) *Postemotional Society*. London: Sage, p. 51.

10 Hochschild, A (1983) *The Managed Heart: Commercialization of Human Feeling*. Berkeley, CA: University of California Press, p. 7.

11 Leidner, op. cit, p. 217.

12 Mann, S (1999) *Hiding What We Feel, Faking What We Don't*. UK: Element Books Ltd, p. 68.

13 Plutchik, R (1980) *Emotion: A Psycho-evolutionary Synthesis*. New York: Harper and Row.

14 Izard, C E (1990) *Emotions, Cognition and Behaviour*. Cambridge: Cambridge University Press.

15 Richins, M L (1997) 'Measuring emotions in the consumption experience', *Journal of Consumer Research*, **24** (2), 127–146.

16 Mudie, P, Cottam, A and Raeside, R (2003) 'An exploratory study of consumption emotion in services', *Service Industries Journal*, **23** (5), 84–106.

17 Hochschild, op. cit, p. 11.

18 Mann, op. cit, p. 39.

19 Hochschild, op. cit, p. 237.

20 Mann, op. cit, p. 40.

21 Lief, H I and Fox, R C (1963) 'Training for "detached concern" in medical students', in Lief, H I, Leif, V F and Lief, N R (eds), *The Psychological Basis of Medical Practice*. New York: Harper and Row, pp. 12–35.

22 Hirschborn, L (1989) 'Professionals, authority and group life: a case study of a law firm', *Human Resource Management*, **28**, 235–252.

23 Mann, op. cit, p. 44.

24 Ibid., p. 44.

25 Ibid., p. 45.

26 Laird, J D (1974) Self-attribution of emotion: the effects of facial expression on the quality of emotional experience, *Journal of Personality and Social Psychology*, **29**, 475–486.

27 Grayson, K (1998) 'Customer responses and emotional labour in discrete and relational service exchange', *International Journal of Service Industry Management*, **9** (2), 126–154.

28 Leidner, op. cit, p. 218.

29 Ibid, p. 30.

30 Mann, op. cit, p. 27.

31 Flanagan, J C (1954) 'The critical incident technique', *Psychological Bulletin*, **51** (4), 327–358.

32 Wagner, R F (1995) 'A study of the critical requirements for dentists', *University of Pittsburgh Bulletin*, **46**, 331–339.

33 Bitner, M J, Booms, B H and Tetreault, M S (1990) 'The service encounter: diagnosing favourable and unfavourable incidents', *Journal of Marketing*, **54** (1), 71–84.

34 Stauss, B (1993) 'Using the critical incident technique in measuring and managing service quality', in Schening, E E and Christopher, W F (eds), *The Service Quality Handbook*. New York: American Management Association, pp. 408–427.

35 Gilbert, D C and Morris, L (1995) 'The relevant importance of hotels and airlines to the business traveller', *International Journal of Contemporary Hospitality Management*, **7** (6), 19–23.

36 Hoffman, K D, Kelley, S W and Soulage, C M (1995) 'Customer defection analysis: a critical incident approach', in Stern, B and Zinkhan, G M (eds), *Enhancing Knowledge Development in Marketing*. AMA Summer Educators Conference Proceedings, pp. 346–352.

37 Chell, E and Pittaway, L (1998) 'A study of entrepreneurship in the restaurant and café industry: exploratory work using the critical incident technique as a methodology', *International Journal of Hospitality Management*, **17**, 23–32.

38 Chung, B and Hoffman, K D (1998) 'Critical incidents: service failures that matter most', *Cornell Hotel and Restaurant Administration Quarterly*, June, 66–71.

39 Chung-Herrera, B G, Goldschmidt, N and Hoffman, K D (2004) 'Customer and employee views of critical incidents', *Journal of Service Marketing*, **18** (4), 241–254.

40 Gremler, D D (2004) 'The critical incident technique in services research', *Journal of Service Research*, **7** (1), 65–89.

41 Bitner *et al.* (1990), op. cit.

42 Bitner, M J, Booms, B H and Mohr, L A (1994) 'Critical service encounters: the employee's viewpoint', *Journal of Marketing*, **58** (October), 95–106.

43 Grove *et al.* (2000), op. cit.

44 Hochschild, p. 47.

45 Ibid., p. 55.

46 Lovelock, C and Wirtz, J (2004) *Services Marketing*. Upper Saddle River, NJ: Pearson Prentice Hall, p. 251.

47 Ibid., pp. 251–256.

48 Bitner *et al.*, op. cit.

49 Moschis, G P and Cox, D (1989) 'Deviant consumer behaviour', *Advances in Consumer Research*, **16**, 732–737.

50 Fullerton, R A and Punj, G (1993) 'Choosing to misbehave: a structural model of aberrant consumer behaviour', *Advances in Consumer Research*, **20**, 570–574.

51 Harris, L C and Reynolds, K L (2004) 'Jay customer behaviour: an exploration of types and motives in the hospitality industry', *Journal of Services Marketing*, **18** (5), 339–357.

52 Fullerton and Punj, op. cit.

53 Zenke, R and Anderson, K (1990) 'Customers from hell', *Training*, 4 February, 25–33.

54 'If You Can't Get Even, Get Mad', a survey and report by advertising agency Publicis, 2005.

55 'The Rebellious Consumer – Rebels with a Cause', Mintel's 2005 British Lifestyles report.

56 Harris, L L and Reynolds, K L (2003) 'The consequences of dysfunctional customer behaviour', *Journal of Service Research*, **6** (2), 144–161.

57 Boyd, C (2002) 'Customer violence and employee health and safety', *Work, Employment and Society*, **16** (1), 151–169.

58 Harris, L C and Ogbonna, E (2002) 'Exploring service sabotage', *Journal of Service Research*, **4** (3), 163–183.

59 Godwin, B F, Patterson, P G and Johnson, L W (1999) 'Consumer coping strategies with dissatisfactory service encounters: a preliminary investigation', *Journal of Consumer Satisfaction, Dissatisfaction and Complaining Behaviour*, **12**, pp. 145–154.

60 Harris and Ogbonna, op. cit.

61 Mudie, P (2000) 'Internal marketing: a step too far', in Varey, R J and Lewis, B R (eds), *Internal Marketing: Directions for Management*. London: Routledge, p. 260.

7

Managing people

Introduction

People who deliver the service are of key importance to both the customers they serve and the employer they represent. To the customer they are in fact part of the product. Their ability and willingness to satisfy, their manner and appearance, all play a part in determining how satisfied the customer is with the service encounter. To the employer, those delivering the service can make or break the organization. On the one hand, they may be the only way that a service brand differentiates itself. On the other hand, they can also be the reason why people do not come back.

In many organizations everything that the front-line employees do is stage managed. They have little discretion or flexibility in the way they offer the service, rather they are restricted to implementing a strict set of rules and procedures. This leaves the jobs deskilled and the workers demotivated.[1] In other organizations front-line employees can be given too much flexibility and responsibility without the commensurate training or rewards.[2]

7.1 Customer contact staff

It has been suggested that, in services, future business success will depend on the level of emotional capital available to an organization.[3] The term *emotional capital* refers to the human resource available and in using the word capital, Lashley advocates human resource be regarded as an *asset* of the business.

Of course, not all services sector employees interact with customers, but those who do heavily influence the customer's service experience. They do this in three ways: they offer cues to the customer to help them assess an otherwise ambiguous situation; they create first impressions; and they create the cognitive framework that shapes the way in which the service is interpreted and evaluated.[4] Staff that interact with customers are often referred to as either customer contact staff or front-line staff.

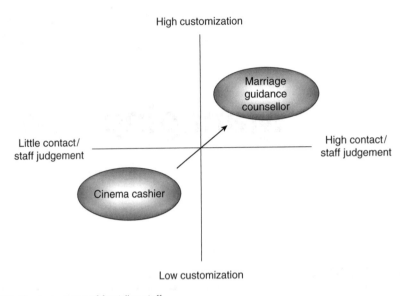

Figure 7.1 The importance of front-line staff
Source: Adapted from Lovelock (1996)[5]

Not every front-line employee plays an equally important role in the delivery of service. Lovelock[5] suggests that the two most significant variables in this respect are the degree to which the service offering is customized and the extent to which customer contact staff exercise judgement in meeting an individual customer's needs (Figure 7.1). The bottom-left quadrant of the figure is where the service is standardized and front-line employees are not empowered to exercise their judgement, front-line staff play a relatively minor role in the service experience, e.g. a ticket cashier at the cinema. On the other hand, front-line staff are very important to service operations in the top-right quadrant. These services are characterized by a high degree of customization and customer contact staff exercizing their judgement in the desire to fulfil customer expectations, e.g. a marriage guidance counsellor. The degree of importance attached to front-line employees in these situations will depend on the specific service being offered.

Front-line personnel are not a homogeneous group. The hotel chambermaid and the plastic surgeon are both front-line employees in that they both deal directly with customers. Some of the skills that are required are common to both jobs. These core skills have become common requirements of all front-line staff regardless of the specific service that they provide (Figure 7.2).

In addition to these essentials, most industries also require some supplementary skills. Front-line staff will only provide a quality service if they possess all the qualities required, both core and supplementary. Historically, those who provided services that required a lot of technical ability got away without the core skills. If a doctor was rude, or kept patients waiting, no one complained. No one accused him of providing a poor service. His position allowed him to behave in this manner. Now, though, even those in the professional services are expected to possess core service skills.

Front-line staff act as another element of communication. They help portray the desired image of the company. If the intended image is one of sophistication then do

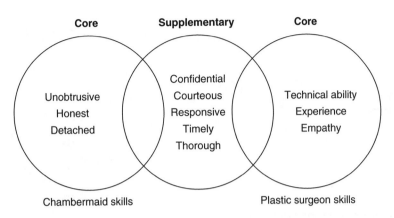

Figure 7.2 Core/supplementary skills

not employ people who chew gum and bite their nails. If it is important that customers empathize with staff then ensure that service personnel are segmented by their personalities so that they meet the customers' requirements. In a department store the total pool of shop assistants should be segmented so that, for example, those serving in the children's department are patient and fun-loving, while those serving in the china department are careful and light of foot.

7.2 Emotional labour

The concept of empathizing with customers, and the impact that displaying this type of emotion might have on front-line staff, was catapulted centre stage by Hochschild[6] in her seminal book *The Managed Heart*. Two types of displayed emotion are often required: these are referred to as surface acting and deep acting. The former, as the name suggests, requires service workers to appear pleasant and empathetic regardless of how they feel. The latter requires the person to 'bow from the heart', so that in addition to expressing desired emotions, they are also expected to actually feel/experience these emotions. Deep acting is management's response to the growing scepticism of customers towards the surface acting, 'have a nice day' approach.

Why does management actively encourage emotional labour? Well because it believes there is a link between this and the company's sales performance. Front-line workers, however, remain sceptical.[7] Indeed management policies can often leave front-line workers subjected to customer abuse,[8] ground staff working for certain low-cost airlines being a case in point. These employees have to attempt to mitigate the dissatisfaction, and the better they are at this, the less management are likely to tackle the causes of the violence they experience.

It has been recognized that if the employee's true emotional feelings are dissonant with what has to be expressed, this leads to stress, declining job satisfaction, and emotional exhaustion.[9] Consider the call centre worker, employed to carry out repetitive tasks in an intensive environment where his or her output can be measured. Some consider this type of work to be the modern-day equivalent of the Dickensian workhouses.[10]

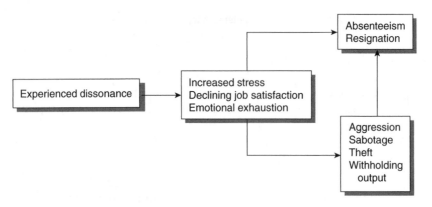

Figure 7.3 Employee response to experienced dissonance

How do employees respond to this stress? Their responses may be neither of the relatively benign outcomes of absenteeism and attrition. Instead, it could lead to the behaviours discussed in Hogans'[11] organizational delinquency concept: aggression, sabotage, theft or withholding output. They identified four personality factors that would determine whether an individual would respond 'antisocially' to feelings of dissonance. These were – hostility to rules, impulsiveness, sense of alienation and social insensitivity. Consequently, if management perceives a high level of dissonance among staff, it would do well to attempt to weed out these personality types in future selection procedures, while at the same time considering ways in which they could redesign the work to help reduce the feelings of dissonance.

Ashforth,[12] building on social identity theory, has suggested that the greater the worker's identification with the service role, the greater his or her willingness to comply with management's emotional display rules. If instead the individual identifies himself in terms of other social groups there is a higher likelihood he will experience emotional dissonance. One can think of the contrast between the student working in a call centre and the budding director working on the set of the latest Hollywood blockbuster.

It is not solely social identity theory that determines the worker's emotional response. People who find it difficult to distance themselves are more at risk of emotional knocks in their work environment. So high involvement (deep acting) may not always be good. Wharton[13] discovered that, contrary to received opinion, women are no more likely than men to suffer negative consequences from the performance of emotional labour. In another gender study, Hochschild[14] found that in jobs where emotional labour was the main human capital sold by the worker to the employer – estimated to be around one-third of all jobs in the USA – 50% of all female employment could be classed as such.

7.3   Empowerment

Hence the perceived benefit of emotional labour is the improvement in customers' service experience and satisfaction, and consequently diminished levels of dissatisfaction and complaints. An associated concept is the one of empowerment, although empowerment is presumed to deliver the dual benefits of enhanced customer satis-faction, *and* increased employee commitment. True empowerment is where front-line/customer contact staff have responsibility to deliver customer satisfaction *and* the authority to customize the service offering in order to do so. Therefore front-line staff have to manage the quality/productivity trade-off.

Empowerment of employees may be easier when they have few rules to follow, i.e. the service delivery process is customized. However, many organizations choose to standardize their operation to help control costs and quality levels. In some organ-izations it may even be appropriate to standardize the whole operation. For instance, McDonald's instructs its counter staff on tray assembly – cold drinks first, then hot, and always put the tray within easy reach of the customer.

However, even in organizations where service delivery is almost entirely stand-ardized the empowerment of front-line employees can help. It can, for instance, pro-vide quicker response times to customer complaints. The employee will not have to find a supervisor who can handle the complaint, and then attempt to explain the cause for the dissatisfaction. Instead the employee can make his or her own decision on the spot about the best way to recover the situation.

Quick response times to customer complaints is a restrictive use of the concept of empowerment. In this context, it plays no part in service delivery. Instead it is placed in a purely reactive role within the service recovery arena.

In those industries where service delivery is to some extent customized, there are even greater opportunities for empowerment. Here the employee can be given the flexibility and authority to meet the customers' needs. They are placed in a proactive role where they anticipate problems and correct them during service delivery.

In addition to the extent to which service delivery is customized, research would suggest that empowerment is also most prevalent in companies that have aban-doned the traditional top-down, control-orientated management model for a high-involvement or high-performance approach. Such companies are characterized by the extent to which information, knowledge, power and rewards are distributed throughout the organization. Bowen and Lawler[15] state that empowerment is:

$$\text{Empowerment} = \text{power} \times \text{information} \times \text{knowledge} \times \text{rewards}$$

Since the formula requires individual components to be multiplied together, if any of the four elements is zero, then empowerment will be zero. The equation reminds management to avoid the common error of giving employees more power without the necessary support to exercise that power. They also note that these pay-offs from empowerment must be set against the resource implications of increased costs for selection and training, higher labour costs, slower service and less consistency in service delivery.

The main benefits of empowerment are:

- Quicker response times to customer needs
- Quicker response times to complaints
- Employees feel better about their jobs and themselves
- Employees interact with customers with more warmth and enthusiasm
- Empowered employees can be a good source of ideas for service development
- Great word-of-mouth advertising and customer retention.

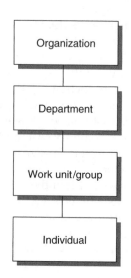

Figure 7.4 Levels of empowerment

Empowerment is not an all-or-nothing concept.[16] It has been suggested rather that it is a continuum ranging from total control to total empowerment. The lowest level being 'suggestion involvement', where employees make recommendations which are not binding on management. The next level is 'job involvement', whereby jobs are redesigned to allow employees scope to use a variety of skills to complete an identifiable task. The highest level entails the distribution throughout the organization of power, information, knowledge, and rewards.

Others believe that managers merely use the rhetoric of empowerment to secure control over their staff.[17] There is certainly a growing scepticism for the concept and an uncomfortable contradiction between emotional labour and empowerment with many managerial techniques aimed at driving customer focus (empowerment) being very good at prescribing and controlling the (emotional) labour process. One commentator has proposed that the increasing uncertainty and fruitless reality of work means that some of the lower Maslow[18] levels are not being met, consequently reducing the probability of empowerment through the higher-order levels.[19] He discusses empowerment for both the individual and the organization. In doing so he is amongst the first to conceptualize the idea of empowerment beyond that of the level of the individual.

At this higher level, work-unit or team performance has been shown to be positively related to the extent of empowerment within the unit. An organizational climate that embraces empowerment policies and practices, e.g. information-sharing, clarity regarding goals, encouragement of autonomous action etc., leads to enhanced work-unit performance.[20]

7.3.1 Organizational climate and culture

So for the empowerment model to work both Taylor's[21] 'command and control' style of management and Weber's[22] rule-ridden organization have to be abandoned.

Instead, management's job becomes the management of emotion. However, as emotion is more organizationally managed, the less it feels truly emotional.[23]

Instead management must build a culture and climate for the organization that elicits the type of emotional behaviours relevant for their service environment. If management is seen trying to 'control' the organizational culture, issues of trust arise.[24] Likewise, organizational climate – being the shared perceptions of what an organization expects, supports, rewards – should support and reward empowered behaviours.

So if management are to leave the development of an appropriate culture to emerge from the staff themselves, and are not to be seen trying to 'control' the culture, they need to ensure that they recruit people with the right values.

7.3.2   Job design

There are two aspects of job design that should be considered in any attempt to empower front-line employees – one is *job enlargement*, the other is *job enrichment*. When people are asked to think of ways that jobs could be enriched they invariably mention things that are really only job enlargements. Enlarging a job means giving the employee more tasks to perform. Herzberg[25] refers to this as 'horizontal job loading', and makes suggestions for ways in which a job may instead be enriched. However, just as not all employees want to be empowered, they do not all want to be enriched. The chequered history of job-enrichment programmes would suggest that the extent to which employees want their jobs to be enriched, depends on the nature of their motivations.

Other aspects of job design that should be considered by those in the organization entrusted with personnel matters are:

- Job specification
- Training and development
- Working conditions
- Appraisal systems
- Promotion prospects
- Salary and benefits.

7.4   Recruitment

In the same way that customers need to build a relationship with the company before they develop loyalty, employees need to form a similar attachment before they become committed. This relationship often begins long before individuals become employees.

Many prospective employees will have been exposed to the external communications of the hiring organization even before they consider working for it (see Chapter 10). They may even be a lapsed or current user of the service. This all plays a part in an individual's decision to work for a particular company.

The company gets another chance to create a favourable impression in its recruitment and selection process. All too often the employer regards this process as a one-sided affair, believing that the onus falls entirely on applicants to make the company want them. This is a somewhat shortsighted approach.

The company wants the best possible recruits. To ensure that it gets them, the company must be prepared to 'tell and sell'. Recruitment communications should contain the following:

- A clear description of the job specification, including job title, reporting structure and main areas of responsibility.
- A statement of any definite requirements, e.g. academic qualifications, years of experience, height (police force).
- Reasons why individuals should consider joining the company.
- A description of the company's culture and mission.

Obviously it is not necessary, or desirable, to include all of these in every piece of communication. For example, many of the large accountancy firms produce glossy recruitment brochures that meet the latter two requirements, and neatly perform the telling and selling functions. On the other hand, specific job advertisements placed in the media may choose instead to focus on the first two requirements. By doing so, they may be able to contain advertising costs.

Recruitment communication is most effective when it attracts the right number of the right type of applicants. The company is wasting time if it ends up interviewing applicants who do not meet the company's job specification. Therefore, recruitment communications should seek to tempt appropriate individuals to apply, but at the same time deter unsuitable applicants.

7.4.1   The pre-employment relationship: selection

The importance of selection in the service industry can be summed up in three statements made by Schneider and Schechter.[26]

1 The climate and culture of an organization is a function of the people who are employed there.
2 Most service organizations require interdependent employee behaviour, and therefore everyone operating in the system must be performing well. Individual excellence will not compensate for poor performers.
3 The best predictor of future behaviour is past behaviour.

A cornerstone of the selection process is the face-to-face interview. This again is a two-way process. It enables the company to present a picture of what it stands for, and what the job entails. It should also give the applicant the opportunity to elaborate on his or her application. The power in the relationship at this time tends to lie with the company. It decides on the interview timing, the format, and the techniques and procedures that will be adopted.

To get the best out of this interchange the organization ought to be testing relevant skills. This means that in addition to the obvious technical skill requirements, the organization should have considered what personal qualities are necessary to do the job successfully. Obviously not all service jobs require identical skills. However,

William George[27] suggests that interpersonal competence and a service orientation are two basic skills that all service personnel should possess.

In the 1960s and 1970s, role-playing scenarios were used to assess these basic skills. However, many applicants found them relatively easy to manipulate, and the assessment of the scenarios was open to wide variations in interpretation.

In an attempt to overcome these weaknesses, some larger organizations in the UK have adopted quantitatively based techniques. These are intended to reduce what Woods and McAuley refer to as 'the halo and the devil-horn effect' of the qualitative scenarios.[28] Psychometric testing is one such technique. In many cases, this test takes a similar form to the traditional IQ tests. The applicant answers a series of multiple-choice questions within a tight time frame. Historically, these tests only managed to remove one of the weaknesses of the behaviouralists' approach – the results were not open to the same level of interpretation as before. Individuals are scored using conventional statistical measurement techniques, i.e. the tests are constructed so that they produce a normal distribution. Individuals are then compared in terms of how they scored on each characteristic relative to the mean. However, the crudeness of some of the early tests meant that the bright applicants who were aware of the skills that the company was looking for could see how to answer the questions in such a way that they would achieve high scores on the appropriate skills.

Nowadays, these tests have become much more sophisticated in design. Applicants attempting to manipulate the test become confused and disorientated by the apparent sameness of many of the questions. For organizations employing large numbers or who have large numbers of candidates, tests can be an appealing option, in that by operating cut-off points the number of candidates can be significantly reduced.

Table 7.1 contains the output from one individual's psychometric tests. The questions that were asked were designed to capture the 31 personality attributes in the left-hand column. Each of the attributes were scored on a 10-point rating scale. So, for example, this individual scored maximum points on the attributes such as Caring, Data rational, Conceptual and Achieving.

Any self-report method like psychometric testing is suspect when the characteristics relate to interactions, because they depend not only on the respondent's honesty (which is usually quite high) but on their self-awareness and understanding of their impact on other people. Studies of emotional intelligence suggest that this is best measured through interview, 360-degree feedback and observation rather than self-report. For this reason the service sector should therefore be careful about using such tests as a screen or for final selection.

Whatever methods are chosen to assess the applicant's suitability, the company must develop a selection system that hires people with the right attitude. Kiger[29] refers to this as 'psychological hardiness', meaning the recruit is optimistic by nature, flexible and has the ability to listen. What the organization is looking for are those individuals whose innate personality and emotional expression matches that which the company seeks to promote. This is becoming increasingly important in service sector recruitment given that customers are becoming far more sophisticated in their 'spotting' of employees with managed hearts. What it needs are 'winners at the front-line not just warm bodies'.[30]

Table 7.1 Psychometric testing variables

Personal attribute	Score
Persuasive	9
Controlling	6
Independent	7
Outgoing	8
Affiliative	5
Socially confident	8
Modest	3
Democratic	5
Caring	10
Practical	6
Data rational	10
Artistic	9
Behavioural	9
Traditional	5
Change oriented	9
Conceptual	10
Innovative	9
Forward planning	9
Detail conscious	5
Conscientious	9
Relaxed	5
Worrying	7
Tough minded	3
Emotional control	6
Optimistic	7
Critical	6
Active	8
Competitive	9
Achieving	10
Decisive	7
Social desirability	7

This individual displayed the personality suitable for senior level management

7.5   Orientation and socialization

Hopefully, the outcome of the recruitment and selection process will be new recruits who are *willing* to perform the tasks that are required of them. The willingness which they bring to the company may well have to be strengthened and moulded.

While the new recruit to a supermarket checkout operator's position will probably have some image of what it is like to sit at an EPOS (electronic point of sale) checkout desk, the image that he or she has will be based on his or her own limited experience as a customer. As a customer, the individual may have had a different perspective. They may have expected it to be quite a sociable job. A former checkout operator describing her job on Channel 4 Television said, 'You never see their faces. All you see are their hands. They might just as well be gorillas.'[31]

Front-line staff are expected to conform to certain role models in the provision of service. This can sometimes mean performing everyday tasks in a slightly different manner because that is what the company wants. An employee may have to shake hands more vigorously, talk more animatedly, or make more eye contact than they otherwise would. Trainers have to work on inhibiting and inducing certain feelings. The overworked nurse is expected to be calm and patient. The swimming pool attendant is not supposed to become irate with the squeals of noisy school children, but remain detached and vigilant.

Naturally, different emotions will be relevant to different service industries. Management must consider what the salient emotional expressions are before it begins to train recruits. If the business is debt collection, then front-line employees will be expected to be nasty to debtors, whereas flight attendants are expected to be pleasant to passengers.[32]

A company strengthens and moulds the recruit's willingness by training. In addition to shaping their willingness, in many cases the training may also serve the purpose of developing their *ability* to do the job. Training programmes that seek to orientate and socialize recruits to an organization have been shown to be more effective in building commitment and productivity than those which do not. The quicker this happens after the employee joins a company the better.

In addition to providing new members of staff with the necessary tools for their jobs, enlightened employers will seek to use the training forum as an opportunity to get its recruits fully 'on board'. It does this by practising 'rites of passage',[33] otherwise known as orientation and socialization. All companies will not adopt identical approaches to this process. After all, the purpose of the transition is to shape the recruit in such a way that he or she handles customers effectively. As Rohlen[34] says, 'What is OK to be practised by the US Army, is not quite so relevant for a high street bank.'

7.6 Orientation

Orientation is the process by which the organization helps the new recruit understand the company and its culture. It is particularly important for those service organizations whose front-line employees meet customers at arm's length from any supervision, back up, or control. In these cases it is vital that the employee has been imbued with the company's values. Most orientation programmes ask the recruit to be a receptive, yet passive, audience for this communication. However, since the desired outcome is for recruits to feel enthused about the prospect of working for the company, it is sometimes necessary to work on building receptivity first.

Senior management involvement in this process usually goes down well. But whatever the chosen route for orientation, the programme should seek to leave recruits with an understanding of the purpose and mission of the company. The organization then has more chance of everyone pulling in the same direction.

Orientation should also seek to communicate any folklore that the company has which demonstrates the culture of the organization. The folklore can be related to a previous employee who made an outstanding contribution to the company's fortunes, or it can be about particular service encounters where the company went to extraordinary lengths to deliver outstanding service.

The contribution that such stories make to orientation is twofold. First, people are more likely to remember the values and goals of the company if they are illuminated with actual situations. Second, these myths and heroes create the impression of a private and elite society that the recruit is privileged to join. Remember, in a service organization, orientation should clearly communicate to recruits the central importance of the customer.

7.6.1   Socialization

Now that the recruit understands the culture and workings of the organization, he or she must be initiated into the workings of its cultural setting. Orientation has told them what to expect in this context, socialization is the process by which they begin to experience it.

Management may build socialization by feeding to recruits the thought that a lot will be expected of them as employees of the company. If the employee does not feel that he or she is living up to expectations he or she will begin to feel guilty. In this case the process of socialization has become internalized in the employee, and management no longer has to rely on coercion to ensure motivation.

Another socialization technique is to make recruits publicly acknowledge these rites of passage. In many communist countries public declarations of commitment were often demanded. It then became more difficult to betray the Party. Similarly, high-pressure selling organizations such as Amway adopt socialization techniques that deliver religious fervour and devotion in the recruits.[35]

Some companies socialize their employees by giving them hands-on dirty work experience. They get management to take part in the service encounter, e.g. McDonald's gets all its new managers to serve customers on the shop floor. Indeed, it asks its advertising agency and all other service agencies that it uses to do the same. The purpose of these role-adoptive scenarios is to give these employees and those in supporting roles a greater understanding of the business.

An area of current controversy in the socialization process is the extent to which individuals have to conform to corporate culture. Schein[36] has developed three basic behavioural responses to socialization:

- Rebellion – rejection of all that is expected
- Creative individualism – acceptance of all crucial behavioural norms
- Conformity – acceptance of everything.

Of course, the response of most employees will fall somewhere between the first and the second categories, or the second and the third. The first and third categories are generally regarded as socialization failures. The middle category is most desirable, but it is a difficult position for an employee to maintain consistently.

The degree to which management seeks conformity depends on the industry in which it operates. If, for example, individuality and innovation are important values (as in hairdressing) then the organization should not seek to make these employees conform.

Individuals who are best placed to work in positions that require individuality and innovation are those who are *intrinsically* motivated.[37] That means that they prefer complexity, novelty, challenge and the opportunity to master a skill in their employment. Conversely, an individual who is *extrinsically* motivated seeks job simplicity and predictability. Such individuals lack initiative. To perform their job they need to be told what to do, and then require continual supervision while doing it. Jobs of this nature are few and far between. Even jobs that on the surface would appear to suit this type of person, e.g. postman, or clerical assistant, normally benefit from someone who can use their intelligence. The postman who recognizes that a letter is wrongly addressed and delivers it to the correct one is performing a better service for his or her customers.

7.7   Gaining commitment from employees

7.7.1   Encouraging motivation

The orientation and socialization processes are designed to foster commitment to the organization on the part of the employee. It is one thing establishing this feeling in new recruits, but once these initiations are over and they are left alone to perform their new role, what will foster commitment are factors like job design (see previous section), role/employee congruity and appropriate feedback.

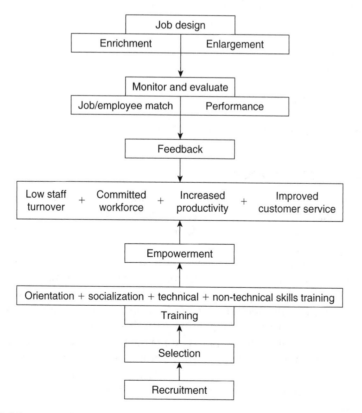

Figure 7.5 Building a committed workforce

To maintain the commitment, the relationship must be carefully nurtured and groomed. Motivation that was built on orientation and socialization programmes during the introductory training may have become quite depleted from everyday bashing at the front-line. So what should the organization do to retain its good staff? And what must it do to keep them committed and motivated?

Organizations can deal with this issue in a variety of ways. Whatever they decide to do, two principles should guide them:

1 Keep the importance of the delivery of quality service and customer satisfaction visible.
2 Top management involvement in the delivery of these goals should also be visible. Not only in terms of what they say, but also in terms of what they do.

A whole variety of techniques designed to foster employee commitment have been proposed.[38] The organization can practise rites of renewal, which seeks to fine-tune the system using the latest organizational development techniques – quality circles, management by objectives (MBO), team building, to name but a few. However, there is substantial cynicism about their effectiveness. Many regard them as a series of gimmicks designed to make management feel good about the fact that they are doing something. This game will often act as a smokescreen leaving the real issues undisturbed. Herzberg[39] believes that the only way to motivate employees is to give them challenging work. He lists the following factors as contributing to motivation:

- Achievement
- Recognition for achievement
- The work itself
- Responsibility
- Growth or advancement.

All the other techniques are at best offering only short-term motivations.

7.7.2   Loyal employees

Fostering commitment can lead to several economic benefits for the organization. Bain and Company have developed a generic model of the benefits that can be associated with employee loyalty.[40] Their model is the result of a ten-year study across a range of industries (Figure 7.6).

In much the same way that loyal customers are more profitable to organizations, loyal employees can create value because recruitment and training costs are reduced. Indeed, Cardy,[41] in proposing the concept of employee equity, suggests that organizations that consider the lifetime value of an employee are much more likely to experience high levels of retained and loyal staff. These employees tend to work more efficiently and effectively. Their experience makes them better at finding, recruiting and retaining customers. Finally, long-term employees are often a good source of both customer and employee referrals. The relative importance of Bain's seven indicators will vary from industry to industry. Indeed, in some industries not all seven will be present.

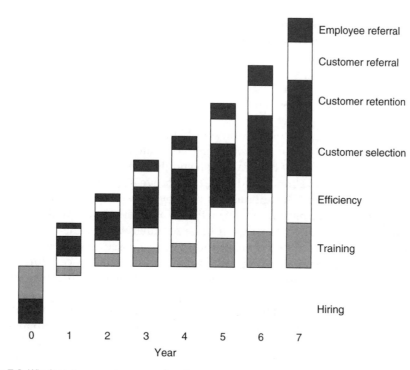

Figure 7.6 Why long-term employees create value
Source: Bain & Co

It has been suggested that an easy first step to improving the loyalty of employees is to conduct an employee/job satisfaction survey.[42] Furthermore, satisfaction, be it that of an employee or a customer, is the result of an individual's perceptions of their experience exceeding their expectations of it. Consequently, the measurement of employee job satisfaction can be conducted along similar lines to that of customer satisfaction (see Chapter 12 for further discussion). Disney conducts an annual employee survey designed to monitor employee morale and satisfaction.[43] It believes that there are three reasons why employees would work harder/continue to provide excellent customer service. They are pay, recognition and additional involvement. So as an organization it is constantly looking for ways to demonstrate to employees how much they are valued. They have service recognition awards, peer recognition awards, attendance awards, milestones for years of service etc.

The employee's contribution to service delivery should be evaluated in two ways:

1 Through employees themselves being given a voice: this is part of the internal marketing concept – if the organization is treating its staff like customers then it must find out their attitudes towards the current organizational practice.
2 Through the customer's evaluation of the service that he or she received.

Employees should ideally be evaluated and remunerated in terms of their contribution to customer satisfaction (evaluate effectiveness rather than efficiency). This follows the principle of 'what gets measured gets done'. If employees know that they are being evaluated in terms of customer satisfaction, then they are more likely to be motivated to provide this satisfaction.

7.7.3 Feedback

Performance monitoring and evaluation should be concerned with the achievement of customer satisfaction. Employees who help to create this satisfaction must know how they fared. The results of the evaluation should be fed back to employees.

In doing so, the organization would hope to improve its performance, and thereby to satisfy more customers. The appraisal of employees can be carried out on a regular or irregular basis. The appraisals can be tied to a review of pay, but they need not all be. Employees will, of course, expect to be remunerated for their efforts, and a performance appraisal is a good time for this to be discussed. It will be most appropriate in those circumstances where pay is related to performance. However, the organization would be foolish to encourage employees to believe that their performance will only be discussed when their pay is up for review.

One feedback mechanism that is growing in influence is that which encourages 'service wisdom'. Employees are venerated for successfully handling situations that were not covered in their service manuals or training sessions. The Holiday Inn's 'employee of the month' scheme or American Express's annual Great Performance Award are examples of this. In exceptional cases, the service encounters that gave rise to the award may become part of the company's folklore.

The feedback process should not be entirely one-way from management to employees. Instead it should be a three-way process between the employee's internal/external customers, his subordinates, and management. Unfortunately this is still only practised by the most enlightened of companies. Most employers still behave as if the employees belong to them. They feel that the employees owe the organization something for being given the privilege of working there, and do not see that they might owe the employees more than their salaries in return for their labour.

7.8 Staff dissatisfaction

Scratch the surface of many service organizations where much of the front-line employees' work has been routinized or dehumanized and you will find in many cases the employees are unhappy with the organization.[44] Why should they attempt to make customers happy when they are not happy themselves?

In transactional analysis these individuals have adopted what Harris,[45] describes as an 'I'm not OK' position. The organization has made them feel 'Not OK', and they take it out on the customers – 'You will not be OK either'. If the service providers are to improve the interaction of these staff with customers, then they have to make them feel, 'I'm OK, the organization's OK, you're OK, and I'd like to help you'. But before the organization can remove the dissatisfaction, it has to be understood. So what makes employees dissatisfied with their jobs?

Many factors have been found to contribute to this problem. These are:

- Role ambiguity
- Role conflict
- Role overload
- Employee/job mismatch
- Performance measured on quantity not quality
- Lack of empowerment
- Lack of a common purpose
- Lack of management commitment.

7.8.1   Role ambiguity

Employees do not understand what management or customers expect of them (see Chapter 2). This situation is improved with role clarity; clearly communicate what individuals must do, and tell them how they are doing. However, telling the individual what you want him or her to do is not enough. It is the employer's responsibility to give the employee the ability to perform the job. This can be achieved by training, leaving him or her a competent and confident performer.

7.8.2   Role conflict

Two or more incompatible sets of pressures impact on the employee's behaviour. This is more likely to arise in situations where the employee is in what Boas Shamir describes as a subordinate service role.[46] In these situations the provider of the service has no more expertise or ability to deliver the service than the ordinary man in the street. The majority of service encounters that take place in fact do so with the employee in this position. Think of the jobs performed by the receptionist in a hotel, the shop assistant, the waiter and the bus conductor. We all feel that we could do them, and this makes us more critical of the service that is delivered.

There are four basic sources of role conflict (Figure 7.7):

- **Customer-siding conflict:** the employee wants to do more for the customer than the organization allows (provide a child's portion at a reduced price).
- **Company-siding conflict:** the employee takes the side of the organization believing that the customer is acting in an unjustified or selfish manner, i.e. refusing to admit late theatregoers during the performance.
- **Company-combining conflict:** the organization expects the employee to satisfy demanding customers and do lots of paperwork and administration besides.
- **Customer-combining conflict:** separate groups of customers have different requirements for the service, e.g. some customers may regard the main job of their coach tour guide to be one of information provision, other members of the party may instead believe that this person is there primarily to keep the tour on time.

So what can the organization do to minimize role conflict?

- Design jobs whose scope is pitched at the abilities of the proficient employee
- If need be, prioritize the multitude of tasks that the employee is expected to fulfil

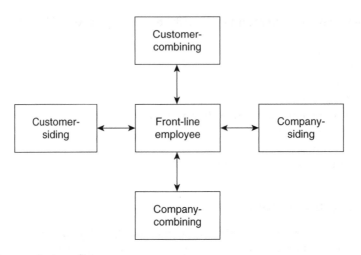

Figure 7.7 Sources of role conflict

- Define these tasks in terms of customers' expectations
- Ensure that performance is measured on those tasks that have been given priority; these should be customer-focused tasks
- Train employees in time management.

7.8.3   Role overload

The name describes the problem! No matter how diligently individuals work they can never do all that is asked of them. They are always behind – causing frustration and dissatisfaction with their performance.

This is most likely to occur where jobs have been badly designed. However, even where the initial job design was excellent, circumstances can change. It may be that the level, or pattern, of demand for the service has changed. If instead of handling equal customer traffic throughout the day, a workforce is faced with periods of relative inactivity followed by periods of intense activity, role overload may result.

Workloads and patterns of demand should be continually monitored and evaluated to reduce the risk of role overload.

7.8.4   Employee/job mismatch

Not every individual performing a front-line service role is an appropriate person for the job. In some cases this is the result of a poor recruitment and selection process. In others, the organization does not really care. It is known that many service companies experiencing high turnover rates among contact staff tend to recruit new staff expediently with little regard for their ability.[47] This is shortsighted, because these individuals probably do not really care much about customer satisfaction. Whatever the job, management should consider the qualities that are necessary to do the job. It should then adopt a selection process that tests for these qualities.

7.8.5   Performance measured on quantity not quality

It can be disheartening for a front-line employee to discover that they work for a company that is more interested in employee efficiency than employee effectiveness, the number of customers that they have dealt with being of more importance than the degree to which these customers were satisfied (see Chapter 10).

7.8.6   Lack of empowerment

Employees who have little flexibility or discretion in the way that they handle customers' demands can find their jobs frustrating. They can be likened to circus animals who slavishly respond to appropriate triggers, with set routines (see previous section).

7.8.7   Lack of a common purpose

Frequently the individual employee that greets the customer feels quite isolated in that position. He can believe that he carries out his job without the full backing either of the other employees in the back office or indeed of the company's management.

What is needed is for the company to have a common purpose and for everyone employed in it to pull in the same direction with the intention of achieving the common goal. One way of doing this is to make customer satisfaction the stated goal, and to make everyone in the company treat the other members of staff that they interact with as if they were customers. They should be encouraged to provide a standard of service to these employees that they would wish to receive themselves.

7.8.8   Lack of management commitment

It is one thing for management to develop a common purpose, and to communicate this mission to all its employees, but it cannot expect this alone to motivate the staff. If employees feel that management say one thing to them and then do another themselves, they are likely to become disenfranchised. As Abraham Lincoln said, 'actions speak louder than words'.[48] So, for example, if part of the stated mission is to improve customer satisfaction, then management should be seen to treat customer complaints seriously.

7.8.9   Role tension

Any of the dissatisfactions discussed above can lead to role tension in the employee. This tension will affect the level of commitment that the individual is willing to make. For an organization to realize the full potential of its employees, it must attempt to build a committed workforce. In a recent study it was found that job tension reduces job satisfaction, which in turn leads to higher rates of absenteeism and turnover.[49]

The greater the tension that employees feel, the less committed to their employers they become. The organization will suffer this lack of commitment, even if it is not to blame for the tension, e.g. discourteous customers can easily make the front-line employee tense. If such an incident is reported to management, which then takes little notice or does not want to get involved, the level of tension will rise. A management that practises internal marketing is now faced with the conflicting interests of these two groups of customers.

7.9   Staff turnover

One way that a dissatisfied employee can deal with his or her dissatisfaction is to leave the organization. There are many companies that accept high rates of turnover as a fact of life in the provision of service. In the 1980s counter staff turnover at McDonald's was 150% and at Burger King it was 250%.[50] Unfortunately, the acceptance of this creates a vicious circle (Figure 7.8).

In such circumstances, management considers that investing in selection and training is a waste of resource. Since employees are likely to leave soon, there is little point in developing their skills; after all, training them just makes it easier for them to find another job. An employer who thinks in this way fails to see that lack of investment in selection and training probably contribute to the high rates of turnover in the first place.

Traditional view = training is an overhead and is costly
Enlightened view = training does not cost

Companies should try to avoid high levels of staff turnover for several reasons. In the first place, the management of these companies tends to be less effective. It spends most of its time trying to fire-fight the current operation, instead of thinking about the future. For companies listed on the stock exchange, this can often result in adverse city comment with a consequent fall in the share price, and therefore value of the company. Curtailed expansion will also mean that the good people who have stayed until now begin to look elsewhere.

Companies with high levels of attrition usually provide poor customer service, because the employees providing the service will not have been doing so for long, they will often have little training, or understanding of the company's values or product. Their apparent lack of confidence in what they are doing often results in lower sales.

High staff turnover also results in extra costs for the company. It has to spend more on recruitment, administration and some basic training. Estimates suggest that separation, replacement and training costs are 1.5 to 2.5 times the annual salary for the person who resigns from their job.[51] In addition, there is a cost implication from the productivity losses that are experienced before new staff are up to speed.

However, while high levels of staff turnover should be avoided, the company should not set as its personnel goal, no staff turnover at all. For one thing, an organization that experiences no attrition goes stale. Fresh blood can bring new thinking and energy to take a company forward. Without this injection the organization can become complacent, and fixed in its view of how things should be done, resisting the challenge of change. Companies whose management has been in place for some time often resist until it is too late. Consider other creatures who once populated this planet, but through a lack of evolution are now extinct.

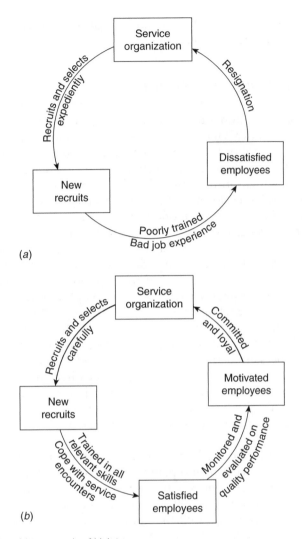

Figure 7.8 The vicious/virtuous cycle of high turnover

Another reason why some attrition should be encouraged is that no matter how expert an organization's selection process is, the odd misfit will manage to slip through the net. In these cases it is always better for the company to let the individual go rather than expend precious resources trying to keep him or her on board in pursuit of a zero staff turnover rate.

So the benefits to the company of building a workforce with low levels of turnover are increased commitment from staff, which in turn leads to increased productivity and better customer service. Organization commitment has been shown to be related to personal variables such as gender and marital status, i.e., personality traits that the company cannot influence. However, it is primarily related to variables that are under the control of the company. For example, the longer an employee has been with an organization, the more committed to it he or she will be. Conversely, the more that employees experience tension and dissatisfaction with their career progression, the less committed they become.

7.10   Internal marketing

There are two possible solutions to excess staff turnover. One focuses on the individual employee, the other deals more with the organization's role. These routes are not proposed as either/or options. To experience the benefits of low turnover the company must tackle the issue from both directions. Taken together, the two routes represent what is known as *internal marketing*.[52] The practice of internal marketing means using the traditional tools of marketing-segmentation, NPD (new product development), market research, promotion, etc. on potential and current employees.

So far our discussion has focused on front-line staff since they are most visible in the delivery of quality service. However, for the organization to operate effectively *all* employees must be pulling in the same direction. There is little sense in selecting and developing excellent front-line staff if they are not supported by those in the back office. While the customer does not see these employees it does not mean that they play an insignificant part in the delivery of a quality service.

All employees who are in the back office should treat the other members of the organization that they deal with as internal customers. Whether they provide direct support to front-line staff, as in the RAC's command control room, for example, which feeds information to its recovery vehicles, or direct support to other back-office staff, as in the accounts department of an hotel, they should behave towards these individuals in the same way that they would if they were external customers. Everyone in the organization must share the responsibility for delivering customer satisfaction.

The traditional interaction between customer and front-line employee can also be extended (Figure 7.9). Given the inseparability of production and consumption in most service encounters, customers actually become involved in the production of the service. Their behaviour (as well as that of employees) affects the outcome. Service organizations would do well to treat their customers as *partial* employees, adopting the same disciplines that we have discussed in this chapter for dealing with employees. The organization should select its customers, and then train them for the service encounter. This training can be given impersonally, e.g. through the company's external communications. They can be used to inform customers of what is expected of them in the service encounter. This tuition can also be given in person, e.g. the health club manager who takes his or her customers round the club and shows them how to use the facilities.

Central to the idea of internal marketing is the concept of the 'internal customer'.[53] This leads to the suggestion that employees should be treated as (internal) customers and that the organization has to consider issues of internal service quality which in turn will impact on internal service retention.[54]

Adopting internal marketing practices was predicted to have a positive impact on business performance. However, the supporting evidence is weak (at best) and some would suggest that internal marketing is merely another cynical tool used by management to control service employees: 'For the employee, as internal customer, it is simply a matter of control and more control. Unlike the "caring" resolve of external

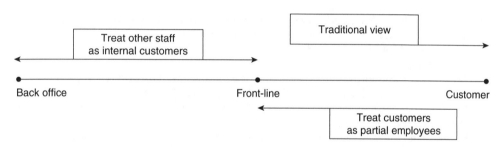

Figure 7.9 Expanding the roles of employee and customer

marketing, internal marketing's instrumental view of the internal customer as a means to an end affords little concern for care and much desire for control.'[55]

Summary

The employees who deliver service are of fundamental importance to both the customer that they serve and the employer for whom they work. In many cases, the source of customer dissatisfaction is in fact, the service employee. The employees in turn, deliver less than acceptable service because they are dissatisfied with the way that their employer treats them. There are many factors that can contribute to this dissatisfaction – those related to their role, to their lack of empowerment, or to the way that management runs the company.

The existence of these problems leads to a lack of motivation and commitment, and often results in a high turnover rate. Management can do several things which should help to reduce the likelihood of these arising. These include recruiting and selecting appropriate employees who match the job specification, training them in both the technical and non-technical skills necessary for the job, developing relevant orientation and socialization programmes, empowering those at the front line and compensating them in some way for the extra responsibility, and monitoring and evaluating their performance in terms of the quality of service that they provide not the quantity. The results should be fed back to employees to aid their development and thereby improve the service.

Finally, while the focus of this is the front-line employee, the same principles should also be adopted for all service employees. Those who do not have to face the customer themselves should be encouraged to regard other employees as their customers, treating them in the same way that they would expect customers to be treated.

References

1 Hochschild, A R (1983) *The Managed Heart: Commercialization of Human Feeling.* Berkeley, CA: University of California Press.

2 Keaveney, S (1988) 'Adding value to services through contact personnel', in Suprenant, C (ed.), *Add Value to Your Service.* American Marketing Association.

3 Lashley, C (2002) 'Emotional harmony, dissonance and deviance at work', *International Journal of Contemporary Hospitality Management,* **14** (5), 255–257.

4   Rafaeli, A (1993) 'Dress and behaviour of customer contact employees: a framework for analysis', *Advances in Services Marketing and Management*, **2**, 175–211.

5   Lovelock, C (1996) *Services Marketing*. Englewood Cliffs, NJ: Prentice Hall.

6   Hochschild, op. cit.

7   Taylor, S (1998) 'Emotional labour and the new workplace', in Thompson, P and Warhurst, C (eds), *Workplaces of the Future*. Basingstoke: Macmillan.

8   Boyd, C (2002) 'Customer violence and employee health and safety', *BSA Publications*, **16** (1), 151–169.

9   Fernie, S and Metcalf, D (1998) *(Not) Hanging on the Telephone: Payment Systems in the New Sweatshops*. London: Centre for Economic Performance, LSE.

10 Bain, P and Taylor, P (2000) 'Entrapped by the "electronic panopticon"? Worker resistance in the call centre', *New Technology, Work and Employment*, **15** (1), 1–18.

11 Hogan, J and Hogan, R (1989) 'How do you measure employee reliability', *Journal of Applied Psychology*, **74**, 273–279.

12 Ashforth, B E and Humphrey, R H (1993) 'Emotional labor in service roles: the influence of identity', *Academy of Management Review*, **18** (1), 88–115.

13 Wharton, A S (1999) 'Service with a smile: understanding the consequences of emotional labor', *Annals of the American Academy of Political and Social Science*, **561**, 158–176.

14 Hochschild, A R (1993) 'Preface' to Fineman, S (ed.), *Emotion in Organisations*. London: Sage.

15 Bowen, D E and Lawler III, E E (1995) 'Organising for service: empowerment or production line?', in *Understanding Services Management: Integrating Marketing, Organisational Behaviour, Operations, and Human Resources Management*. New York: Wiley, pp. 269–294.

16 Collins, D (1996) 'Control and isolation in the management of empowerment', *Empowerment in Organisations*, **4** (2), 22–39.

17 Roth, W F (1997) 'Going all the way with empowerment', *The TQM Magazine*, **9** (1), 42–45.

18 Maslow, A (1954) *Motivation and Personality*. New York: Harper and Brothers.

19 Wilson, T (1997) 'Empowerment – beyond the rhetoric', *Training Officer*, **33** (6), 182–185.

20 Siebert, S E, Silver, S R and Randolph, W A (2004) 'Taking empowerment to the next level: a multiple-level model of empowerment, performance, and satisfaction', *Academy of Management Journal*, **47** (3), 332–349.

21 Taylor, F W (1911) *The Principles of Scientific Management*. New York: Harper and Brothers.

22 Weber, M (1946) *The Theory of Social and Economic Organisation* (trans. A M Henderson and T Parsons) New York: Free Press.

23 Rafaeli, A and Worline, M (2001) 'Individual emotion in work organizations', *Social Science Information*, **40** (1), 95–123.

24 Ogbonna, E and Harris, L C (1998) 'Managing organizational culture: compliance or genuine change?', *British Journal of Management*, **9**, 273–288.

25 Herzberg, F (1968) 'One more time: how do you motivate employees?', *Harvard Business Review*, Jan–Feb, 53–62.

26 Schneider, B and Schechter, D (1982) 'Development of a personnel selection system for service jobs', in Brown, S, Gummesson, E and Edvardsson, B (eds), *Service Quality: Multidisciplinary and Multinational Perspectives*. Lexington, MA: Lexington Books, pp. 217–236.

27 George, W (1990) 'Internal marketing and organisational behaviour: a partnership in developing customer-conscious employees at every level,' *Journal of Business Research*, **20**, 63–70.

28 Woods, R H and Macauley, J F (1989) 'RX for turnover: retention programmes that work,' *Cornell Hotel and Restaurant Administration*, May, 79–90.

29 Kiger, P J (2002) 'Why customer satisfaction starts with HR', *Workforce*, **81** (5), 26–32.

30 Schlesinger, L A and Heskett, J L (1991) 'Breaking the cycle of failure in services management', *Management Review*, Spring, 17–28.

31 Supermarket Cashier (1992) 'Custom-eyes critical eye', Channel Four television series.

32 Rafaeli, A and Sutton, R I (1990) 'Busy stores and demanding customers', *Academy of Management Journal*, **33** (3), 623–637.

33 Van Gennep, A (1960) *Rites of Passage*. Chicago: University of Chicago Press (originally published by Emile Mourry, Paris, 1909).

34 Rohlen, T P (1973) 'Spiritual education in a Japanese bank,' *American Anthropologist*, **75**, 1542–1562.

35 Macdonald, C A and Sirianni, C (1996) *Working in the Service Society*. Philadelphia: Temple University Press.

36 Schein, E H (1988) 'Organisational socialisation and the profession of management', *Sloan Management Review*, Fall, 53–65.

37 Malone, T W (1997) 'Is empowerment just a fad? Control, decision making, and IT', *Sloan Management Review*, Winter, 23–35.

38 Lawler, E E, Mohrman, S A and Ledford, G E (1995) *Creating the High Performance Organisation: Impact of Employee Involvement and Total Quality Management*. San Francisco, CA: Jossey-Bass.

39 Herzberg, op. cit.

40 Reicheld, F F (1996) *The Loyalty Effect*. Cambridge, MA: Harvard Business School Press.

41 Cardy, R L (2001) 'Employees as customers?', *Marketing Management*, **10** (3), 12–13.

42 Rust, R, Stewart, G L, Miller, H *et al.* (1996) 'The satisfaction and retention of frontline employees: a customer satisfaction measurement approach', *International Journal of Service Industry Management*, **7** (5), 62–80.

43 Jerome, L and Kleiner, B H (1995) 'Employee morale and its impact on service: what companies do to create a positive service experience', *Managing Service Quarterly*, **5** (6), 21–25.

44 Bell, C R and Zemke, R (1988) 'Do service procedures tie employees hands?' *Personnel Journal*, September, 77–83.

45 Harris, T (1970) *The Book of Choice*. London: Jonathan Cape.

46 Shamir, B (1980) 'Between service and servility: role conflict in subordinate service roles', *Journal of Human Relations*, **33** (10), 741–756.

47 Schlesinger, L A and Heskett, J L (1991) Breaking the cycle of failure in services management', *Management Review*, Spring, 17–28.

48 Lincoln, A (1856) Cited in *Oxford Concise Book of Proverbs*. Oxford: Oxford University Press.

49 Rogers, J D, Klow, K E and Kash, T J (1994) 'Increasing job satisfaction of service personnel', *Journal of Services Marketing*, **8** (1), 14–26.

50 Woods, R H and Macauley, J F (1989) 'RX for turnover: retention programmes that work', *Cornell Hotel and Restaurant Administration*, May, 79–90.

51 Solomon, J (1988) 'Companies try measuring cost savings from new types of corporate benefits', *The Wall Street Journal*, 29 December, B1.

52 Gronroos, C (2000) *Service Management and Marketing*. Chichester: Wiley.

53 Bruhn, M (2003) 'Internal service barometers: conceptualisation and empirical results of a pilot study in Switzerland', *European Journal of Marketing*, **37** (9), 1187–1204.

54 Naude, P, Desai, J and Murphy, J (2003) 'Identifying the determinants of internal marketing orientation', *European Journal of Marketing*, **37** (9), 1205–1220.

55 Mudie, P (2003) 'Internal customer: by design or by default', *European Journal of Marketing*, **37** (9), 1261–1276.

8

Demand and capacity management

Introduction

In service industries the matching of capacity and demand is particularly difficult. There is either too much demand for the capacity, putting a strain on resources, or too little demand, giving rise to unused capacity and a loss in revenue. This is known as the *perishability factor*, whereby revenue from a unit of capacity, e.g. a hotel bedroom that's not sold on a particular day, is lost forever, unlike a product that if unsold can be stored in a warehouse for sale at a later date. Therefore services need to develop some understanding of demand patterns. While the level of demand can sometimes be outwith the organization's control, strategies are available for measuring demand, along with capacity, with a view to bringing them into balance.

One technique that is becoming highly significant for demand and capacity management in the service sector is that of yield or revenue management. By setting different prices for different time periods organizations seek to increase the yield or revenue from the service.

One problematic symptom of excess demand is queuing. Whilst reservations and advance booking can mitigate its occurrence, in some situations it still occurs and will remain so with the inevitable frustrations for customers.

8.1 The basic problem: perishability

If a manufacturer of cars, washing machines or furniture fails to sell some of its products on a particular day or over a certain period they are stored for sale at a later date when demand increases. For organizations providing a service, e.g. hotels, trains, their 'product' in the form of rooms and seats is not capable of being stored. Where a hotel room on a particular day and a train seat on a particular journey lies empty the revenue that could have been gained is lost and can never be regained. The 'products' have in effect perished. The situation is the same for services such as counselling where the unit of capacity is time. Perishability is a significant issue for services then and can best be summed up as follows:

- If demand far exceeds capacity it cannot be met as in manufacturing, by taking goods from a warehouse.
- If capacity far exceeds demand the potential revenue from that service is lost.

Where service capacity is largely fixed and demand is subject to variation, organizations can experience any of the following situations:[1]

- Excess demand – the level of demand exceeds maximum available capacity
- Demand exceeds optimum capacity – the service is less than adequate
- Demand and capacity are well balanced – this is the level of optimum capacity
- Excess capacity – demand is below optimum capacity.

From Figure 8.1 it is evident that the level of capacity utilization will impact on the quality of service. As the name implies, the optimum is the best level in most cases for all parties concerned – customers, employees and the organization. Operating at maximum capacity, however, or even beyond as with some transportation services, is seen as a desired feature of some service situations, namely nightclubs and bars. (The trend is now for 'vertical bars', standing room only, where most of the tables and chairs are removed allowing a much higher number of customers to enter.) Otherwise services must aim to occupy that optimum capacity zone. There has been little comment as to where it lies. For an airline it is said to range from 65 to 75%[2] and for most services the optimal capacity appears to be between 70 and 90%[3] of maximum

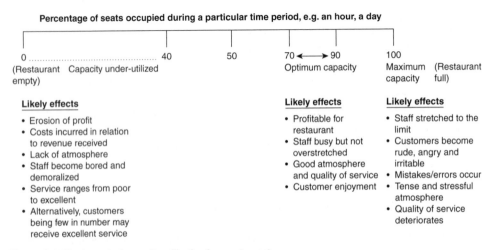

Figure 8.1 The impact of capacity utilization in a restaurant

capacity. Where specifically it may lie will be conditioned by the service type or situation. Customers, in general, could be said to feel happier if less than all the seats on a train or in a restaurant were occupied. Equally from the organization's viewpoint operating at the maximum means there is no slack to allow for addressing a range of problems that may arise, e.g. demanding customers, employee errors, diagnostic difficulties (car repair). Just how much of a challenge arriving at the optimum can be is illustrated by the matter of how many patients a doctor should see in one hour.

8.2   Service capacity: resources and assets

Service organizations draw on the following resources and assets in varying degrees depending on the type of service:

- Physical facilities designed to house customers, the obvious ones being hotels, hospitals, aeroplanes, schools. Each facility will be defined in terms of number of rooms, beds, seats and classrooms.
- Physical facilities designed for processing customers and their possessions, examples would include washing machines (launderette), computer technology (banks), X-ray equipment (hospitals), turnstiles (football stadium).
- Labour is a key element in the provision of service, e.g. waiters in a restaurant, cabin crew on an aeroplane, tellers in a bank. A number of services rely heavily on labour where the service comes to the customer, as in breakdown services, cleaning, gardening, roof repair, postal services.
- Time is a resource that serves as the basis upon which several services may be sold, e.g. a consultant, lawyer, plumber, car repair, counsellor.

There will inevitably be periods when capacity is under-utilized. On the other hand, a service's capacity will come under strain when demand is high. In such circumstances the flexibility of that capacity to meet demand will be tested.

8.3   Service demand

To anticipate and alleviate pressures on capacity, services need to have, as clearly as possible, an understanding of demand patterns. Two questions come into play. First, by how much does demand vary or fluctuate? There may be extreme variation to very little. Secondly, is the variability able to be predicted? If a predictable cycle or pattern is detectable its duration may be as follows:

- One day (varies by hour)
- One week (varies by day)
- One month (varies by day or week)
- One year (varies by month or season).

The causes of these cyclical variations may be many and will vary by type of service. Causal factors for a bus service are likely to be employment/school hours, shopping behaviour and entertainment. As there is a degree of stability to these factors

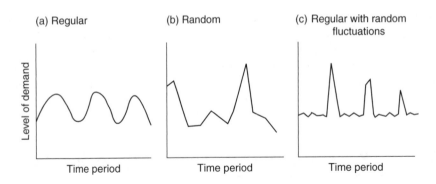

Figure 8.2 Demand patterns

demand will be largely predictable and vary by hour, less so by day. Consequently the bus company is able to schedule its fleet in tune with demand. Some services – health, breakdown, roofing, insurance – will be subject to random and extreme fluctuations in demand caused by factors outwith their control, e.g. weather, outbreak of illness. Overall, the demand patterns for specific organizations and across the service sector are not available for public consumption. However, it can be stated that demand for most service organizations will exhibit one of the following patterns (Figure 8.2).

8.4   Managing demand and capacity

Originally two strategies were suggested for managing demand and capacity: the first would involve adjusting capacity to match demand (defined as 'chasing demand') and the second, altering demand to match available capacity (known as 'level capacity').[4]

1 **Adjusting capacity to match demand**
   A number of options are available for consideration:
   - Extend the opening hours – this is not an option open to all service organizations. Where it is possible it is likely to occur only when demand levels are regarded as particularly excessive.
   - Encourage employees to work harder – the requirement here is usually that of processing more customers per hour or per day. Although a mark of efficiency (more output from existing staff), service quality for customers may deteriorate.
   - Cross-train employees – enables organizations to operate with fewer staff. Instead of being confined to handling few responsibilities staff are equipped to manage a variety of tasks and activities. It amounts to a move in the direction of job enlargement and some might say job enrichment, increasing employee motivation, satisfaction and morale. Not all employees will welcome it, particularly where there is seen to be little increase in commensurate rewards. The type of service and the organizational culture will be two prominent factors that need to be taken into account prior to such a move.
   - Recruiting part-time employees – this is an option low in cost and potentially one that can be achieved quickly. Organizations should, of course, ensure that

part-time employees be given the same support and encouragement as given to full-time staff.

- Add facilities – usually in the form of table, chairs or other equipment. Just how much scope there is for this will depend on the initial configuration and layout designed to communicate a specific atmosphere and/or level of service. Adding facilities may change both.
- Hire or share facilities or equipment – may be in the form of additional physical space or vehicles required either on a temporary or recurring basis.
- Using customers as productive resources – up to this point all attempts at adjusting capacity have involved manipulating internal resources and assets. However some have suggested that organizations should regard customers as 'partial employees' and make a contribution to productive capacity.[5]
- Outsourcing (already referred to in Chapter 2) – for small to medium-sized organizations, in particular, calling on outside assistance is a valuable option in trying to meet market demand. Typical areas for outsourcing are technological and marketing support, employee recruitment and training, and Web development. Large organizations also outsource. Consider the recent case of British Airways and the outsourcing of its inflight catering to Gate Gourmet. Competitive pressures in the airline industry had forced this move. Unfortunately, the demand for lower costs led to industrial action by Gate Gourmet employees.

The above options, then, are aimed at increasing capacity to absorb demand. However, for service organizations there will inevitably be periods of time where capacity is under-utilized. Such a situation will remain so if attempts to encourage demand during these periods prove unsuccessful. It has been suggested that slack time be used 'productively as a time to train new employees, do maintenance on the equipment, clean the premises, prepare for the next peak and give the workers some relief from the frantic pace of the peak periods'.[6]

2 **Altering demand to match available capacity**

Whereas capacity management is a response to demand, demand management is an attempt to shift demand. Given the relative inflexibility of capacity organizations may seek to smooth demand by reducing the variability and fluctuation of existing patterns. Organizations can turn to the marketing mix for stimulating demand during periods of spare capacity or shifting demand during periods where capacity is operating at or near maximum. Of the '4 Ps' price and, to a lesser extent, place, offer the most potential in this area.

- Manipulate price – this will be discussed in more detail in the following section on 'Revenue Management'. The central role of price is to discourage too many customers from using the service during 'peak demand' periods and encourage more customers to select 'off-peak' periods. On price alone this strategy will only work if enough customers can be attracted by the lower prices available during low demand periods. Leisure, hospitality and transportation services would appear suited to this approach. However this strategy of price differentiation is, it is argued, not without risk. Customers may become acclimatized to the lower prices and expect them whenever the service is used. Equally there is risk to the organization's image in that lower prices may attract undesirable customers.[7] This would be particularly relevant for a service that regards itself as more upmarket or exclusive.

- Offer a mobile service – for a number of reasons consumers have welcomed the emergence of mobile services where the provider takes the service to the customer rather than or in addition to the customer having to visit the provider in some fixed location. Libraries have used this approach for many years, the service being particularly valued by the disabled and those living in remote locations. Other services that have found mobility an effective method of managing demand include breakdown and maintenance, blood donation and catering.
- Communicating with customers – the provision of information as to when demand is, or is likely to be, high appears to be a strategy not well adopted by service organizations. In particular for customers in our 'call centre society' it can be especially frustrating. Waiting is a feature of modern day society and will be addressed later in the chapter.
- Changing the service offer – for most organizations this is not an option. What they offer remains fixed. Where services with a sizeable facility like hotels experience significant seasonal fluctuations however, action may be taken to encourage varied usage of the facility when capacity is under-utilized.

■ 8.5 Aligning demand and capacity: the options

Due to the relative inflexibility of service capacity coupled with the variability of service demand, aligning the two remains a challenge. Relatively recent writing,[8] incorporating the original thinking,[9] suggests four options are available to service organizations in determining a relationship between demand and capacity. They are:

- **Provide** – where sufficient capacity is available at all times to meet peak demand. This may mean periods of excess capacity but that is to be preferred to a situation where business is lost due to insufficient capacity.
- **Match** – where attempts are made to anticipate demand pattern so that capacity levels can be changed to accommodate. It would involve careful scheduling of work as well as considering sub-contracting or outsourcing.
- **Influence** – where demand patterns are changed, if possible, to obtain effective utilization of capacity. Responsibility for changing demand will lie with marketing deploying elements of the marketing mix as appropriate.
- **Control** – where capacity remains fixed in service situations that are unique and high cost resources are needed to provide the level of service expected. Consequently, variation in demand needs to be kept to a minimum.

Each of these options in relation to an actual demand pattern is shown in Figure 8.3.

Actual demand in Figure 8.3 is presented as more of a random rather than regular fluctuation across the six time periods. The basic question that arises is:

- What level of capacity should be maintained to satisfy the demand? Should a company provide excess capacity to improve customer service or minimize excess capacity to maximize resource utilization.[10]

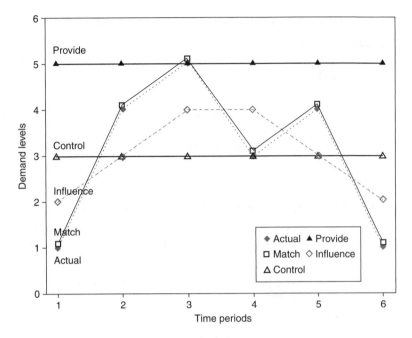

Figure 8.3 Demand management strategies – hypothetical
Source: Crandall and Markland (1996)[10], reproduced with permission from the Production and Operations Management Society

The following two options characterize the original thinking:[11]

- The 'match' option (managing the capacity) is shown as parallel to, but slightly higher than, the actual demand lines. This option is more easily managed with employees than equipment and facilities.
- The influence option attempts to smooth the actual and match capacity by shifting the peak demands to the low demand periods. Variable capacity then becomes less of a problem. It is slightly higher in low demand periods and slightly lower in high demand periods.

The more recent thinking embraces two further options:

- The provide option shown as the straight horizontal line at the top of Figure 8.3 presupposes that enough capacity is available to meet even the peak demands. It could be thought of as a wasteful option as resources will inevitably be under-utilized, particularly through periods 1, 4 and 6.
- The control option is shown as the horizontal line in the middle. It is designed to meet average demand, using waiting lines or some other means of accommodating excess demand until capacity is available.

One piece of research[12] of selected service industries suggests an overall preference for the provide and match options over those of influence and control. Two broad reasons are advanced: companies' desire to improve customer service and the notion that companies understand how to change capacities better than they understand how to change demand patterns.

8.6   Yield management (also known as revenue management)

8.6.1   Definition

From the discussion so far it should be clear that service organizations face a challenge in terms of managing demand and capacity. Yield management is a technique designed to address that challenge. It is defined as 'provision of the right service to the right customer at the right time for the right price'.[13]

8.6.2   Where can yield management be applied?

Yield management is not (yet) suitable for all service organizations. Application has been most successful in services that have the following characteristics:[14]

- Relative fixed capacity – e.g. once a hotel has rented out all its rooms further demand cannot be met without substantial capital investment
- Perishable inventory – a major constraint for services is time or more specifically time during which a unit of capacity is available. If a hotel room (unit of capacity) is not sold for a particular date the revenue that would have been gained is lost
- Segmented markets – where the market for a service can be segmented according to certain criteria, e.g. price sensitivity
- Fluctuating demand – where the adoption of various pricing approaches enables the reduction of peaks and valleys in variable demand. Success in this regard results in more effective utilization of capacity
- Services that can be sold in advance through reservation systems – allows for better use of capacity
- Low variable to fixed cost ratio – in service pricing some contribution must be made towards fixed cost. The low level of variable cost, e.g. cleaning a hotel room, coupled with discretion in pricing means that the revenue expected from selling it is invariably greater than if it was not sold. That is why yield management is usually regarded as a profit-enhancing strategy.

Users of yield management fall broadly into three categories:

1 Sophisticated – airlines and large hotel chains are regarded as the classic users employing complex information systems and computer models for the purpose of analysing and predicting consumer demand patterns.
2 Moderate – theatres, trains, hairdressers, small/medium hotels use less advanced systems and technologies in the deployment of classic yield management techniques.
3 Potential – restaurants and golf courses are current and notable examples of services ready for yield management were it not for, in both cases, variability and unpredictability over the duration of service. For yield management to work there must be a fixed length of time within which the service is consumed.

8.6.3 How does yield management work?

Yield management works by recognizing and applying the following key elements.

Time

Time – when a service is consumed, e.g. hour of the day, day of the week, month of the year, is the key element in terms of determining how much a customer is likely to pay and consequently the yield that accrues to the organization. The sensitivity of customers as to when they consume the service is of prime importance in yield management. In addition to the times of consumption, the timing of any reservation may decide the price to be paid.

Demand – to enable yield calculations and assessments to be made, services need to classify demand periods and the variations between them. One possible classification can be seen in Figure 8.4.

In total there are 32 demand periods in Figure 8.4 (4 seasons [×] 2 days of week [×] 4 times of day). For yield management purposes it is a question of whether each of the 32 cells merit unique treatment in terms of price levels and customer profiles. Criticism has been made of the airline industry for its increasing fine-tuning of segmentation and combinations of fares, rules and conditions, only to find that '60–80 per cent of these products never generated a single sale of a seat to a customer'.[15]

Price discrimination – in conjunction with time, mentioned earlier, customers are also sensitive to price. Where a customer needs to use a particular service, e.g. the railways during, say, a peak period (time-sensitive), that customer will be willing to pay more (price-insensitive). The converse then is where a customer is unconcerned over, say, the time of travel (time-insensitive) and consequently will enjoy a discounted price if an off-peak period is selected (price-sensitive). Although time and demand levels are the main causal factors or rate fences in price discrimination, other factors (as we shall see) permit variation in pricing.

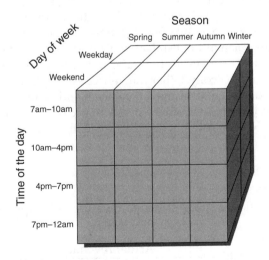

Figure 8.4 Variations in demand by time period

Rate fences

The price discrimination strategy or variable pricing as mentioned above should have some logic to it. To achieve this, yield management sets what is known as rate fences at time of usage. These are rules or conditions designed to make clear the reason for either a particular price or price differences in general. To be successful it is felt that customers need to perceive price differences as justified and fair. Where two customers are using the same service (a particular rail journey) there can be a difference in the price that each customer has paid. The customer paying the higher price may regard this situation as unfair. However, particular rate fences in this instance are designed to offer an explanation. For example, the customer paying the cheaper price has booked a seat in advance or falls into a category of customer (pensioner, student) which qualifies for a lower price. Although time of service usage is a major rate fence in yield management, other conditions or qualifications are in operation depending on the type of service. A number of rate fences of two types have been cited for restaurants:[16]

1 **Tangible rate fences**
   - Table location
   - Party size
   - Menu type
   - Presence or absence of certain amenities (e.g. bread on the table)
2 **Intangible rate fences**
   - Group membership or application
   - Time of day or week
   - Duration of use
   - Timing of booking
   - Walk-in or reservation
   - Type of reservation (guaranteed or not).

Another service industry open to yield management type activity is the opera. The 'value' of each seat is determined and priced according to what the customer is willing and able to pay. Seats vary in terms of 'place utility'. In other words, all the seats do not deliver the same experience. Seat location then becomes a rate fence. Box 8.1 illustrates the seating plan of English National Opera. In line with seat location and differentiated experience, prices for the stalls and dress circle are higher than those for the upper circle and balcony. Other rate fences are in place qualifying for a price concession, e.g. students, children aged between 5 and 16 with an adult, senior citizens, tickets unsold three hours before a performance (standby tickets) and standing tickets (all seats have been sold but standing available at the back of the Dress and Upper Circles).

Yield measurement

The basic yield statistic is a straightforward measure. It is expressed as follows:

$$\text{Yield} = \frac{\text{Actual revenue}}{\text{Potential or Maximum revenue}}$$

Box 8.1 Seating plan – English National Opera

Seating plan

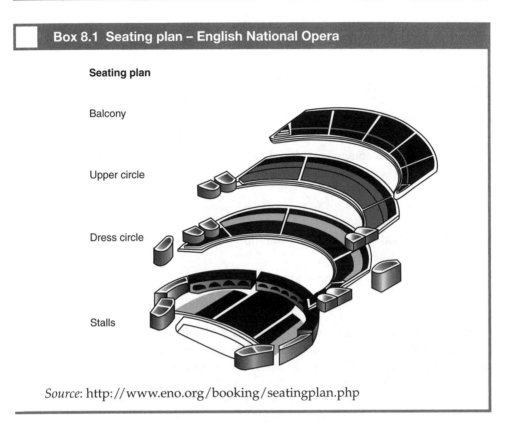

Balcony

Upper circle

Dress circle

Stalls

Source: http://www.eno.org/booking/seatingplan.php

Revenue potential is the revenue that could be secured if 100 per cent of capacity is sold at the maximum price possible. In more detail, yield is a function of price efficiency and capacity used, namely:

$$\text{Capacity utilization} \times \text{Price efficiency}$$

where

$$\text{Capacity utilization} = \frac{\text{Units of capacity sold}}{\text{Total units of capacity}}$$

and

$$\text{Price efficiency} = \frac{\text{Actual price}}{\text{Maximum price}}$$

(Note: terminology can vary according to industry, e.g. hotel capacity is occupancy rate, transport capacity is load factor, hotel price is rate, and so on.)

If we consider the hotel industry, yield would be found from:

$$\frac{\text{Rooms sold}}{\text{Rooms available for sale}} \times \frac{\text{Rate (price) of rooms sold}}{\text{Rate potential}}$$

For example, a hotel with 280 rooms sells in one night 140 rooms at £80 and a further 70 rooms at the maximum rate of £200. The yield would be

$$\text{Yield} = \frac{140}{280} \times \frac{80}{200} + \frac{70}{280} \times \frac{200}{200}$$

$$= 0.5 \times 0.4 + 0.25 \times 1$$

$$\begin{array}{cccc} \text{occupancy} & \text{price} & \text{occupancy} & \text{price} \\ \text{percentage} & \text{efficiency} & \text{percentage} & \text{efficiency} \end{array}$$

$$= 0.2 + 0.25$$

$$= 0.45 \text{ or } 45\%$$

$$\text{Maximum yield} = 280 \times £200 \text{ (total number of rooms} \times \text{maximum rate)}$$

$$= £56\,000$$

$$\text{Actual yield} = £56\,000 \times 45\%$$

$$= 25\,200 \; (140 \times £80 + 70 \times £200)$$

In reality a hotel's capacity will be composed of a mix of rooms at varying prices. Suppose, in the example above, that 95 rooms are priced at £200 (maximum rate) and the remaining 185 at £80 (maximum rate), the maximum yield would be £33 800 (95 [×] £200 + 185 [×] £80). The percentage actual yield is 74.5% (£25 200 divided by £33 800). Price efficiency is maximized at 1 or 100%. On the other hand, average capacity utilization across the two categories of room is:

$$0.75 \text{ or } 75\% \qquad \left(\frac{140}{185} + \frac{70}{95} \text{ divided by } 2 \right)$$

With the above example in mind, measures have been established for measuring success in yield management (see Box 8.2).

Box 8.2 Revenue per available time-based inventory unit (REVPATI)

- **Airline:** Revenue per available seat mile
- **Hotel:** Revenue per available room night
- **Car rental:** Revenue per available car pay
- **Restaurant:** Revenue per available seat hour
- **Function space:** Revenue per available square metre per day part
- **Golf course:** Revenue per available tee time

Source: Kimes (2002)[17]

An example from the airline industry[18] illustrates the calculation of revenue per available seat mile with the additional consideration of cost. To begin with, operational expenses are calculated for each flight and then divided by the number of available seats on that flight. This means each seat has a fixed cost associated with it.

To make this figure even more meaningful the cost is then broken down to cost per kilometre. Therefore, each flight has an available seat kilometre (ASK), which is computed by multiplying the number of seats on the aeroplane by the distance of the flight. For example:

Boeing 747 with 400 seats
Flight: London to Johannesburg (10 000 kilometres)
$\therefore$ ASK = 4 million (400 $\times$ 10 000)

Full cost of flight = £210 000
$\therefore$ Cost per ASK = 5.25 pence per seat per kilometre
(£210 000 divided by 4 million)

To find out if the yield on revenue of the above flight is good, bad, or indifferent a further calculation is required. The marketing team needs to know the revenue per passenger kilometre (RPK) of each flight. Using the same flight and costs as above, the RPK would be worked out as follows:

380 passengers on board
Total revenue is £247 500

Total passenger kilometres = 380 $\times$ 10 000

$$= 3 800 000$$

Thus RPK = 6.5 pence, which gives a yield of 23.8% over the ASK.

The conclusion drawn was just how marginal airline operations can be. The challenge for the airline is one of managing the mix of passengers on the different classes.

8.7   Waiting and queuing

8.7.1   Why waiting matters

'Waiting is frustrating, demoralizing, agonizing, aggravating, annoying, time consuming and incredibly expensive.' This view of waiting is offered in an advertisement for Fedex, an American parcels carrier. Since one of the company's selling propositions is that they can deliver goods to customers sooner than their competitors, it is not surprising that they emphasize the disadvantages of waiting. However, it is clear that many service customers do find waiting a tiresome problem – to avoid which they are often prepared to pay extra. In James Gleick's book *Faster* we are invited to read about 'the acceleration of just about everything'.[19] In the book we read about fast food, Internet booking, and the chaos that occurs when speed is not matched by reliability – a problem we can see everyday at airports when people miss connections or are delayed because of a shortage of staff at check-in desks.

In a competitive environment the ability to provide a service without waiting confers two kinds of advantage. The first appeals to the customer – speed is one of the key service qualities which gives one firm an advantage over another – an advantage which sells cars in stock, fast food (even at the expense of taste) and photo-processing 'while you wait'. The second kind of advantage is operational – avoidance of waiting is often avoidance of waste. For example, an airliner which spends less time at an airport turn-round can make more trips, and more profit, in a day. In logistics increased speed in the supply chain means that goods for sale spend less time between factory and consumer, which improves cash flow, as well as increasing sales.

Waiting may be a lead time delay, between placing an order (or perhaps describing a symptom to a doctor) and delivery of the goods, or receiving appropriate medical treatment. 'Lead time' is the gap between signalling a demand, want or need – in commercial terms, generating an order – and satisfactory completion, or fulfilling the order. An efficient organization tells the customer what the lead time will be, meets the deadline consistently, and offers a faster response than competitors. Reducing lead time is one of the key efficiency aims of modern business. In services it is often achieved by self-service – for example by inviting hotel guests to help themselves from a breakfast buffet rather than wait for a waiter to take an order and later deliver it. In hospitals the ability to reduce waiting time between identifying the need for an operation and actually performing it is a key performance indicator – as well as being a matter of life and death.

In many service systems waiting often shows in the physical presence of a crowd of people, often in vehicles, waiting because the system is congested. Too many people (and very often too many cars) have arrived at the same place at the same time, and the system cannot cope. The people waiting, whether on foot or in vehicles, 'tail back' from the point where the flow is disrupted, and it is this 'tail-back' which gives a waiting line the name 'queue' – the French word for a tail.

8.7.2   Queues – waiting given shape

When customers flow through a service system, as they do when they travel, or check into a hotel, or arrive at a restaurant for a meal, then the need to wait often takes the shape of standing in a queue – 'waiting in line' as it is termed in the USA. There are three main causes of queues. They are:

1   The need to halt a flow of people or vehicles for a transaction. Transaction processes include selling tickets, having documents checked, passing through security and immigration checks, and being sorted into categories.
2   The slowing of a flow because there is a physical constraint which slows things down. This constraint is usually called a bottleneck, and if you up end a bottle of water you can see why. Bottlenecks occur because several flows converge (as at road junctions or transport interchanges) or because of some infrastructure limitation, like a narrow bridge crossing a river which divides a city.
3   Queues occur because people arrive before the service is open for business. Such queues include those waiting for a bus driver to arrive and open the doors, those outside shops waiting for opening time, and people waiting in areas of famine for food donations. This last example gives the reason why many service opening time queues occur. A queue ensures 'first come first served', which is particularly important if there is a belief that there will not be enough to serve everybody who waits.

The need to queue occurs frequently in service systems where customers do not order service in advance, as is true of commuter journeys by public transport, shopping in supermarkets, and driving down a city street at a busy time. In such situations the arrival rate of customers is often likely to exceed the capacity of the service system to handle the flow of people, especially at peak times. People who wait for service may find themselves in a crowd, or in a funnel-shape group moving towards a sales point, or in a panic-stricken stampede running towards an emergency exit. Forming an orderly queue is often the fairest and most efficient way to serve those who wait.

8.7.3   The reason for queues

Organizing a waiting group to form an orderly queue, or (as Americans put it) 'wait in line', has many advantages. The first is that it gives to those who wait the visible fairness of 'first come first served'. So long as there is no queue-jumping then the first person in the queue ought to be the first person to arrive, and the first person to be served. The importance which people in the queue give to this idea is very obvious if you look at the kind of queue that forms (often waiting all night) to get the best chance of bargains in the January sales of major department stores. Because there are, quite deliberately, not enough of the best bargains for everyone in the queue, who is first in the queue matters a great deal. When there are enough goods for everybody in the queue, then first come first served is a matter of equalizing the wait. In addition a queue lets people see 'where they stand' so they can make some sort of guess about how long they will wait. Queues have other advantages as a shape of waiting. They permit space to be used efficiently, as you can see when you observe two orderly lines of vehicles waiting to go through a 'bottleneck', such as a junction where two streams converge. If the vehicles stay in line, the space is used efficiently, and the 'throughput' is maximized. If drivers start jockeying for position, chaos develops, tempers rise and the speed of traffic falls.

Slow moving queues usually form for several 'supply side' reasons. The first is that the halt for processing takes a long time. This may be that the process is necessarily complicated or time-consuming, as is often the case when people are booking diverse travel tickets for future travel. Queues waiting for processing are often long because there are not enough servers to meet demand, even when peaks of demand are predictable. Two common solutions to processing queues are to encourage pre-booking (especially by purchasing on line) and adjusting supply by multi-skilling staff, so a customer service assistant can be switched from enquiries to check-in tasks. Processing often has to be careful to protect revenue or to prevent hazards, such as the ability to put bombs in airliner baggage. Waiting can be reduced by employing more service staff, by speeding or simplifying the processes (e.g. by using 'smart cards' for security), and by self-service systems, such as fast ticket machines. Bottlenecks are often very difficult to cure because the infrastructure limitation would be very expensive to remove, or because the very feature which impedes the flow is cherished for its charm. It would be possible, although costly, to build a four-lane motorway through the centre of the city of York, but to do so would destroy the appeal of the old city. Queues prior to service start times are often caused by the fear of shortages. In affluent societies they have most commonly been reduced by solving the problem of shortages. Another approach is by rationing, so that those who arrive first get no more than those who arrive later. We should note that some shortage queues are created deliberately, like those for bargain price goods in department store sales.

There are 'demand side' reasons why queues form. The most common reason is that services cannot be stored, but demand fluctuates, which is why there is often a price discount for booking early, especially on services that are likely to have unused capacity. We commonly find that the total demand for service in a working day is matched by the total capacity of the service, but that there are peak times when the number of customers exceeds the system's capacity, and queues form. Peaks occur because the demand for service is derived from other social and economic habits, such as the desire to fly from busy airports on the day before public holidays. Peaks may occur once or twice a day, or seasonally, such as at Christmas. Related to peak demands are surges. A surge is the term used to describe the sudden arrival of a large group of customers not related to peak times, but often having an identifiable cause. To take a simple example, the arrival of a coach party at a country inn will cause a surge of demand. This surge will probably have been recognized by the reservation of tables in the dining room, but the desire for a pre-lunch drink may cause a surge of demand at a bar designed to serve a local clientele. Two other demand side phenomena should be noted. The first is that the total demand for the service may exceed total supply, so there are queues at most times of day. An economist would describe this situation as one of disequilibrium and it often exists in services where there is no price mechanism to regulate demand.

Another demand problem which should be noted is that of panic – often amongst those fleeing from danger. In a smoke-filled nightclub or airliner the best way to get people out safely is to form orderly lines flowing through as many exits as possible. Reality shows us that in such situations people sometimes stampede, fight, freeze, or ignore routes to safety which could have been used.

8.8 Queuing: a behavioural perspective

A number of behavioural principles or propositions governing queuing and waiting have been proposed.[20, 21] They can be summarized as follows:

- Uncertainties – there is nothing worse from a customer's point of view than not knowing how long you will have to wait. People must be given an indication of how long they should expect to wait and it should err on the side of caution. For example, it is obviously better to say 'you will be seen in 20 minutes' or 'the take-off will be delayed by 30 minutes' where the wait is anticipated by the service provider to be less in both instances. Promising a wait of less than its predicted actual duration should be avoided at all costs. The worst thing to say would be 'We'll be with you soon' or 'The delay in departure will not be long'. In these cases the risk of customer dissatisfaction is increased because their expectations have been raised.
- The essential characteristic and apparent attractiveness of the appointment system are its complete lack of uncertainty. Unless you arrive early, there is no waiting involved as people expect to be taken at their allotted time. What is not always understood or tolerated is why a service does not adhere to the appointment schedule. A hairdresser will usually keep to the schedule while the local GP may not. The explanation lies in the greater degree of uncertainty and unpredictability surrounding patient needs in the doctor's surgery.

- Explanation – the length of a delay can be given meaning if people are told the reason(s). There are innumerable reasons for delay but the important point is that customers will make a judgement as to whether it is reasonable, acceptable, or justifiable. One might speculate that failure to inform customers is as much to do with avoiding unnecessary ridicule and censure. Train companies revelations that a particular type of snow or leaves on the line, or excessive heat, can cause severe disruption are usually met with incredulity and annoyance, particularly as there appears to be nothing that can be done about it. There is nothing more frustrating from the customer's viewpoint than serving points, e.g. in post offices, banks, supermarkets, suddenly closing without any explanation, or where service employees are seen to be 'sitting idly by' while the queues get longer. Ideally an explanation of the real cause of the delay should be given, but in the real world organizations may decide to give out either no reasons or ones deemed more acceptable to the customers.
- Anxiety – this feeling can often be the consequence of uncertainty and no explanation. It is the product of thinking 'I'll never be seen to', which with the advent of appointments and take-a-number systems is less frequent. However, it can be felt when standing far back in a very long queue entering a capacity-constrained facility, e.g. a pop concert, a football match. Organizers can eliminate it with the reassurance that 'everyone will get in'.
- Boredom – waiting can be incredibly boring. If organizations can offer some desirable distractions that take customers' minds off the time the response might well be one of 'how time flies'. There has not been a great deal of imagination generated in this area. Successfully filling unoccupied time is a difficult exercise and an area where there is enormous scope for experimentation and development. Quite often customers take it upon themselves to fill in time by befriending each other.
- Pre-process versus in-process – this is partially related to the previous point in that although customers have to wait they want to feel as soon as possible that progress is being made towards the service commencing. The obvious example is being given a menu on sitting down for a restaurant meal. The important point is that customers need to feel they are involved as quickly as possible. Anything the provider can do to fill in the customers' time before the core service begins will achieve that objective.
- Value – in general people value their time, so what they are waiting for has to be worth it. What customers define as 'valued' is as diverse as the reasons for delay mentioned earlier. It is not simply a matter of what is valued being seen as something highly priced. Long waits are endured to obtain an important prescription from a doctor. People camp out overnight or wait many hours to obtain entry to various forms of entertainment. The wait is very much seen in terms of 'it's worth it'.
- Equity – people correctly feel aggrieved if the first come first served (FCFS) and first in first out (FIFO) systems are not observed. The take-a-number procedure operated by many services is a good example of FIFO. It works well when all customers' transactions require about the same amount of time, but not where markedly different amounts of time are in evidence. There are instances where FIFO and FCFS would seem to be violated, e.g. an emergency arrival at a hospital, but this is an example where customers accept non-observance of the rule.

Sometimes what seems to be a breaking of the equity rule is understandable. For example, a person waiting in a restaurant for a seat witnesses a party of four entering and being given a table straight away. The single person may feel a sense of injustice but the restaurant owner cannot be expected perfectly to match his fixed capacity of seating arrangements with the unpredictability of customer demand patterns. Equally a customer in a department store may feel frustration when telephone callers receive priority service. An occurrence such as this can be avoided through the adoption of proper procedures.

8.8.1 Applying queuing theory

We have seen that many queues occur because of the need to halt a flow for processing. This is a problem to which queuing theory can usefully be applied. Queuing theory is the application of the mathematics of probability to the likelihood of queues. Those managing systems wish to ensure that the maximum duration of queues stays within given limits, because they do not wish to exceed the zone of tolerance of the customers, who may renege if queues are too long. The second desire is to ensure that serving staff (and their associated equipment) are efficiently utilized, so there is a wish to avoid situations where there is no waiting at all because staff have nothing to do. To solve this problem the managers of the system can employ mathematical models. These models may become quite complex, but they all start with two basic sets of data: the average arrival rate, denoted by λ (the Greek letter lambda) and the average service rate, denoted by μ (μm). From these two statistics a value for the traffic intensity, shown by ρ, can be derived. Traffic intensity can best be thought of as the average utilization of the service facility with the formula:

$\rho = \lambda/\mu$ (note $\lambda < \mu$, otherwise we can end up with an infinite queue).

Asking the question 'how many … ?' we have the two formulae:

$$M_q = \rho^2/(1 - \rho) \text{ and } M_s\rho/(1 - \rho)$$

where M_q is the average number of items in the queue and M_s is the average number of items in the system.

Asking the question 'how long to wait … ?' requires the following formula:

$$W_q = \rho/(\mu - \lambda) \text{ and } W_s = 1/(\mu - \lambda)$$

where W_q is the waiting time in the queue and W_s is the waiting time in the system.

Worked example: Customers in a supermarket join a single queue at an average rate of 30 per hour and are served at an average rate of 35 per hour. Find the average:

1 Number of customers waiting to be served (m_q)
2 Number of customers in the system (m_s)
3 Time spent queuing (w_q)
4 Time spent in the system (w_s)

Solutions: $\rho = 0.857$.

1 $(0.857)^2/(1 - 0.857) = 5.14$, i.e. 5 customers
2 $(0.857)/(1 - 0.857) = 5.99$, i.e. 6 customers

3 $(0.857)/(35 - 30) = 0.1714\,h$, i.e. $10.28\,min$
4 $1/(35 - 30) = 1/5\,h = 12\,min$

Summary

Service providers face a particular problem when it comes to demand management and capacity utilization. Unlike manufacturing, service organizations cannot stockpile their 'output' in a warehouse and wait for demand to materialize.

Demand for services can fluctuate in such an unpredictable way that capacity is either unable to cope, or grossly under-utilized. Achieving a match between demand and capacity is therefore a difficult goal to achieve. Services will vary in terms of how easily capacity can be adjusted. A number of options are available for making capacity more flexible, two of which are gathering interest, namely using customers as productive resources, and outsourcing. Demand represents more of a challenge. Among the options here, variable pricing remains attractive.

A technique attracting attention is that of yield or revenue management. By applying a number of key elements you will have gathered a basic understanding of how this technique works. No matter how successful yield management is, there still remains the residual matter of customers having to wait and queue. This is simply a feature of service for which there appears to be no available solution. However, attending to the behavioural principles governing queuing and waiting should focus your mind on how to make this phenomenon as comfortable and fair as possible for customers.

References

1 Lovelock, C (1994) *Product Plus*. New York: McGraw-Hill, ch. 16.
2 Heskett, L, Sasser, W E and Hart, C W L (1990) *Service Breakthroughs: Changing the Rules of the Game*. New York: Free Press, p. 139.
3 Kurtz, D L and Clow, K E (1998) *Services Marketing*. New York: John Wiley and Sons, p. 346.
4 Sasser, W E (1976) 'Match, supply and demand in service industries', *Harvard Business Review*, Nov.–Dec., 133–140.
5 Mills, P K and Morris, J H (1986) 'Clients as partial employees: role development in client participation', *Academy of Management Review*, **11** (4), 726–735.
6 Sasser, op. cit.
7 Zeithaml, V A and Bitner, M J (2003) *Service Marketing*. New York: McGraw-Hill, p. 421.
8 Crandall, R E and Markland, R E (1996) 'Demand management – today's challenge for service industries', *Production and Operations Management*, **5** (2), 106–120.
9 Sasser, op. cit.
10 Crandall and Markland, op. cit.
11 Ibid.
12 Ibid.
13 Smith, B C, Leimkuhler, J F and Darrow, R M (1992) 'Yield management at American Airlines', *Interfaces*, **22** (1), 8–31.
14 Wirtz, J, Kimes, S E, Theng, J H P and Patterson, P (2003) 'Revenue management: resolving potential customer conflicts', *Journal of Revenue and Pricing Management*, **2** (3), 216–226.
15 Duneavy, H and Westermann, D (2004) 'Future of airline revenue management', *Journal of Revenue and Pricing Management*, **3** (4), 380–383.

16   Kimes, S E, *The '4-C' Strategy for Yield Management*. Centre for Hospitality Research at Cornell University, Ithaca, NY.

17   Kimes, S (2002) 'Tourism Revenue Management Programme', Stirling Management Centre, 27–29 November.

18   Ingold, A and Huyton, J R (1997) 'Yield management and the airline industry', in Yeoman, I and Ingold, A (eds), *Yield Management*. London: Cassell.

19   Gleick, J (1999) *Faster*. London: Abacus, p. 1.

20   Larson, R C (1987) 'Perspectives on queues: social justice and the psychology of queuing', *Operations Research*, **35** (6), 895–905.

21   Maister, D H (1985) 'The psychology of waiting lines', in Czepiel, J A, Solomon, M R and Suprenant, C F (eds), *The Service Encounter*. Lexington, MA: Lexington Books, D C Heath and Company.

9

Service communications

Introduction

Today's environment is fiercely competitive. It is therefore not enough to develop a service for which there is known demand. It is not enough to say that a good service will sell itself. The service must be communicated to the target market in order to generate and develop a loyal customer base. While communications can be planned before the service is ready for consumption, they should certainly not be implemented. With the ever-increasing variety of media channels, and the proliferation of brands, marketing communications must be planned and implemented in an integrated fashion.

9.1 Integrated marketing communications

In previous times, there were more limited opportunities for ways in which a company could communicate with its audiences. There were also generally fewer brands in any market sector, meaning that it was relatively easier for the brand to be seen and heard (and remembered). It is estimated that today the average person is exposed to 1300 advertising messages every day.[1] However, today's multi-brand markets and diverse and numerous ways of talking to consumers means that it becomes increasingly important that every piece of communication works optimally.

One key way in which the marketer can optimize communications is to integrate them. This is often referred to as integrated marketing communications (IMC). So that all communications, whether internal to the organization or external to its various stakeholder groups, share the same 'tone of voice'. Whether the consumer is viewing an advertisement or talking to a call centre that is handling the company's customer helpline, or whether it is the manner in which complaints are handled and service is recovered, there should be little doubt that the communications come from the same company.[2]

Two companies that are particularly good at communicating with one tone of voice are Orange the telecommunications provider, and First Direct, which provides banking services (see Figures 9.1 and 9.2). In each case, the tone of voice communicated is more profound than what the company looks like. It also talks about what type of company it is: what its values are and what it believes is important in its market.

Figure 9.1 Orange advertisement: consistent tone of voice

Figure 9.2 First Direct advertisement: consistent tone of voice

When Orange first launched its service with the strapline 'The future's Orange' it also had a member of staff called Director of Futurology. It used its communications to build an image of the brand as one at the cutting edge of mobile communications without forgetting that the average user was no technophile.

Figure 9.3 Co-operative Bank Advertisement: distinctive and consistent tone of voice

First Direct turned banking on its head when it was the first to launch a purely telephone banking service. It took as its priority the needs of the time-pressured consumer for whom traditional banking hours were increasingly inconvenient.

Another bank that has adopted a unique tone of voice is the Co-operative Bank, now known as CFS (Co-operative Financial Services). It has a strong corporate and social responsibility policy (often referred to as a CSR policy). They are the only high street bank with a published Ethical Policy that states where they will and will not invest customers' money. They also speak out and campaign for changes on issues they know from research that their customers feel strongly about. They have campaigned for trade justice and for safer chemicals. The use of CSR policies to communicate corporate brand values is increasingly common.

9.2   The role for communications

Communication can *add* value to the service in the eyes of the consumer. This is one of its key benefits. In many cases this will enable the provider to charge a premium over that of competitors. Advertising is one of the most visible ways through which an organization communicates with its customers. In 2003 service organizations in the UK spent some £3246 million on television and press advertising (Table 9.1). This expenditure has grown significantly in recent years, both in absolute terms and also as a share of total advertising in the UK.

Table 9.1 UK service sector advertising expenditure, 2003

Industry	£000
Retailing and mail order	917 000
Financial services	683 000
Travel and transport	290 000
Household stores	217 000
Entertainment	444 000
Government	201 000
Business-to-business	494 000
Total	3 246 000

Source: AC Nielsen MEAL

9.3   Services communication

The key differences between products and services should be taken into account in considering service communication as follows:

- **Simultaneous production and consumption:** The layout, shop facia and the appearance and manner of the staff are critical communication variables. So too is communicating the role that the consumer is expected to play in the production of the service they want to consume.

Figure 9.4 Kwik-Fit advertisement: the communication of a guarantee

- **Intangibility:** Service providers should attempt to reduce the risk to the consumer of buying an intangible product by providing tangible clues about the service offering. These clues come from all aspects of corporate communication.
- **Heterogeneity:** This, too, leads to greater perceived risk. Again communications can help to reduce this factor. It may be appropriate to communicate a service guarantee (Figure 9.4) or promise, or to demonstrate how well trained your staff are.
- **Perishability:** Many promotional tools, e.g. advertising, sales promotion and direct marketing, have a role to play in shaping demand. This is one of the most

challenging aspects of service management and arises from the fact that services cannot be inventoried.

Each of these variables have previously been discussed in greater detail in Chapter 5.

Flowing from this there are five key aspects of communication for the service marketer:

- The role of personal selling
- The importance of internal marketing communications
- The management of expectations
- The provision of tangible clues
- Word-of-mouth communications.

9.4   Key communication variables

9.4.1   The role of personal selling

Service delivery often involves human encounter, whether face-to-face, or more remotely via the telephone. The way in which that encounter develops can determine whether the customer walks away feeling pleased, satisfied, annoyed, or victimized. Although the customer's expectations help determine levels of satisfaction, the encounter itself will invariably play a significant part in determining satisfaction. The person who delivers the service is often actually part of the service itself. He or she is not merely facilitating the exchange of a product that is already fully developed and is waiting to be picked from a shelf. Waiting staff in a restaurant deliver not just food but customer satisfaction.

Research conducted by John Bateson for his book *Managing Services Marketing*[3] concluded that personal selling and image-creating strategies were the communications tools most often used by service organizations. He notes that organizations must choose their contact personnel carefully and train them to interact effectively with customers.

The role of personal selling is not the same for every service organization. The partner in a large accountancy firm will be performing quite a different personal selling role from that of a checkout operator in a supermarket.

In attempting to mould the interpersonal skills of contact personnel, service managers should ask themselves the following questions:

- Which staff are customer-facing? It's not just traditional sales staff that 'sell' the service.
- What other functions do they fulfil?
- What ought they to be communicating about the service?
- On what dimensions do consumers judge the standard of service delivery?
- What factors shape expectations of each service encounter? Are they related to service complexity? To frequency of use of the service?
- Is it more appropriate for customers to be offered a customized or a standardized response? (Of course, service delivery varies not only among people but also within people. We all have our good and bad days. On a good day customization

will probably result in an improved service offering. However, on a bad day, stand-ardized service has a greater chance of achieving satisfied customers.)

If some thought is given to these factors, then the communication function of contact personnel has a greater chance of being effective.

Personal selling is often the most important variable in the development of expect-ations. No matter what the advertising communicates, or what the consumers' friends say, their expectations will be shaped by any personalized communication that they receive from the company. If your hairdresser tells you that the colourant that he or she has used will last for eight weeks then that is how long you expect it to last. If a store sales assistant tells you your purchase will be delivered the follow-ing day then that is what you expect. Frontline employees have to be trained to understand that it is important to develop *realistic* expectations in consumers how-ever tempting it may be to over-promise.

9.4.2   Call centres

Service companies are increasingly conducting some of their personal selling remotely via telephone, with a growing number outsourcing this to call centres. In the early days such centres were generally tasked with handling customer helplines and in the area of service recovery. In other words, they were more involved with cus-tomer retention than recruitment.

It is estimated that the UK call centre industry has grown by almost 250% since 1995, with 5320 contact centres and almost 500 000 people employed at the end of 2003. The industry is forecast to grow to almost 650 000 agent positions by 2007.[4]

However nowadays an increasing number of call centres passively handle initial customer enquiries and more proactively seek new business. In both cases the indi-vidual is playing an important role in helping to generate business and in the absence of any body language or other visual clues, the attitude and accent of the operator becomes important. Jamie Oliver (the celebrity chef) answers the telephone when you phone his restaurant, Fifteen. Even though it is only a voice-recorded message telling you the opening hours and how to get to the venue etc., it is a very powerful use of remote personal selling.

9.4.3   The importance of internal marketing communications

The importance of the employee in the delivery of a quality service means that they should not be ignored when it comes to considering who the relevant communica-tion targets are (see Chapter 7 for further discussion of the importance of service employees). The most prolific writer in this field, Leonard Berry[5,6] makes this point.

There are certainly internal pieces of communication that can help improve employees' job performance. Traditionally the mission statement was regarded as a critical tool in this respect. However, nowadays more dynamic tools such as internal newsletters – often transmitted via email – staff forums and awaydays are vital. Indeed, some larger organizations with geographically dispersed staff have begun to employ business television. Dedicated programmes produced by the internal com-munications team are broadcast via satellite to centres where staff congregate to view.

It is important with all of these tools to build dialogue into the process. Internal communications can no longer be regarded as a way of the organization communicating to employees with no feedback mechanisms. Companies need to listen as well as to inform.

The employee can also benefit from external corporate communications which appear to be aimed at the consumer. There are several reasons for this.

First, many services are delivered through a geographically dispersed network of branches and outlets. Employees have little contact with head office. In this case external communications can help to maintain their commitment to the organization. It can also help remind them of the corporate culture that was imbued during their induction.

It may serve as a reminder or a reassurance of what the organization expects of them, or, as Zeithaml states, 'if [the communication] features employees doing their jobs, it communicates to them that they are important'.[7] However, the proposition that these communications are more effective if they use actual employees rather than professional actors could be refuted. An aspirational or more grounded role model may be more appropriate and effective. Recently B&Q the hardware retailer has used staff in its external communications to good effect (Figure 9.5).

Finally these communications can help to manage customers' expectations and in so doing they can communicate with employees about what to expect from their customers.

9.4.4   Managing expectations

Communicating with the customer about what to expect of the service is important. If expectations can be managed so that customers have more realistic expectations of the service delivery then their expectations are more likely to be met. American Express informs its card holders that 'Membership has its privileges'. Customers then come to look for their privileges.

Czepiel, Solomon, and Suprenant[8] note that most problems about customer satisfaction relate to expectations exceeding service delivery. Satisfied customers result from the service experience fulfilling expectations (see Chapter 5 for a fuller discussion). This is why the management of these expectations is so important. External communication is only one of a number of variables that are influential (Figure 9.6). It is, though, perhaps the most easily controlled.

Raising expectations through communications can increase the risk of customer dissatisfaction. It may be tempting to over-promise in order to get business through the door. However, the repercussions often outweigh any initial benefit.

Delta Airlines at one time vowed 'We're ready when you are', and Holiday Inns told its customers 'No surprises guaranteed'. Both companies had to revise their communications because they were over-promising. Consumers' expectations were raised and then not fulfilled: they did not expect any delays if they travelled with Delta, nor were they happy when Holiday Inns did indeed produce some surprises.

In the UK in the 1980s, the recently denationalized rail company British Rail fell into the same trap by advertising the fact that 'We're getting there', when it was obvious to the commuting public that British Rail was patently *not* getting there. 'The wonder of Woolies' is yet another example from the same era. This advertising

Figure 9.5 B&Q advertisement: using staff in communications

led consumers to re-evaluate their expectations of these services, but it led them to revise them upwards, which in turn led to increased levels of dissatisfaction. Organizations began to realize that while this practice may encourage new business it does not encourage repeat business.

External communications that help develop expectations may involve a 'look behind the scenes' approach. This enables organizations to demonstrate all the effort that they go to in order to provide the service. This has been a popular theme with utilities companies.

Another approach is to provide customers with a script or scenario of the likely service encounter. Financial services and airline companies have used this approach in the past. Both strategies work well on television. They use this medium to its full potential, allowing characters to develop in live-action situations.

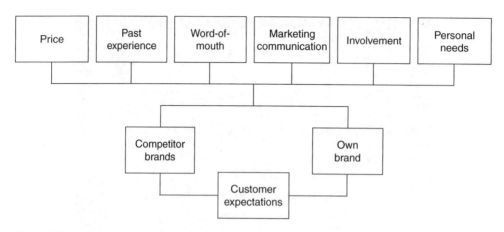

Figure 9.6 Developing customer expectations

Most literature on this subject actually suggests that the role of communication is to revise consumers' expectations downwards. This arises from the view that consumers set themselves unrealistically high expectations in the first place.

However, a more challenging task for the service marketer is to develop and maintain a quality service that meets or exceeds most consumers' expectations. Product manufacturers that are regarded as being leading-edge companies in terms of delivering quality products such as Motorola and NEC now take as their manufacturing goal Six-Sigma quality. This is a means of measuring how close production comes to total quality.

Six-Sigma quality means that there are only 3.4 defects per million parts produced. Motorola may soon adopt an unheard-of-goal of 60 defects or less for every billion components it makes. Some Japanese manufacturing companies attempt to go further by manufacturing to zero defects. Toyota have introduced the concept of *poka-yoke*, which aims to make the workplace mistake-proof, i.e. to manufacture to total quality.[9] So rather than externally aiming to reduce expectations these organizations instead internally aim to raise quality.

While this is more readily achievable in product marketing, service marketing should not ignore this potential strategy. Indeed, it may be a way of sustaining a competitive advantage. Future developments will certainly see more companies aiming to reduce the gap between expectations and delivery by tackling the issue internally as well as externally.

9.4.5 Tangible clues

The less tangible the generic service, the more powerfully and persistently the judgement of it gets shaped by the packaging. As Levitt states,[10] 'Metaphors and symbols become surrogates for the tangibility that cannot be provided or experienced in advance.'

The consumption of services is often associated with high levels of risk. Much of this risk stems from the intangible nature of services. It is not just the fact that the service cannot be touched in the same way that a product can. It is also that consumers often find it difficult to comprehend what they are being offered. This risk can be reduced by the provision of tangible clues that relate to the service offering.

In a restaurant, the use of starched napery will communicate to customers that it is a quality establishment. Similarly, a bellboy on the steps of a hotel says something of its up-market positioning. These tangible clues make the nature of the service more easily understood.

If any of these signposts are to be used in professional communications then care must be taken to select those that are *relevant* to consumers. They should be built around parts of the service offering that are key motivators for purchase.

Legal & General, the insurance company, practise this to good effect with the use of their multi-coloured umbrella. They offer protection from life's uncertainties, and with this the prospect of a brighter future. The umbrella as a tangible clue communicates this effectively (Figure 9.7).

Figure 9.7 The Legal & General logo

9.4.6 Word-of-mouth communication

Personal recommendation is a powerful communication vehicle in the service sector. The importance that consumers attach to word-of-mouth endorsement by their peer group arises from their need to reduce risk from the intangible and variable nature of services. It has been demonstrated to be many times more effective a tool of persuasion than traditional advertising. Service marketers must learn to capitalize on this tool. So how should they do this? The following list presents some of the options:

- **Introduce a friend scheme:** Encourage current users to inform others of the good service. (American Express offers current card holders a case of wine if they introduce a friend.)
- **Testimonials:** Use satisfied customers' experiences in advertising.
- **Persuasion of opinion formers:** Use PR to target opinion leaders or early adopters.
- **Promotional items:** Promotional items can provide tangible clues implying 'club' membership. The Open Golf Championship umbrella, or the Wimbledon sweatshirt are examples of this.
- **Appointment of brand ambassadors:** These are people employed by the company whose remit it is to build personal relationships with customers and other stakeholders.

- **Feedback:** Incorporate it into the communication of a comprehensive complaints procedure. 'If you're happy with what we do tell them [friends etc.], if you're not tell us.'

Recently, some services marketers have taken the concept of personal selling a stage further in their recruitment of new customers. Recognizing the potency of word-of-mouth communication, they have covertly paid for individuals to 'pose' as consumers and extol the virtues of the brand in question, rather like the street traders who whip up desire for the goods on display by employing people to 'buy' the various scents, cigarettes etc. as if they were contraband goods.

9.5   Corporate identity

In many cases, consumer purchase decisions are based on the organization that a service is bought from rather than a specific brand; for example British Airways may have attempted to segment their service offering into Business Class, First Class, Holidays etc. (they have dedicated brand teams working on each of these segments) but we expect that most people still see themselves as buying from British Airways. For this reason the development of a corporate identity becomes important. It is also beneficial to develop an image that gives the organization a focus since there are many variables working against the projection of a cohesive image.

There are many factors that contribute to the building of corporate image; Figure 9.8 illustrates the main ones, some of which are discussed in more depth in Chapters 4 and 7. Obviously not all services will use every mechanism; not many solicitors are seen to deploy carrier bags as part of their corporate image, nor will many restaurants run fleet vehicles. Whatever channels are chosen to promote the corporate identity, the

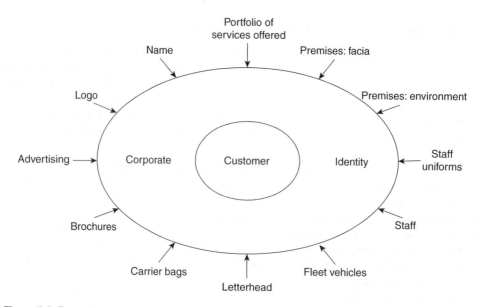

Figure 9.8 External corporate communications

task is to create a cohesive image that communicates an appropriate message. To manage this process efficiently and effectively it is important that the identity is carried synergistically across all communications.

9.5.1   Naming the service

What should a service name communicate? It is often felt that the best names communicate the key benefit that the service offers: Creased Lightning for an ironing service, Typerite for a typing service.

If the marketplace is competitive or the key benefit is different for different groups of consumers then the name should attempt to convey creatively the service that is offered, e.g. Branching Out for a florist, or The Potting Shed for a garden centre.

At a third level, it may be that this cannot be done creatively and so the generic service name is incorporated (often alongside the owner's name) e.g. Martin's Removals, or Fraser's Launderette. The three levels of naming are illustrated for a service that unblocks drains;

Drain Kleer	main benefit communicated
Blockbusters	service creatively communicated
P. N. D. Drainage	service generically communicated

All these approaches are superior to those names that give consumers no hints about the service that is offered. They are easier for consumers to remember because the name itself generates a visual image. These images complement the verbal name and leave the consumer with a more fully developed picture of the company.

The human brain finds it easier to store and retrieve words or names when they also have a visual prompt. This was researched by Lutz and Lutz,[11] whose results confirmed that an interactive image facilitates recall of the company or brand name better than a non-interactive image.

The service name can develop verbal interactive imagery. The interaction is between the company name and the service that is provided. We live in an over-communicated society. We are producing more information and absorbing less of it. So the easier we make it for consumers to remember the company name the more chance we have of being successful. A good example of this approach to brand naming comes from the US toy retailer 'Toys R Us'. The name itself tells consumers that it is a toy retailer, while the 'R' written backwards in the logo may be just the way that a child would write it.

As Berry, Lefkowith and Clark[12] state, there are four key characteristics that a service name should possess:

- Distinctiveness: identifies supplier and distinguishes from competition
- Relevance: conveys service benefit
- Memorability: understood and recalled with ease
- Flexibility: scope to cover business expansion.

We have also witnessed a growing trend towards the contraction of companies names to initials. So, we have seen British Midland International re-brand as BMI;

Channel 4 became C4; BBC Childrens Television to CBBC; the Royal Bank of Scotland to RBS. This could be attributed to the growth in text messaging, the increasingly sound-bite nature of communications, or more generally the faster pace of life where any simplification/contraction of information that still communicates the message will be preferred.

9.5.2   Designing the logo

The logo can take this process a stage further. It can help consumers to form a picture of the company by presenting them with visual clues of the service that is on offer. A good logo helps both the company and its customers. It enables the company to have more impact in its desire to imprint a memorable picture on the consumer's mind. This in turn means that consumers do not have to work as hard to create an image for themselves as they did when presented with a name only. This is described as

Figure 9.9 Smile.co.uk advertisement

pictorial interaction by Lutz and Lutz.[13] Remembering the picture also means remembering the company name (for example, Figure 9.9).

The corporate identity of British Airways has been reversed three times in the past three decades. In the 1970s the public image of British Airways had been one of a nationalized industry ravaged by strikes and inefficient management practices. The logo that was in place during this period reflected the company image. It was designed at the time of the amalgamation of BEA and BOAC, and in attempting to incorporate design elements from each of those companies the design solution arrived at was a compromise. The logo projected a solid image, yet it lacked any feeling of movement that might be expected of a travel company.

In 1984 British Airways launched a new corporate logo which was intended to reflect the company's new culture. The revised logo represented a significant step forward. BA's new management, working towards privatization, wanted to convey a much more dynamic image. The logo was expected to assert BA's superiority to staff, customers and potential investors. The design certainly captures movement, and helped to project the image of a progressive company, driving forward in the travel business.

In 1997 the corporate identity was revised again. This time, the desire was to reflect globalization of the airline. Radical changes in the industry (the emergence of supergroupings, the growth of low-cost niche carriers and changes in the regulatory environment) have all played a part in the redesign of the corporate identity, at the heart of which is the creation of more than fifty images which appear on everything that bears the British Airways name. These are designed to be representative of different countries throughout the world, thus adding a dimension of global identity to this British carrier.

The company's corporate palette of red, white and blue has been brightened and lightened, more closely drawn from the British union flag than the 1984 scheme. This is intended to reflect the airline's British heritage. The name 'British Airways' has been depicted using a softer, rounder typeface, and a new three-dimensional Speedmarque has evolved from the flat red Speedwing symbol of 1984 (see Figure 9.10).

9.5.3 The uniform

For many service organizations today, the corporate look is incomplete unless all front-line staff are dressed by the company. This can serve three purposes. First, it helps customers to identify those individuals who are in fact employees of the company. To fulfil this signalling function, the uniform must have 'stand-out'. A good example of distinctive corporate clothing is that worn by most of the airlines' steward staff.

These uniforms are also usually good at fulfilling the second objective: that of communicating an appropriate corporate image. So the bright orange trendier garments worn by Easyjet reflects the corporate 'style' of the company. In contrast, the conventional rather constricting oriental wear worn by cabin crew on Thai Airways positions the employees in a more traditional servile capacity. In the days of restricted air travel, the 'hostess' would be dressed so that the male passengers (and most of them were men!) spent their airborne time fantasizing about the hostess

British airways

BRITISH AIRWAYS

BRITISH AIRWAYS

Figure 9.10 The evolving corporate logo of British Airways

rather than thinking about the dangers of flying. The girls were there to provide reassurance. Nowadays cabin staff are there to be efficient and professional and their uniforms reflect this change in approach. As Jean Phillips of the Wensum Corporate Company notes, 'When developing a corporate clothing range for an organization, not only does one take into account clothing design and company identity, but one equally needs to focus on the working environment. Generally speaking, too many companies lose sight of this major requirement.'[14]

And finally, the uniform serves the purpose of suppressing individuality.[15] Idiosyncrasies in behaviour and appearance are much less obvious when an individual is in uniform. In effect, uniform clothing promotes uniform behaviour. This happens partly because the employee feels a part of the organization and partly because the customer expects the employee to act out the image.

9.6   Branding services

How are communications developed? In many cases the initial stage of the process is to develop a brand image. Brands have continued to increase in importance in services marketing throughout the 1990s and early part of the twenty-first century. This trend is expected to continue since:

- There is an increasing proliferation of brands within service sectors. Service markets are becoming more competitive.
- It has been shown to be up to five times cheaper to retain current customers than to attract new ones.[16]

- Service life cycles are becoming shorter. New service development thus assumes a greater importance. The risks of product launches are reduced in the context of umbrella branding.
- The service itself may offer no unique and sustainable tangible benefit – this can be added by development of brand imagery.

9.6.1   Brand image development

In Chapter 1, the concepts of core and augmented service were discussed. The competitive marketplace experienced by most services companies today means that the development of an augmented service offering is key to the sustained success of the venture. The development of a relevant, and salient, image for the brand is one of the key ways in which augmentation can take place. Many of the other means for augmenting service can be easily copied and consequently any advantage gained is often short-lived.

The process should begin with an assessment of the benefits that accrue to users of the service. Preferably these should be unique. With no branding of the service at this stage, these benefits are more likely to be functional in character, that is a car hire firm will get you from A to B, an hotel will provide you with a good night's sleep. However, in the development of an augmented service, an assessment of the social and psychological benefits that also accrue is necessary.

Market research may well have to be conducted in order to understand the consumer response. The outcome of this stage is an understanding of what consumers regard as the key attributes of the service; for example, a social benefit to an executive of hiring a car may be that he or she will look more professional, or more of a big time player, to the client if seen arriving at a meeting by hire car rather than by public transport. A psychological benefit for the executive may be an enhanced feeling of self-importance.

A social benefit derived from staying at a prestigious hotel may well be the company that the guest expects to keep. A psychological benefit could be the pampering/indulgence of the whole experience. It is from an understanding of these benefits that communications are built. They should highlight what it is that motivates people to use the service. By attaching your brand name to the most important motivator(s) you begin to give consumers reasons to prefer your brand over that of your competitors, that is, you begin to build brand preference (Figure 9.11).

An effective communications strategy should attempt to take consumers swiftly from the position of brand non-recognition to that of brand preference. There is little advantage in consumers knowing of your service if they do not act on this knowledge.

Brand rejection amongst those who recognize (brand aware) the brand but do not try it occurs when your communications message is not motivating. It may not be motivating to those who are not target consumers. That is not a problem. What is more worrying is when the rejectors are within your target. Research must be undertaken to establish who are the rejectors. If it is the latter group then they must be further researched to understand the reasons why.

Consumers who are brand indifferent need more motivation. In many cases this arises because the service has not been experienced. Sales promotion techniques aimed at inducing trial should be considered.

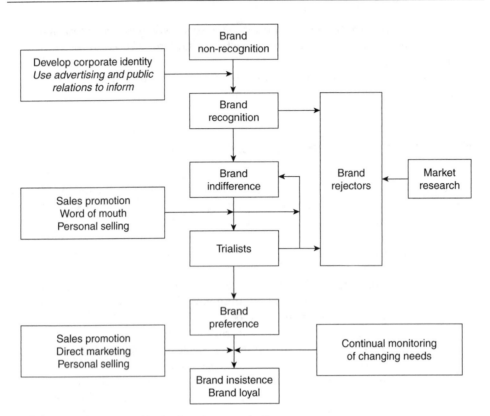

Figure 9.11 Developing brand loyalty through communications

Brand insistence/loyalty is every marketer's dream. So how do you get there?

- Encourage repeat purchase using sales promotion/loyalty programmes. This makes consumers familiar with your service which in turn diminishes risk. It is also known that if you can persuade a customer to purchase on three successive occasions he or she is much more likely to remain loyal. This is attributed to the habitual nature that the purchasing occasion has developed.
- Ideally the company would use the data gathered during the loyalty programme to customize future loyalty-building promotions. Many of the major UK retailing chains – Tesco, Sainsbury's, Boots – are skilled at this.
- Introduce penalties so that the cost of changing brands is high. Financial institutions, particularly the building societies, practise this to good effect. If you decide to move to a company that offers a lower rate of interest, then the original lending company will charge you a penalty for doing this. This financial penalty will often mean that there is no longer any pecuniary advantage from making the change. (For further discussion, see the section on relationship marketing in Chapter 11.)
- Recently some companies have seen the removal of penalties as a way of differentiating themselves from the competition. However, like many other service improvements, if it proves motivating to consumers, then other companies are likely to copy.

Table 9.2 Setting advertising objectives to address service variables

Service variable	Advertising objective
Intangibility	Provision of tangible clues
	Reduce risk
	Provide reassurance
Heterogeneity	Customization
	Reduce risk
	Provide reassurance
Inseparability	Staff focus: selection, training etc.
	Customer empathy
Perishability	Use advertising to manage demand (price offers, selling off the page etc.)

- Keep your current customers satisfied by developing and sustaining a unique service advantage. As Dobree and Page[17] state, branding is one key method of addressing the problem of competitive advantage. Branding is often the best way of sustaining a competitive advantage. A competitive advantage built solely on functional benefits is much easier for competitors to copy.

Recent studies suggest that it is becoming increasingly difficult to keep customers loyal and many markets are experiencing higher rates of switching behaviour than in the past.

9.7 Advertising the service

The advertising of services is often more complicated than for products. In many cases this is due to the intangible nature of the offering. The advertising has to evoke the likely experience of the user, which in turn introduces a second complication. The service can often be unique to each buyer, as is the case for most professional services. The service will be a bundle of attributes that will not all be offered to every buyer at every purchase occasion.

9.7.1 Setting advertising objectives

One approach to the setting of advertising objectives and strategy is to consider the four variables that are used to describe the difference between services and products. In the past, writers have suggested which of the variables they believed to be the most important. Shostack[18] thought that the provision of tangible clues was advertising's biggest task. Urwin[19] believed that presenting an emotional appeal to consumers was the biggest challenge, and for Parasuraman, Zeithaml and Berry[20,21] reliability was the factor most important for the advertising to communicate.

It is our opinion there is no single correct approach. The advertiser should choose the variable that causes consumers most concern in the purchase of the particular service and attempt to overcome their preconceptions (Table 9.2).

For example, in the film industry the most important variable is likely to be the perishability of the service. Demand for the service normally declines with the length of time that the film has been on the market. The purchase of financial

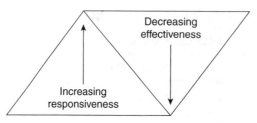

Figure 9.12 Trade-off between key attributes: film processing

services, on the other hand, is often fraught with uncertainty due to the intangible nature of the service.

Another approach to the setting of objectives is to seek answers to the following questions at the beginning of the development process:

- What is it that motivates consumers to use my service?
- What is it credible to communicate to them in this context?
- Can I deliver what I promise?

In other words, in developing the communication the advertiser has to consider 'What, to Whom, How, When, and Where?'

Setting the advertising objective answers the first of these questions. It determines what the advertising is intended to communicate. This in turn should feed back into the question of consumer motivations. Ideally, the advertising should have as its objective the communication of the key motivator. This motivator will be different for different services. Note, however, that the same motivator often applies to more than one service.

This is a simplification of the process. What happens if there is more than one key motivator? Take, for example, a film processing service. Consumers might say that key motivators are responsiveness and effectiveness (see Figure 9.12). However, there is a trade-off here. Doing things faster usually results in more mistakes. We are assuming here that the service provides every key attribute that the consumer regards as important in their selection of a service brand in that particular market. If it does not, then the company should attempt to develop these if a long-term presence in the market is anticipated.

9.7.2   Setting advertising strategy

The next step is to arrive at an advertising strategy. This determines how the objective will be communicated. Setting the objective will not in itself set the strategy. Figure 9.13 illustrates the main factors to be considered in the development of an advertising strategy.

9.7.3   Campaign evaluation

The development of advertising is not a one-off job. After the campaign has run some attempt must be made to assess its effectiveness. Part of this process should be an examination of the continuing relevance of the original objective and strategy. While

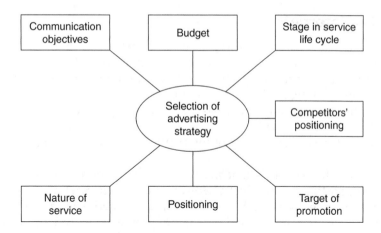

Figure 9.13 Factors affecting selection of advertising strategy

the most efficient use of advertising monies is often to develop a single-minded campaign that can run and run, e.g. British Airways, the changing nature of the competition and/or consumers can sometimes lead to the need to revise plans. The only way in which this can be determined is by continually monitoring the market.

9.7.4   Advertising professional services

The 1980s witnessed a relaxation in the control and regulation of professional services advertising. It began in 1985 with a test case brought by opticians. Research in the USA had shown that the restriction of advertising worked against the interests of consumers because it generally led to higher prices. The absence of advertising left consumers with insufficient information on which to base their brand choice. The case was decided in the opticians' favour and this led to an Office of Fair Trading Report in 1986 which lifted many of the remaining restrictions on other professional services.

In addition to the methods of promoting services that have already been mentioned, there is another tool that is popular with those in professional services. It is known as a promotional survey.

The organization commissions research into something that it believes will interest their customers. So, for example, an advertising agency might find that its clients would be interested in changing consumer behaviour. The agency will then promote the survey like a new product with headline PR in the trade press and more detailed coverage in individual presentations. These presentations are then used as soft-selling occasions.

The basic idea is to do something that current and/or potential clients will value. It need not be research. It may just focus on your field of expertise. A law firm could arrange a seminar with prominent legal brains on employment law, for example.

Historically there has been some feeling that the successful professional organization does not need to advertise. To do so reflects adversely on their standing in the industry. This belief may not be as prevalent today as it has been in the past. However, the importance of interpersonal contact and respect means that any form of promotion that brings potential clients face to face with the service provider should be encouraged.

9.7.5   The Internet

The Internet was developed in the 1960s by CERN in Switzerland as a communications network that would survive a nuclear attack. During the 1970s, universities around the world adopted the technology for communicating with one another. It was not until the 1980s that the business community began to recognize the potential of the Internet and there has since been explosive growth in both the number of organizations with their own website and the number of consumers accessing the Internet. The number of Internet users has been estimated as high as 1 billion.

Unlike most other channels that marketing uses to communicate, the Internet presents the opportunity to conduct a two-way dialogue, in real time, 24 hours a day. Initially, most people visited websites for information and entertainment, and corporate sites were designed to deliver brand propositions and product/service details. Increasingly, however, customers have been willing to buy services over the Internet. This is known as e(electronic)-commerce. They are also using the medium for commenting on an organization's performance.

So the World Wide Web presents enormous potential in assisting the deployment of a relationship marketing strategy: it enables customers/organizations to communicate on a one-to-one basis; it can build brand relationships; act as a channel to market; and provide a customer service function. In doing so, it is bringing about profound changes in consumer, and business-to-business buying behaviour. Service companies such as banks, hotels and airline companies have already re-engineered their business to incorporate Web technology into their processes.

Summary

In the communication of services there are five key variables that are important to marketers. They are: personal selling, word of mouth, targeting employees in external communications, managing expectations through communications, and using communications to provide tangible clues about the service. Tangible clues about the service offering can be given in all sorts of ways. Indeed, most aspects of corporate identity help to provide tangible clues. The service personnel, their uniform, the company logo, its advertising etc. all contribute to the impression that customers have of the company, and therefore help to shape their expectations.

For many companies the development of communications begins with the development of a brand image. Because there is often no discernible difference between brands in the market, the image can become the single differentiating factor. By creating an image of the service that is relevant to the market, the company has the potential to develop a loyal customer base. Customer loyalty is a worthwhile goal. For one thing, it usually results in greater profits.

In most cases advertising will be used to communicate the brand image. The advertising of services presents two unique problems. First, the service experience is not identical for every customer. In fact, in many cases each customer receives a service that no one else ever experiences. Second, the intangible nature of service leaves the advertising with the job of attempting to evoke the likely experience of the user.

References

1 Forbes, G (2001) *We're Still Living in TV Times*. Cookham, Berkshire: Chartered Institute of Marketing.

2 Lindell, P G (1998) 'You need integrated attitude to develop IMC', *Marketing News*, 26 May, p. 5.

3 Bateson, J E G (1989) *Managing Services Marketing: Text and Readings*. New York: Dryden Press.

4 CWU Research (2004) *The UK Contact Industry: A Study*. London: Department of Trade and Industry.

5 George, W R and Berry, L (1981) 'Guidelines for the advertising of services', *Business Horizons*, **24**, 52–56.

6 Berry, L (1987) 'Big ideas in services marketing', *Journal of Services Marketing*, Summer, 5–9.

7 Zeithaml, V A (1990) 'Communicating with customers about service quality', in Bowen, D E, Chase, R B and Cummings, T G (eds), *Service Management Effectiveness*. San Francisco, CA: Jossey-Bass.

8 Czepiel, J A, Solomon, M R and Suprenant, C F (1985) *The Service Encounter.* Lexington, MA: Lexington Books.

9 *International Business Week* (1991) 'Questing for the best', 2 December, 18–23.

10 Levitt, T (1981) 'Marketing products and product intangibles', *Harvard Business Review*, May–June, 94–101.

11 Lutz, K A and Lutz, T J (1978) 'Eliciting strategies: review and implications of research', in Hunt, H K (ed.), *Advances in Consumer Research*. Ann Arbor, MI: Association for Consumer Research.

12 Berry, L L, Lefkowith, E and Clark, T (1988) 'In services – what's in a name', *Harvard Business Review*, Sep.–Oct., 28–30.

13 Lutz and Lutz, op. cit.

14 Telephone conversation with Jean Phillips, Managing Director of the Wensum Corporate Company, 1992.

15 Nathan, J and Nicholas, A (1972) 'The uniform: a sociological perspective', *American Journal of Sociology*, **77**, 719–730.

16 Dobree, J and Page, A S (1991) 'Unleashing the power of service brands in the 1990s', *Management Decision*, **28** (6), 14–28.

17 Ibid.

18 Shostack, G L (1977) 'Breaking free from product marketing', *Journal of Marketing*, April, 73–80.

19 Urwin, S (1975) 'Customised communications – a concept for service advertising', *Advertising Quarterly*, Summer, pp. 28–30.

20 Parasuraman, A, Zeithaml, V A and Berry, L L (1988) 'Servqual: a multiple item scale for measuring consumer perceptions of service quality', *Journal of Retailing*, Spring, 12–40.

21 Parasuraman, A, Berry, L L and Zeithaml, A (1991) 'Understanding customer expectations of service', *Sloan Management Review*, Spring, 39–48.

10

Performance measurement

Introduction

Organizations need to know how well they are performing, not only in an absolute sense but relative to:

- Predetermined standards set out in organizational goals and objectives
- Competitors (if there are any)
- Customer expectations
- Resources deployed (capital, labour, materials, energy, information).

Performance appraisal will inevitably mean undertaking some form of measurement. Questions will be asked about:

- What is being measured
- How it is being measured
- Why it is being measured.

Two areas in particular help in addressing the issue of organizational performance. They are productivity and customer retention.

10.1 Productivity

Productivity is a measure of relationships between an input and an output namely:

$$\text{Productivity} = \frac{\text{Output}}{\text{Input}}$$

It is a standard measure that has been used by manufacturing industries for a very long time, where, for example:

$$\text{Total Productivity} = \frac{\text{Total outputs}}{\text{Sum of all inputs}}$$

The real difficulty lies in aggregating a range of partial measures into a composite measure for the whole organization. In other words, how the organization's total output and the value added are explained by the mix and deployment of resources. As total productivity, therefore, can be difficult to determine and fail to detect specific explanations for poor performance, a number of disaggregate measures are used:

$$P = \frac{\text{Production}}{\text{Machine hours}}$$

$$P = \frac{\text{Production}}{\text{Number of employees}}$$

$$P = \frac{\text{Sales}}{\text{Number of square feet}}$$

$$P = \frac{\text{Passenger miles (railway)}}{\text{Number of guards}}$$

Output is, of course, influenced by a host of factors such as the level of automation, the quality of raw materials, scheduling of labour, layout of operations and customer behaviour. The danger of using only one partial measure of productivity in the form of labour input is that poor performance may wrongly be attributed to unproductive workers. The explanation may quite easily be found in poor materials and equipment, poor layout and awkward customers. Ball, Johnson and Slattery[1] give an example of the range of productivity measure in the hotel industry (Table 10.1).

Nowadays the term performance indicator is often used to describe productivity measures. Given the distinctive characteristics of services, the pursuit of productivity measurement is a challenging one. It is a topic that generates a great deal of attention. Exhortations are often made about the need to increase efficiency (as distinct from effectiveness) and invariably this is supposed to be achieved by getting more output from the same input or getting the same output from less input. Inevitably, calls are made for more output from less input!

Labour is a major input in any organization (particularly a service) and the focus for this call for increased productivity has been, and still is, 'blue-collar' workers. Their counterparts, white-collar workers, have escaped being subjected to productivity measurement. Increasingly, however, the picture is changing. The performance of white-collar workers is being measured, although the term 'performance indicator' seems to take precedence over productivity.

It is generally agreed that it is much easier to measure productivity on an assembly line than in a service business where the 'product' is often the customer's intangible experience. Services, themselves, will of course vary in terms of how susceptible they are to measurement and the form that measurement will take[2] (Figure 10.1).

Table 10.1 Example ratios of hotel productivity

	Physical measures	Physical/financial measures combined	Financial measures
Labour measures	$\dfrac{\text{Kitchen meals produced}}{\text{No. kitchen staff}}$	$\dfrac{\text{Restaurant revenue}}{\text{Hours worked in restaurant}}$	$\dfrac{\text{Banqueting revenue}}{\text{Banqueting payroll}}$
	$\dfrac{\text{Housecount}}{\text{Total employee hours}}$	$\dfrac{\text{Total room sales}}{\text{Total reception employees}}$	$\dfrac{\text{Hotel revenue}}{\text{Total management salaries}}$
	$\dfrac{\text{Restaurant covers}}{\text{Hours worked in restaurant}}$	$\dfrac{\text{Total room sales}}{\text{Chambermaid day}}$	$\dfrac{\text{Total added value}}{\text{Hotel payroll}}$
Energy measures	$\dfrac{\text{Total guest rooms}}{\text{Total kilowatt hours}}$	$\dfrac{\text{No. cooked meals}}{\text{Total cooking costs}}$	$\dfrac{\text{Hotel revenue}}{\text{Total energy cost}}$
Capital measures	$\dfrac{\text{Total hotel customers}}{\text{Square foot of hotel}}$	$\dfrac{\text{No. rooms sold}}{\text{Total capital expenditure}}$	$\dfrac{\text{Net profit after tax}}{\text{Equity capital}}$
Raw material measures	$\dfrac{\text{Chips prepared (lb)}}{\text{Potatoes used (lb)}}$	$\dfrac{\text{No. bar customers}}{\text{Cost of liquor used}}$	$\dfrac{\text{Food revenue}}{\text{Cost of food consumed}}$
Total factor measures	$\dfrac{\text{No. satisfied hotel customers}}{\text{Total no. hotel customers}}$	$\dfrac{\text{Housecount}}{\text{Cost of contributing resources}}$	$\dfrac{\text{Net profit after tax}}{\text{Cost of contributing resources}}$

Source: Ball *et al.* (1986)[1]

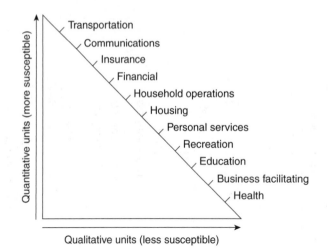

The diagram shows a right triangle. The vertical axis is labelled "Quantitative units (more susceptible)" and the horizontal axis is labelled "Qualitative units (less susceptible)". Along the hypotenuse, from top to bottom, are listed:

- Transportation
- Communications
- Insurance
- Financial
- Household operations
- Housing
- Personal services
- Recreation
- Education
- Business facilitating
- Health

Figure 10.1 Productivity of services: susceptibility of output to measurement
Source: Rathmell (1974)[2]

Established productivity measures are less easily applied as one moves from the left to the right of Figure 10.1. Measuring productivity in a transportation service poses fewer problems than in a counselling service. For a transportation service, input (e.g. driver hours) and output (e.g. tonne-miles) and the relationship between the two offers a clear measure of productivity. For a counselling service, quantitative input and output measures and the relationship between the two are not so readily available. Counselling involves advice and human relationships, and because of that, understanding the process and impact of such a service is far from straightforward. It is a service where the proper application of knowledge and skills should take precedence over attempts to apply input/output ratios.

10.2   The productivity framework

To develop our understanding of productivity we need to add to the ideas of input and output already mentioned (see Figure 10.2). There are two words featured in Figure 10.2 that are frequently mentioned in everyday discussion but often without clear understanding of their meaning. They are used loosely and often interchangeably. The words are, of course, efficiency and effectiveness. The meanings will become clearer as we look at some examples. However, in general they can be defined as follows:

- **Efficiency:** the rate at which inputs are converted into outputs, e.g. calls per sales representative; customers served per catering assistant. The emphasis is often on quantitative measurement and the objective is one of securing the maximum output from the minimum input.
- **Effectiveness:** the extent to which purposes/goals are achieved, e.g. the number of productive and profitable calls per sales representative and the nature of customer relationships established and fostered; the number of satisfied customers served per catering assistant. The emphasis is on qualitative measurement and the objective one of meeting customer needs and delivering service quality.

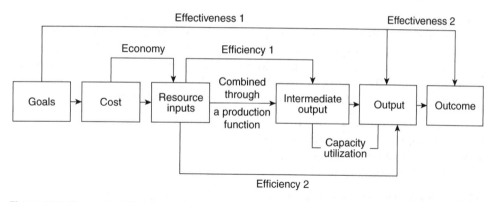

Figure 10.2 The productivity framework

The distinction between efficiency and effectiveness has been defined as 'doing things right' (efficiency) and 'doing right things' (effectiveness).[3] What this amounts to is that efficiency is 'the rate at which inputs are converted into outputs' and effectiveness is 'the extent to which purposes are being achieved'.[4]

Figure 10.2 offers a guide to developing an understanding of the various elements and their relationships:

- **Economy:** the cost of selecting and hiring people, materials and equipment and conversion through training and installation into resource inputs capable of providing service. It is not a measure of performance, but can have an impact on the level of performance.
- **Efficiency 1:** the ratio of inputs to intermediate outputs, e.g. the cost per unit of capacity (cost per place in a private nursing home) or cost per anticipated level of demand (cost per meal prepared in a hotel).
- **Production function:** all the resources (staff, buildings, equipment, consumables) are combined to produce intermediate outputs, i.e. the capacity to produce the relevant service (school places, hospital beds, train seats, restaurant seats).
- **Efficiency 2:** the ratio of inputs to outputs, e.g. the cost per college graduate or cost per number of meals sold in an hotel.
- **Capacity utilization:** the ratio of intermediate output to final output, i.e. how good is management at converting the intermediate output into customer take-up. For example, what percentage of seats will be taken up by customers in a restaurant or what percentage of places will be taken up in a residential home. For services in general, and in particular where advance preparation is involved (meals in a restaurant), accurate demand forecasting will become part of effective marketing management.
- **Effectiveness 1 and 2:** there is no overall agreement as to how effectiveness should be defined. Is it to be in terms of 'output' or 'outcome'?

Output means the service actually delivered to customers. Outcome, on the other hand, is the impact which the service may have on the recipients. It is the quality of the service delivered and its effectiveness in meeting users' needs or achieving its underlying purpose (Audit Commission)[5]. For example, a college educates students (output) but has a certain responsibility for graduate employability and destination (outcome). A management consultancy produces a report and advises a client (output) but has a certain responsibility for the impact of the report on the performance of the client company (outcome). In both cases, however, the outcome measure is not completely under the control of the service provider.

For many services, output is defined in a straightforward manner, as in:

- Number of commuters transported
- Number of home help clients assisted
- Number of restaurant meals served
- Number of admissions to a leisure centre.

What is missing is any reference to the quality of service delivered.

Some services simply have no output or outcome that can practically be measured in quantitative terms; for example, a counselling service.

If the output of a process appears to defy identification with precision, a surrogate measure of output may be used. For example, the true output of the police service could be its contribution to the maintenance of a peaceful, crime free, ordered society, or a public library's true output might be the contribution it makes to expanding the knowledge base of, and to entertaining, the constituent community. As both of these outputs are likely to prove difficult to quantify, proxy measures in the form of 'percentage of reported crime solved' and 'ratio of loans to book stock' are used.[6]

The difficulties surrounding the measurement of output and outcome has led to the development of a different approach which is known as process productivity. It has been argued as being a more realistic and expedient measure.[7] How well the service is delivered is, arguably, a better way for a service like health, where it is difficult to measure changes in health status and where factors other than medical care affect health outcome.

10.3 Improving productivity

Given the standard ratio there are, in theory, five ways to increase productivity:

1 Output increases faster than input
2 Output remains unchanged with fewer inputs
3 Output increases from the same inputs
4 Input decreases more than output
5 Maximum increase in the ratio through an ideal combination of outputs and inputs.

Whatever method is selected, the true test will be the effect on the quality of service delivered. Improved productivity must, therefore, take into account effectiveness as well as efficiency. A number of practical steps can be taken to improve productivity in terms of efficiency and effectiveness:

1 Careful cost control, driven by a management desire to become 'leaner and fitter'
2 Job design – management and employees in pursuit of productivity improvements must attempt to answer questions such as:[8]
   - What work do we do?
   - How do we do it?

- Why do we do it this way?
- How can we do it better?

3 Replace human labour with automation
4 Improve employee motivation:
   - How do employees perceive the organizational culture?
   - Do they feel part of the organization?
   - Are rewards commensurate with the tasks done?
5 Select people more predisposed for productivity, for example the predisposition of an air traffic controller is more important than that of a security guard in a low-crime area
6 Isolate, and even extend, the back office so that the benefits of manufacturing technology can be achieved
7 Schedule resource deployment to match fluctuations in the level of customer demand
8 Involve customers more in the production and delivery of service
9 Make sure that highly skilled employees are not doing jobs that could be undertaken by less fully trained staff.

10.3.1 Practical examples: some undesirable consequences

In the drive for greater efficiency, productivity increases may produce an adverse effect:

Example 1: a 300-bedroomed hotel has reduced the number of chambermaids from 30 to 20 as a result of a productivity drive. There are to be no changes in time to do the job and materials/equipment available. The result is a reduction in the cleanliness of rooms, in particular those occupied by families who leave the room very untidy.

Example 2: an insurance company decides to measure the productivity of its employees by client satisfaction. As a result, the claims department rapidly settled claims and nearly bankrupted the company.

Example 3: a hospital increased patient throughput by decreasing the average duration of bed occupancy. Efficiency could be said to have increased. However, to achieve this efficiency, the hospital selected patients offering the likelihood of shorter lengths of stay. Fundamentally, a faster throughput may increase efficiency but at what cost to full and lasting patient recovery (effectiveness). An increase in the number of early deaths would certainly increase efficiency!

What these examples clearly demonstrate is an overriding concentration on increases in quantity and cost reduction. The consequence is an adverse effect on service quality. Greater efficiency is achieved by increasing the numerator (faster turnover of patients) while maintaining the denominator or maintaining the numerator and decreasing the denominator (fewer chambermaids).

There is often a tension between the drive for efficiency and the achievement of effectiveness[9] (Figure 10.3). A service can be efficient but ineffective; alternatively it

	Ineffective	Effective
Inefficient	Die quickly	Survive
Efficient	Die slowly	Thrive

Figure 10.3 The contrast between efficiency and effectiveness
Source: Brown (1987)[9]

can be effective but inefficient. This can be illustrated by a hypothetical emergency ambulance service:

> One can envisage an ambulance with a highly trained crew that is very efficient and dashes about from accident to accident promptly, treating injured persons with expert skill, placing them in the ambulance and rapidly driving them to the nearest hospital, then racing off to service yet another emergency. The unit would be extraordinarily efficient if it handled two such emergencies in an hour or about sixteen in an eight hour shift. However, it would be utterly ineffective if the actual number of emergencies in the area averaged twenty per shift. This would be an example of a highly efficient service that is utterly ineffective; more ambulances are needed. Alternatively, one can conceive of a very effective ambulance service where no one has to wait more than five minutes to receive expert medical attention, ambulances are promptly dispatched, and many lives are saved. However such a service may be extremely inefficient, if in fact it is staffed with so many ambulances and crews that most of them sit around doing nothing for hours on end because there is little demand for their service.[10]

10.4   Consumer participation and productivity

As the consumer is the central character in the provision of service, the question arises, 'What contribution can the consumer make to the delivery of an efficient and effective service?' To test the impact of the consumer's contribution to service productivity, consider the four following real-life service scenarios.[11]

Scene 1: a major hotel:
Guest A called the desk right after check-in to report a burned-out light bulb and an absence of hot water; both were fixed in an hour. Guest A also slept better, as the hotel assigned him a quiet room when he identified himself as a light sleeper.

Guest B did not communicate to management until check-out time, when he complained that there was no hot water and he had to read in the dark; he was overheard by new guests checking in, who asked if the hotel was undergoing a disaster.

Scene 2: an airline flight from New York to Los Angeles:
Passenger A arrives for the flight with a portable tape player and tape, with a large supply of reading material, and wearing warm clothes. Passenger A also booked a special meal ahead of time.

Passenger B, who arrives empty-handed, becomes annoyed when the crew runs out of blankets and magazines, complains about the lunch and starts fidgeting after the movie.

Scene 3: office of a professional tax preparer:
Client A has organized the necessary information into categories that will help the accountant.

Client B has a shoe box filled with papers, including laundry receipts mixed in with cancelled cheques.

Scene 4: a health club:
When a new aerobics instructor includes a routine that seems hard to follow. Member A modifies the steps and adjusts the pace to allow for her individual physical limitations.

Member B complains that the routine is too hard to follow and suggests that the instructor be fired immediately.

Reflecting on the four scenarios, two related questions are worth remembering:

1 How many of the Customer B type are there around?
2 What can a service provider do to encourage more of the Customer A type?

In trying to turn the service consumer into a valued participant in the service delivery process, the service provider must recognize the following factors and how they could be managed:

- Consumer predisposition, e.g. personality, attitudes, values – may be difficult to change
- Consumer potential commitment/willingness to become involved – low to high
- Consumer knowledge and skills – how easily can they be developed if need be?

In addition to the degree of consumer involvement, the service provider must consider the nature of consumer involvement, i.e. when, where and how in the service delivery process will customer involvement occur? From self-service at a restaurant or petrol station through to interactions with a doctor, teacher or accountant, the potential for exploiting improvements in productivity can be substantial. Whatever changes in service delivery are proposed, the consumer must be the major beneficiary.

10.5 White-collar productivity

The working day for blue-collar workers is often prescribed down to the finest detail (tasks to be done and time taken to do them). For white-collar workers, what they do and how much time they spend doing it, is often left to their own judgement. Within the blue-collar category the tasks are largely standardized and repetitive, e.g. railway porter, catering assistant, bus driver, street sweeper. The white-collar category, on the other hand, includes a diversity of jobs with differing sets of authority, responsibility and duties. Ruch sought to clear up the problem of the white-collar category by isolating two relevant dimensions.[12]

1 The amount of discretion involved – not the amount of skill, but the degree to which there is a specified procedure to follow in the performance of the job. For example, the hotel receptionist's job is not highly skilled but judgement may be required in handling the different customer enquiries and complaints. On the other hand, the dentist's job is a highly skilled procedure in contrast to the procedure for handling complaints. It would be easier to measure, therefore, the productivity of the dentist (number of fillings, extractions per dentist) than the hotel receptionist's performance in handling customer enquiries and complaints. The general rule is that the less discretion there is in the job, the easier it is to measure. The dentist's job, in productivity terms, is, therefore, more akin to the blue-collar worker.
2 The degree to which there is a physical product involved in the process. For the McDonald's cook or the dentist there is a tangible output that can be counted and checked for quality (the hamburger and the filling). The hotel receptionist's job has to be experienced, as once it is performed, the evidence disappears. There is no output left to count or check for quality. The general rule is that the more there is a tangible output, the easier it is to measure.

There are problems then in measuring white-collar productivity:[12]

● Difficulties in determining the output or contribution
● Tendency to measure activities rather than the results, e.g. number of reports created says nothing about the quality of these reports
● The input may not show up in output until some time later; there is a lagged effect
● Quality of output is even more difficult to determine than quantity
● Distinction is often not made between efficiency and effectiveness; the white-collar worker may be efficient at developing reports but ineffective by not having enough to do, attending unproductive meetings, or assigned work outside the area of expertise
● White-collar workers are not accustomed to being measured.

Although there are difficulties, effort should be made to measure white-collar productivity. The inputs may be relatively straightforward, e.g. number of hours worked, number of hours paid, resources used. It is the process and the output that pose the difficulties. The following issues are worth consideration:

● Creativity of white-collar employees in the sense of developing and implementing new ideas
● Efficiency and effectiveness of the utilization of the working day – this is an overriding factor upon which everything else depends
● Satisfaction level of the customers – care needs to be exercised since no matter what the white-collar worker does, the customer may remain dissatisfied, e.g. lecturer and student, doctor and patient
● Ability to handle non-standard situations, i.e. crisis management
● Communication skills and success in keeping people properly informed.

The above list is by no means exhaustive but simply indicates the kind of analysis that needs to be undertaken.

The single greatest challenge facing managers, according to Drucker[13] is to raise the productivity of knowledge and service workers. He stresses that for all their diversity in knowledge, skill, responsibility, social status and pay, knowledge and service workers are remarkably alike in terms of:

- What does and does not work in raising their productivity.

The first lesson that came as a rude shock, according to Drucker, is that the replacement of labour with technology does not, by itself, raise productivity. The key to raising productivity is working smarter rather than harder or longer. Drucker believes that fundamental questions need to be asked if the productivity of knowledge and service workers is to be raised. For example:

- What is the task?
- What are we trying to accomplish?
- Why do it at all?

Drucker bemoans the fact that in many professional service jobs, e.g. nursing, teaching, a great deal of effort and time is taken up with paperwork and meetings, much of which contributes little if any value and has little if anything to do with what these professionals are qualified and paid for. The result is job impoverishment rather than enrichment and a reduction in motivation and morale.

Drucker recognizes that for a good many service jobs, e.g. making hospital beds, handling insurance claims, performance is defined on a quantity basis, very much like production jobs. The application of industrial engineering techniques will determine how long it should take, for example, to make up a hospital bed properly. For other service jobs, e.g. knowledge-based, raising productivity, in Drucker's view, requires asking 'What works?' plus analysing the process step by step and operation by operation.

Process is the subject of an approach that could achieve for office productivity what just-in-time techniques did for manufacturing practice. Business process redesign (BPR) looks at procedures and the way things are organized. BPR is attracting the interest of large service organizations looking for new ways of raising productivity and cutting costs. By simplifying the workflow and reducing the number of stages involved in a procedure, BPR can speed up customer service and involve fewer staff.

The development of schemes relating pay to individual performance has grown dramatically in recent years. According to one survey,[14] 47% of private sector companies have performance related pay (PRP) schemes for all non-manual grades and a further 21% were using it for some non-manuals. There was no significant difference between manufacturing and service industries, but there was a difference between the public and private sectors. In the public sector 37% of organizations in the survey were operating PRP schemes for some of their non-manual grades, but only 6% covered all non-manuals. Non-management grades in the public sector were significantly less likely to be covered by PRP than in the private sector, and those employed in senior management. Management and professional occupations were nearly twice as likely to be eligible for PRP in the private sector as those in the public sector.

The supporters of PRP put forward a number of reasons for introducing it, e.g. it's a motivator, it improves quality and productivity and it's fair. The evidence in support of these claims is inconclusive. Instead, it can be argued that the actual assessment of performance is open to charges of unfairness. Questions are raised about who does the assessment and how it is done. Furthermore is PRP appropriate to all organizational cultures? Even if it is appropriate, how far can PRP help to promote changes in organizational culture? Can it make organizations more customer performance oriented through improved productivity and service quality?

The challenge of implementing PRP is arguably greater for service organizations than their manufacturing counterparts. There is more uncertainty in terms of process and output and factors outside their employees' control may figure prominently in service situations, e.g. infinite variety of possible breakdowns in the service delivery system, difficulties in managing customers.

Some jobs or tasks may not easily lend themselves to concrete performance measures. It is easier to evaluate if hard quantifiable, technical measures can be set. However, softer measures, e.g. related to communication skills, should also be encouraged.

It is argued that PRP is a distinct improvement on previous incentive schemes. According to Kessler and Purcell,[15] 'the link between pay and performance remains as obscure as ever and further research is necessary to throw some light on this vexed issue'.

Of course, the most radical question of all in any discussion of white-collar productivity would be, 'Why not give the workers a say?' Giving subordinates a 'voice' in formal performance evaluation of their bosses can prove invaluable as a source of feedback for everyone concerned.[16] Employees can be asked their view of how effective the bosses are in, for example:

- Providing feedback on performance
- Looking for ways to improve existing systems
- Taking action on urgent requests
- Keeping people well informed
- Handling a disruptive employee.

Care must be exercised over what to appraise and how to do it. Some might question the accuracy of subordinate appraisals. To some extent this misses the point. Their true value is in offering a view of management performance from those directly affected by it. That view can then be compared with management's view of itself. One study[17] found that managers who perceived themselves to be effective at 'providing clear instruction and explanation to employees when giving assignments', were not perceived as such by those persons supposedly on the receiving end of the instructions!

Involving employees in management appraisal can influence their own productivity as well. What they believe and say about management's expectations of them may hold the key to explaining levels of productivity. The 'Pygmalion in Management' view suggests that most managers unintentionally treat their subordinates in a way that leads to lower performance than they are capable of achieving.[18]

The way subordinates are treated is very much influenced by management expectations of them. The result is that high expectations lead to high productivity and low expectations lead to low productivity. However, expectations must, in the view of the subordinate, be realistic and achievable.

A concluding comment about white-collar productivity: it is not so readily observable and measurable as blue-collar productivity, e.g. the bricklayer is both easily observed and measured – number of bricks laid per hour; whereas a nurse comforting a patient after a major operation may not be viewed as productive activity in the conventional wisdom.

10.6   Service productivity as a relationship between input and output

Efficiency and effectiveness in a service organization are measured in terms of inputs and outputs. But unlike manufacturing or extractive industries, service is a process with customer involvement. Understanding the process is fundamental to explaining the relationship of inputs to outputs. This process, and the inputs and outputs, can be portrayed as approximating to a triangle. The base could be a point (making it truly a triangle) or as wide as the top (making it a square) (Figure 10.4).

An example will serve to illustrate. Colleges take in students who have expectations. After a period of time one output will be student satisfaction. The width of the base will indicate what percentage of those who have entered were satisfied at the finish with what they received. In this case (Figure 10.4) the percentage satisfied would be of the order of 25%. The dotted line would represent a situation where all the customers who used the service were satisfied. Of course, in addition to determining how many customers were satisfied, consideration would have to be given to how satisfied they were. Notwithstanding dropouts and failures, the percentage satisfied will serve as a measure of how effective the process they have gone through has been. This kind of analysis could apply to many services, e.g. hotels, package holidays, rail commuters.

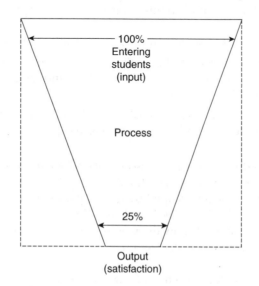

Figure 10.4 The service triangle: percentage satisfied

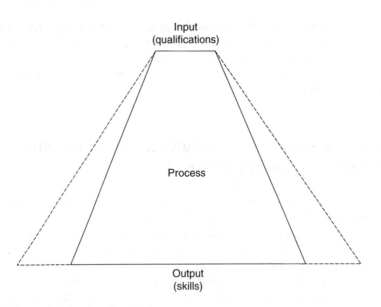

Figure 10.5 The service triangle: value added

Equally, the triangle could be portrayed another way (Figure 10.5). This time the emphasis is on the value added by the process. Students enter with qualifications, e.g. A-levels, and finish with a qualification. But how effective has the process been in developing skills and abilities valuable for entering the world of work? The wider the base (dotted line) the more effective the process has been. Unlike the percentage satisfied measure, the value-added approach is more difficult to determine.

Heaton[19] suggested that the productivity of service organizations could be calculated as the product of four operating functions: input, processing, output or follow-up, and timing and coordination. He applied this to the unusual example of a mental hospital:

Input: 30% of those admitted do not require hospitalization – gross rating then of 70%.

Processing: only 50% of those needing help receive it due to overcrowding, under-staffing and a general lack of skills, understanding and care – gross productivity measurement is then 35% (50% × 70%).

Output or follow-up: on release, only 20% are offered appropriate follow-up and assistance due to limited outpatient services – gross productivity measurement is now 7% (50% × 70% × 20%).

Timing and coordination: There is a time and place for everything; too little too late is as wasteful as too much too soon. Of the 7% only 50% were admitted, treated and released at the proper time and helped by the proper agencies – gross productivity measurement is now 3.5% (70% × 50% × 20% × 50%).

Therefore, out of an initial 100 only three or four were effectively helped. It is hardly the mark of an effective service organization.

Analysis similar to Heaton's is a must for service organizations as it focuses on the process and facilitates understanding of the progress from the input to the output stage. As with the college example mentioned earlier, there will be a number of variables that require investigation. Some of these will be under the control of the service organization and others may be more difficult to control. The nature and deployment of employee skills, materials and equipment are far more controllable than the customers' behaviour and demand levels.

10.7   Customer retention and lifetime value

10.7.1   The retention perspective

The traditional role of marketing has been to win customers. Little attention or effort was devoted to keeping them. This preoccupation with customer acquisition rather than customer retention has been criticized as a 'leaky bucket' approach to business. So long as new customers are acquired to replace those existing customers lost through the hole in the bucket, success in the form of sales is achieved.

It has been estimated that most organizations lose significantly more than 30% of their customers before or at the time of a repurchase decision, mainly through poor service; and the only reason market shares do not drop is because competitors are usually in the same position and are losing customers to their rivals.[20] What all this means is that there is a high turnover of dissatisfied customers searching for a company that they can trust and have faith in. As one observer points out:

> It has always been incredible to me how insensitive companies can be to their customers. Most of them don't seem to understand that their future business depends on having the same customer come back again and again.[21]

Support for retention over acquisition came in a report[22] claiming that a reduction in customer defections by just 5% across a range of service industries generates an increase in profits anywhere from 25 to 85% (for an illustration of the profit impact of customer retention see Appendix 10.1). More recent work has confirmed the earlier finding.[23] Two previously unidentified factors evidently explain such an impact on profits.[24] The first factor is the customer volume effect – the bigger the leak of customers from the bucket, the harder a company must work to fill it up and keep it full. Consider two companies, one with a customer retention rate of 95%, the other with a rate of 90%. The leak in the first company's bucket is 5% per year and the second company's leak is twice as large, 10% per year. If both companies acquire new customers at the rate of 10% per year, the first will have a 5% net growth in customers per year, while the other will have none. What this means is that the first company will double in size over 14 years. while the other will have no growth at all (see Appendix 10.2 for calculations). The second factor is the profit per customer effect – this is more difficult to see than the customer volume effect but evidently the effect on profits is even bigger.

10.7.2   Retention rate and average customer lifetime

The measurement of customer loyalty is known as the 'customer retention rate'. As a company's retention rate improves, the average 'life' of a customer increases. For example, if a company can find a way of increasing its average retention from an

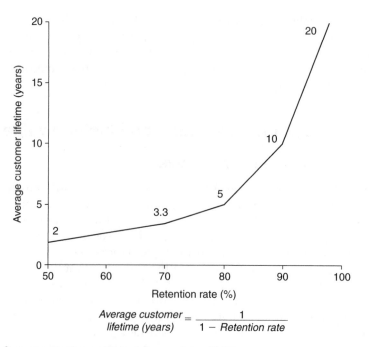

$$\text{Average customer} \atop \text{lifetime (years)} = \frac{1}{1 - \text{Retention rate}}$$

Figure 10.6 Customer-retention model: impact on customer lifetime
Source: Bain & Co.

annual 80% to 90% it will actually double the average customer lifetime from 5 to 10 years (Figure 10.6).

If it retains 80% of its customers it will have had to replace all of them over a 5-year period (5 × 20%). If it retains 90% it will lose just half of them over the same period (5 × 10% = 50%). Increase in retention is one means of increasing profitability.

10.7.3   Why loyal customers are more profitable

According to international management consultants Bain & Co., a number of factors are deemed important for understanding profit enhancement from customer loyalty. The factors cited are:[25]

- **Acquisition cost:** money has to be invested to bring in new customers, e.g. cost of selling, advertising etc.
- **Base profit:** all customers buy some product or service and the prices they pay are usually higher than the company's costs; the longer you keep a customer, the longer you will earn this base profit
- **Per customer revenue growth:** customer spending tends to accelerate over time
- **Operating costs:** as customers get to know a business and company employees get to know their customers, efficiencies in doing business arise and thereby reduce costs
- **Referrals:** satisfied customers are more likely to introduce new customers to the company through word-of-mouth recommendation
- **Price premium:** satisfied customers are often willing to pay premium prices to a supplier they know and trust.

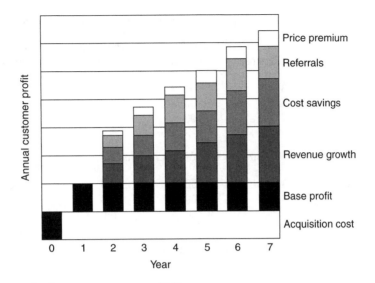

Figure 10.7 Why loyal customers are more profitable
Source: Bain & Co.

Figure 10.7 illustrates the root causes of, and their respective contribution to, increased profitability over time.

A key criticism made of the customer retention concept is that customer longevity does not always result in significant profitability improvement.[26] Bain & Co.'s response has been that 'Our position has never been that simply increasing retention rates will magically produce profits. For example, foolish investments to retain hopelessly unprofitable customers would destroy profits. Our point is that substantially higher profits require high retention. Therefore, understanding the link between retention and profits is essential.[27] The argument revolves around the types of customer retained'. One critic (of Bain & Co.'s argument) gave the following example to illustrate the point:[28]

Three types of retail banking customer:

    A customers: acceptable annual contribution
    B customers: unacceptable but positive annual contribution
    C customers: negative annual contribution

In the first quarter of year 1:	1000 new customers
In the second quarter of year 1:	500 lost money (Type C) 200 made a little but not much (Type B) 300 were strong contributors (Type A)
By the end of year 3:	500 customers left:
Of the 500 initially unprofitable:	150 remain
Of the 200 who made a little:	100 remain
Of the 300 strong contributors:	250 remain

Type A customers now make up to 50% of that total, as against 30% at the beginning.

Table 10.2 Customer retention and profitability: comparison of average annual contributions

	Customer	Number of customers	Profit per customer (£)	Total profit (£)
Year 1, quarter 2	A	300	250	75 000
	B	200	50	10 000
	C	500	(150)	(75 000)
		1000		10 000
	£10 000 ÷ 1000 = £10 per customer			
End of year 3	A	250	250	62 500
	B	100	50	5 000
	C	150	150	(22 500)
		500		45 000
	£45 000 ÷ 500 = £90 per customer			

The resulting improvement in profitability has been caused by the departure of Cs, not by the change of status of Cs to Bs and Bs to As.

If an A customer is worth £250 a year, a B customer is worth £50 per year and a C customer is worth £150 a year, what change has there been in the average annual contribution between early in year 1 and the end of year 3? Table 10.2 tells us that the average annual contribution has gone from £10 to £90 owing to the rise in the proportion of A customers, the most profitable type.

10.7.4   Lifetime value of a customer

To understand the full impact of defections, companies must calculate the lifetime value of a customer. It is defined as the total revenue received from a customer during his or her 'lifetime' with a company, less the costs of servicing and marketing. In effect, the total profit received from having that customer over time. Where there is a difficulty in calculating profit, contribution margin (revenue minus variable cost) or sales revenue can be used.

In general terms, lifetime value of a customer can be calculated as follows:

$$\text{Lifetime value} = \text{Average transaction value}$$
$$\times \text{ Frequency of purchase}$$
$$\times \text{ Customer life expectancy}$$

To take a simple example, just one loyal customer paying an average £100 per week over 10 years for office-cleaning services would be worth £52 000 to the provider.

A relatively simple scenario using contribution margin (CM) as the financial measure of success will demonstrate lifetime value in practice[29] (Table 10.3). From an initial acquisition of 1000 new buyers, the lifetime value over a 12-year period is determined.

In year 1 the company acquires 1000 new buyers. The average contribution margin per buyer (CM/buyer) is £1 owing to a large proportion of the contribution margin having been used to cover the cost of new customer acquisition. Therefore, the

Table 10.3 Lifetime value

	1	2	3	4	5	6	7	8	9	10	11	12
							Acquisition year					
Buyers	1000	250	150	105	84	67.20	53.76	43.01	34.41	27.53	22.02	17.62
Retention (%)		25	60	70	80	80	80	80	80	80	80	80
Contribution margin (CM) per buyer	£1	£20	£20.40	£21.01	£21.85	£22.95	£24.09	£25.30	£26.56	£27.89	£29.28	£30.75
CM % increase		2%	2%	3%	4%	5%	5%	5%	5%	5%	5%	5%
Total CM	£1000	£5000	£3060	£2206	£1836	£1542	£1295	£1088	£914	£768	£645	£542

Source: Wang and Splegel (1994)[29]

total annual contribution for these buyers is £1000. The following year, 250 of the original buyers made repeat purchases from this company. The average contribution per customer increases to £20. The increase in the contribution margin is due to the significant decrease of variable marketing costs by the second year. Over subsequent years we witness an increase in the average contribution per buyer due to the improving quality of repeat customers. From year 6, a contribution margin of 5% is sustained till year 12. The lifetime value of this customer group over the 12 years is £19 896, being the sum of the 12 yearly contribution.

10.7.5 Present value

The problem with Table 10.3 is that we are unable to make direct comparisons between the cash received in year 12 and that received in year 1 in terms of how much each is worth. Clearly £542 received today is worth much more than £542 received in 12 years' time. In fact £542 invested today for 12 years at an annual interest rate of 10% would give a cash amount of £1701 (i.e. £542 $\times$ 1.10^{12}). We have in effect converted today's money (£542) into an equivalent amount (£1701) 12 years in the future by using a rate of interest.

A better way of making all the cash flows comparable is to bring all of them back to today's values rather than to project forward. The technique uses the same logic but in reverse: the objective is to find an equivalent present value for any future cash flow. Instead of applying compound interest we apply a negative interest rate to reduce the future value to the present value. This negative interest rate (or discount rate, as it is called) is the annual cost associated with having to wait to receive the cash. The present value (PV) of a future sum as given by the formula:

$$PV = \frac{1}{(1 + R)^n}$$

where R equals the rate of interest per period and n the number of the periods to be discounted. Returning to Table 10.3 and using a standard discount rate of 10%, the £19 896 in cumulative contribution translates to a present value of £13 111 (Table 10.4).

What does this £13 111 mean? It gives some sense of how much this customer group is worth in today's money. Furthermore, it guides the amount that can be spent today on acquiring customers. Spending sums today in excess of £13 111 on acquiring customers would do little for the company's profitability.

The above calculations and frameworks form the basis for what can become a complex, intricate process. What is at issue here is growth and profitability. The task of balancing what is spent on customer acquisition with what is spent on retention will require knowledge of returns from spending in terms of acquisition and retention rates and subsequent present values. In essence all companies face the following questions:

- How does the current rate of acquisition/retention compare with the highest possible number of customers that could be acquired/retained?
- How would the acquisition/retention rate respond to variations in expenditure allocated for acquisition/retention?

Table 10.4 Present value

Year	Total CM £	Discount factor	Present value £
1	1000	$1/1.10^1$	909.1
2	5000	$1/1.10^2$	4132
3	3060	$1/1.10^3$	2298.9
4	2206	$1/1.10^4$	1506.6
5	1836	$1/1.10^5$	1139.9
6	1542	$1/1.10^6$	870.4
7	1295	$1/1.10^7$	664.5
8	1088	$1/1.10^8$	507.5
9	914	$1/1.10^9$	387.6
10	768	$1/1.10^{10}$	296
11	645	$1/1.10^{11}$	226
12	542	$1/1.10^{12}$	172.6
			13 111.1

- Who are our most profitable customers and why? Is it one or a mixture of factors such as customer characteristics, loyalty behaviour, response to marketing stimuli etc.

Summary

Productivity is an issue that has been around for some time. It is concerned with the efficiency of converting inputs into outputs. For service organizations, unlike manufacturing, productivity management is more difficult. This is because the input, process and output are not always susceptible to objective definition and measurement.

A number of steps can be taken to improve productivity but care must be exercised when devising an efficiency programme because effectiveness may diminish as a result.

Consumers play a pivotal role in services. Strategies must therefore be devised for developing consumer participation in the drive for increased productivity. In doing so, recognition must be given to the difficulties involved in obtaining this participation.

Productivity measures have usually been applied to blue-collar employees but white-collar employee performance and the impact of technology are becoming more important in the pursuit of efficiency and effectiveness.

In addition to the quest for increased productivity, organizations are seeking to retain customers in preference to the traditional way of acquiring them. The attractiveness of this approach has accelerated since evidence showed increasing returns from customer retention. However, it has also been recognized that not all long-term customers are profitable. Nevertheless, with the increasing emphasis on database technology and loyalty cards, the opportunity for establishing the economics of loyalty is self-evident.

▮ Appendix 10.1   Customer retention

A service organization has made available the following information:

Starting point – at current levels of retention, cross-sales and referrals

Key data:

Marketing budget, acquisition	£2 325 000	
Marketing budget, retention	£0	
Total number of customers	50 000	
Average acquisition rate	33.75	(weighted average = 31.5)
Total, new customers p.a.	15 750	
Average retention rate	71%	(weighted average = 70.5)
Total, customer lost p.a.	(14 750)	
Growth/decline in customer file	1000	
Growth/decline in customer file	2.0%	
Average customer lifetime	3.29 years	(weighted average = 3.4)
Average profit contribution per cust. p.a.	£300	

Segmentation	Segment 1 18 to 29	Segment 2 30 to 39	Segment 3 40 to 49	Segment 4 50 plus
Revenue per customer, p.a.	£400	£500	£650	£750
Servicing costs per customer, p.a.	£250	£320	£400	£480
Acquisition costs per customer	£70	£100	£220	£250
Cross-sales ratio (1 to …)	1.07	1.22	1.31	1.12
Referral ratio (1 to …)	1.05	1.13	1.18	1.31
Total customers per segment	5000	20 000	15 000	10 000
Retention rate per segment	60%	70%	75%	70%
Acquisition rate per segment	50%	35%	25%	25%
Lifetime per customer, years	2.50	3.33	4.00	3.33
Customers acquired p.a.	2500	7000	3750	2500
Customers lost p.a.	(2000)	(6000)	(3750)	(3000)
Growth in customer file p.a.	500	1000	0	(500)
% Growth in customer file	10%	5%	0%	−5%

At stage 2:   Marketing expenditure switches from
100% acquisition to
75% acquisition and
25% retention. We assume that this will increase retention by
5% in all segments (i.e. one in 20 more customers will be retained)

We also assume that this will encourage

10% more cross-sales to occur and
7.5% more referrals to occur

Key data:

Marketing budget, acquisition	£2 325 000	changing to £1 743 750
Marketing budget, retention	£0	changing to £581 250
Total number of customers	50 000	
Average acquisition rate	25.5	(weighted average = 23.7)
Total, new customers p.a.	11 850	
Average retention rate	73.75%	(weighted average = 75.5)
Total, customers lost p.a.	(12 250)	
Growth/decline in customer file	(400)	
Growth/decline in customer file	(0.8%)	
Average customer lifetime	3.965 years	(weighted average = 4.186)
Profitability per annum	£300	

Segmentation	Segment 1 18 to 29	Segment 2 30 to 39	Segment 3 40 to 49	Segment 4 50 plus
Revenue per customer, p.a.	£400	£500	£650	£750
Servicing costs per customer, p.a.	£250	£320	£400	£480
Acquisition costs per customer	£70	£100	£220	£250
Cross-sales ratio (1 to …)	1.07	1.22	1.31	1.12
Referral ratio (1 to …)	1.05	1.13	1.18	1.31
Total customers per segment	5000	20 000	15 000	10 000
Retention rate per segment	65%	75%	80%	75%
Acquisition rate per segment	38%	26%	19%	19%
Lifetime per customer, years	2.86	4.00	5.00	4.00
Customers acquired p.a.	1900	5200	2850	1900
Customers lost p.a.	(1750)	(5000)	(3000)	(2500)
Growth in customer file p.a.	150	200	(150)	(600)
% Growth in customer file	3%	1%	−1%	−6%

Question

Determine the impact on profit from stage 1 to stage 2

Stage I

Customer value	Segment 1 18 to 29	Segment 2 30 to 39	Segment 3 40 to 49	Segment 4 50 plus
Profits in year 1 from core product sales	£80	£80	£30	£20
Profits in subsequent years from product sales	£150	£180	£250	£270
Total net profit per customer from product sales	£305	£500	£780	£650

Customer value	Segment 1 18 to 29	Segment 2 30 to 39	Segment 3 40 to 49	Segment 4 50 plus
Profit from cross-sales over lifetime	£21	£110	£242	£78
Profit from referrals	£15	£65	£140	£202
Total customer value	£341	£675	£1162	£930

Summary

Customer value	Segment 1	Segment 2	Segment 3	Segment 4
Total customer value in segment	£1 705 000	£13 500 000	£17 430 000	£93 00 000
Customer value contributed p.a.	£682 000	£4 050 054	£4 357 500	£2 792 792
Total customer value across all segments				£41 935 000
Total annual customer value across all segments				£11 882 346

Stage II

Customer value	Segment 1 18 to 29	Segment 2 30 to 39	Segment 3 40 to 49	Segment 4 50 plus
Profits in year 1 from core product sales	£80	£80	£30	£20
Profits in subsequent years from product sales	£150	£180	£250	£270
Total net profit per customer from product sales	£359	£620	£1030	£830
Profit from cross-sales over lifetime	£28	£150	£351	£110
Profit from referrals	£19	£87	£199	£277
Total customer value	£406	£857	£1580	£1217

Summary

Customer value	Segment 1	Segment 2	Segment 3	Segment 4
Total customer value in segment	£2 030 000	£17 140 000	£23 700 000	£12 170 000
Customer value contributed p.a.	£707 790	£4 285 000	£4 740 000	£3 042 500
Total customer value across all segments				£55 040 000
Total annual customer value across all segments				£12 775 290
At 100% of marketing budget spent on acquisition				£41 935 000
At 75% spent on acquisition, 25% spent on retention				£55 040 000

The impact on profit is an increase of 31% from stage 1 to stage 2.

Appendix 10.2   The customer volume effect

Growth rate $r\%$ per annum (r expressed in decimal form)

Initial number of customers $= A$

At the end of year 1 the number of customers $= A + Ar$

$= A(1 + r)$

At the end of year 2 the number of customers = the number of customers at the beginning of year 2 + number acquired during year $2 = A(1 + r) + A(1 + r)r = A(1 + r)(1 + r) = A(1 + r)^2$

At the end of year 3 the number of customers = the number of customers at the beginning of year 3 + number acquired during year $3 = A(1 + r)^2 + A(1 + r)^2 r = A(1 + r)^2 (1 + r) = A(1 + r)^3$

At the end of year n the number of customers $= A(1 + r)^n$

Over what period of time will the firm double in size?

If the initial number of customers is A, we wish to solve

$$A(1 + r)^n = 2A \qquad (1 + r)^n = 2A/A \qquad (1 + r)^n = 2$$

Taking logs of both sides

$$\log(1 + r)^n = \log 2$$
$$n \log(1 + r) = \log 2$$
$$n = \frac{\log 2}{\log(1 + r)}$$

A range of net growth customers per year and how long it will take to double in size is considered below:

Net growth (%)	Calculation	Years
2.5	$\dfrac{\log 2}{\log 1.025}$	28.07
5.0	$\dfrac{\log 2}{\log 1.05}$	14.20*
10.0	$\dfrac{\log 2}{\log 1.10}$	7.27
20.0	$\dfrac{\log 2}{\log 1.20}$	3.80

* Example in text

References

1   Ball, S D, Johnson, K and Slattery, P (1986) 'Labour productivity in hotels: an empirical analysis', *International Journal of Hospitality Management*, **5** (3), 141–147.
2   Rathmell, J M (1974) Marketing in the Service Sector. Winthrop, Cambridge, MA.
3   Drucker, P (1973) *Management: Tasks, Responsibilities, Practices*. New York: Harper and Row.
4   Butt, H and Palmer, B (1985) *Value for Money in the Public Sector*. Oxford: Blackwell.
5   Audit Commission (1989) 'Managing services effectively', *Performance Review*, **5**, December.
6   Whynes, D K (1987) 'On assessing efficiency in the provision of local authority services', *Local Government Studies*, Jan.–Feb., 53–68.
7   Mersha, T (1989) 'Output and performance measurement in outpatient care', *Omega*, **17** (2), 159–161.
8   Heskett, J L, Sasser, W E and Hart, C W L (1990) *Service Breakthroughs*. New York: Free Press.
9   Brown, R. (1987) 'Marketing – a function and a philosophy', *Quarterly Review of Marketing*, **12** (3 and 4), 25–30.
10 Savas, E S (1978) 'On equity in providing public services', *Management Science*, **24** (8), April, 800–808.
11 Goodwin, C (1988) ' "I can do it myself": training the service consumer to contribute to service productivity', *Journal of Service Marketing*, **2** (4), 71–78.
12 Ruch, W A (1982) 'The measurement of white-collar productivity', National Productivity Review, Autumn, 416–426.
13 Drucker, P F (1991) 'The new productivity challenge', *Harvard Business Review*, Nov.–Dec., 69–79.
14 Cannell, M and Wood, S (1992) *Incentive Pay: Impact and Evolution*. London: National Economic Development Office and Institute of Personnel Management.
15 Kessler, I and Purcell, J (1992) 'Performance related pay: objectives and application', *Human Resource Management Journal*, **2** (3), 16–33.
16 Bernadin, H J and Beatty, R W (1987) 'Can subordinate appraisals enhance managerial productivity?', *Sloan Management Review*, Summer, 63–73.
17 Mount, M K (1984) 'Supervisors, self and subordinate ratings of performance and satisfaction with supervision', *Journal of Management*, **10**, 121–130.
18 Livingston, J S (1988) 'Pygmalion in management', *Harvard Business Review*, Sep.–Oct., 121–130.
19 Heaton, H (1977) Productivity in Service Organisations. New York: McGraw-Hill.
20 Smith, S (1994) 'Building loyalty through communications', *Marketing Business*, November.
21 Davidow, W H (1986) *Marketing High Technology*. New York: Free Press.
22 Reichheld, F F and Sasser Jr, W E (1990) 'Zero defections: quality comes to services', *Harvard Business Review*, Sep.–Oct.
23 Reichheld, F F (1994) 'Loyalty and the renaissance of marketing', *Marketing Management*, **15**.
24 Reichheld, F F (1996) *The Loyalty Effect*. Cambridge, MA: Harvard Business School Press.
25 Ibid.
26 Carroll, P (1991/92) 'The fallacy of customer retention', *Journal of Retail Banking*, **xiii**, 4.
27 Reichheld, F F (1991/92) 'The truth of customer retention', *Journal of Retail Banking*, **xiii**, 4.
28 Carroll, 'Fallacy of customer retention'.
29 Wang, P and Splegel, T (1994) 'Database marketing and its measurements of success', *Journal of Direct Marketing*, **8**, 2.

11

Relationship marketing

☐ Introduction

Organizations can grow business by attracting new customers, losing fewer customers and doing more business with existing customers. A combination of the latter two is generally a more efficient way of utilizing resources.[1]

Many studies have shown that marketing strategies that focus on customer retention, deliver improved profitability for the service provider.[2,3] This has resulted in a paradigm shift in the theory and practice of marketing, and a further branch of marketing known as relationship marketing has evolved.

The practice of relationship marketing relies on an organization's ability to identify, target, communicate and reward valuable customers, and is built from the foundations of quality service.

▮ 11.1   A twenty-first century approach to marketing

Such is the fiercely competitive nature of virtually all markets today that most companies operate in markets characterized by oversupply. Under these conditions, if a service does not satisfy, the customer can move on to find another company whose service does. In recent years there has been a refocusing of marketing away from customer acquisition to that of customer retention. If the company is to benefit from retaining customers, customers will also seek to benefit from giving their loyalty to the company. The refocusing on retention is predicated in the belief that improved economic benefits will be delivered.[4] Furthermore, in order to build retention the service provider must build relationships with those who consume the service. The practice of relationship marketing is designed to deliver retention through the development of a number of 'bonds' between organization and customer.

██ 11.2   What is relationship marketing?

For starters, it is more than retention marketing. It is an approach to the practice of marketing that should be adopted right at the beginning of the service life cycle. So, in the early years where trial and acquisition of customers are usually the goals uppermost in the marketing manager's mind, it would be shortsighted to miss the opportunities for relationship-building even then. Zeithaml *et al.*[5] state:

> Relationship marketing is a philosophy of doing business, a strategic orientation, that focuses on keeping and improving current customers rather than on acquiring new customers.

We, however, do not advocate the *either* acquisition *or* retention position. A company following a relationship marketing approach does not imply it is no longer interested in customer acquisition. What it means is that in seeking to acquire new customers the company should target those individuals/companies that it expects to want to do business with over time – and then begin to build a relationship from day 1. This is not a one-night stand.

11.2.1   Relationship marketing: a historical context

If one looks at the parallel developments of marketing thought with the economic situation in the second half of the twentieth century, the evolution to a relationship marketing paradigm is not unexpected.

After the end of the Second World War, most markets were characterized by a lack of supply and excess demand. Companies sold what they could make. There was no listening to the 'voice of the consumer' and adapting product/service offerings to satisfy their requirements. This approach is known as **product orientation** and is typified by Henry Ford the American car manufacturer's famous statement: 'They can have any colour as long as it's black.'

By the time we get to the 1970s many markets are exhibiting excess supply. To survive, companies now have to fight for customers. They have to listen to and meet customers' needs/wants. They learn how to segment and differentiate their offerings. This is **market orientation**.

However, by the 1980s, most companies had adopted a market orientation and the plethora of similar products/services offering often indistinguishable benefits led companies to seek other means of securing an advantage over competitors. Companies developed a **competition orientation**, where they sought to outperform competitors through value-chain savings, a differentiated route to market, etc.

Increasing variety-seeking behaviour from consumers and an expectation of a continual stream of service innovations coupled with advances in technology lead to

Marketing Methods

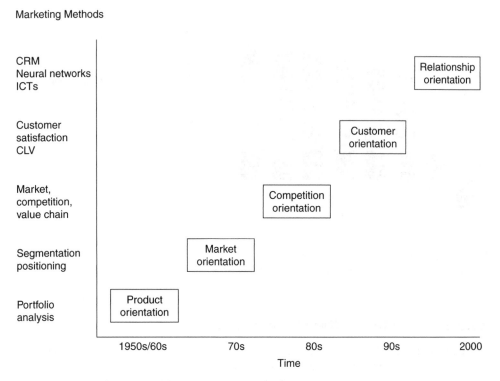

Figure 11.1 Evolution of relationship marketing paradigm

the 1990s being characterized by a renewed marketing focus on the customer. This **customer orientation** was driven by a desire to fulfil the expectations of homogenous groups of customers, often resulting in marketing to increasingly smaller groups of buyers.

The **relationship orientation** is a natural extension to that of customer orientation. For many companies, they have so much invested in strategies designed to meet a customer orientation that they want to hold on to these customers and optimize their relationships. In many cases technology is allowing marketers to engage in 24/7, real-time dialogue with customers – a far cry from the 9 to 5 monologue of the 1950s.

11.3   Why follow a relationship marketing approach?

Many benefits have been shown to accrue to those companies that adopt a relational approach. For one, there are the economic benefits. Such benefits arise from either *increased revenue* or *lower costs*. In a seminal study, Reichheld and Sasser[6] analysed the profit per customer over time in several service industries. Their findings demonstrated that the longer a customer was with a service provider the more profitable they became. Four key reasons for this profit improvement were identified in their study.

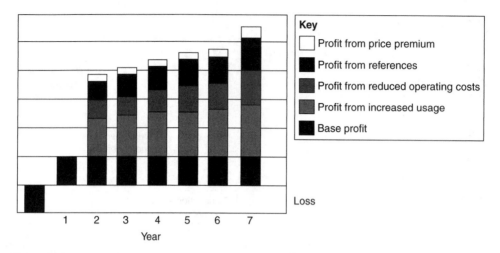

Figure 11.2 Development of value categories in the course of customer relationship
Source: Reichheld and Sasser (1990).[2] Reprinted with permission from *Harvard Business Review*

11.3.1   Benefits to the service provider

- Relational customers tend to increase their purchases over time, either because they are consolidating their purchasing onto a preferred supplier or because their own business/family has grown and there is a need for more.
- Experienced customers tend to make fewer demands on the supplier and fewer mistakes in their operation of the service. So productivity is improved and operating costs are reduced.
- Long-term satisfied customers will engage in positive word-of-mouth recommendation, thereby reducing the marketing spend necessary to attract new buyers.
- There is less need to offer price promotions to this group. Indeed these customers are likely to be less price-sensitive than others (which does not mean they have no price sensitivities).

Using Reichheld's categories, Bain & Co., the international management consultancy, tracked the growth in profit attributed to each of these four factors over a 7-year period[7] (see Chapter 10). Further proof of the economic impact of a relationship strategy can also be found in a further study conducted by Bain & Co. which analysed the impact on profit from a 5% increase in the retention or loyalty rate. Profit impact was calculated by comparing the net present value (NPV) of the profit stream from the average customer life at current retention rates, and then the NPV for the average customer with 5% higher retention rates.

Enormous variations between markets were evident, with an estimated 95% profit improvement in advertising agencies, down to a more modest 35% increase in the software market.

In addition to economic benefits, establishing long-term relationships with customers leads to improved levels of trust and commitment.[8] These can play a powerful role in consumer acceptance of new service initiatives, and also in increased tolerance of occasional services failures.[9]

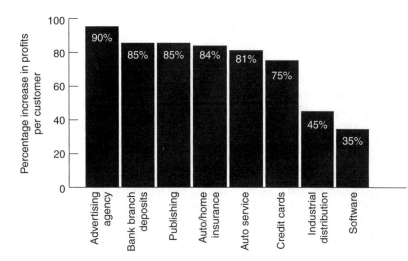

Figure 11.3 Profit impact of a 5% increase in customer retention
Source: Reichheld (1994).[3] Reprinted with permission from *The American Marketing Association*

▇ 11.4   Benefits to the customer

The benefits arising from a relational approach do not solely accrue to the service provider. There are also customer benefits. These fall under three main headings: confidence benefits, social benefits and special treatment benefits:

- **Confidence benefits** arise from feelings of trust or comfort, or conversely from fewer feelings of anxiety, with the service provider. Of the three types of benefit, confidence benefits have been found to be the most important to customers.[10]
- **Social benefits** often arise when the customer receives more than the technical benefits of the service: the local restaurant that remembers where you like to sit, the hairdresser that knows (and asks after) your family. In such cases, there is a more intimate dimension to the customer's relationship with the service provider than with many others. The service provider has become part of the customer's (life) support system. Such relationships are not confined to consumer services. They can also be present in business-to-business markets. Indeed it has been suggested that professional service companies need to be careful not to let staff form specific intimate relationships with clients since they could be vulnerable to customer attrition if they lose these members of staff.[11,12]
- **Special treatment benefits** include such things as getting preferential treatment, as with the loyalty schemes operated by most major airlines. A Silver or a Gold Card holder with British Airways, for example, is much more likely to get a seat upgrade than a passenger with either a Blue Card or no card at all. Upgrades are also used by car hire companies to reward their relational customers. The service provider may make concessions that would not be made otherwise – late drop-off at the dry cleaner, no bank charge for exceeding an overdraft limit. Interestingly, of the three categories of customer benefit, special treatment benefits are regarded as least important by consumers.

11.4.1   Customer loyalty

It would be misleading to suggest that until the concept of relationship marketing emerged, marketers were solely focused on one-off transactions. The majority were also interested in fostering customer loyalty.

Loyalty is more than repeat purchasing. Organizations can often (certainly in the short-term) bind customers through economic and structural bonds that make it costly for a customer to switch. In recent years many players in the financial services industry, particularly mortgage companies, have been accused of making the process of switching to another lender both expensive in terms of early redemption payments, and also costly in terms of time spent filling out lengthy paperwork. On occasion, the customer faced with such obstacles may simply opt to continue to patronize the original company, but it would be wrong to consider this repeat/continuing purchasing to be evidence of loyalty. Such a state has come to be known as spurious loyalty.

Customers with true, premium or intentional loyalty have in addition to repeat purchasing behaviour a strong positive attitude/attachment to the company. Such people will be advocates of the company and will exhibit a level of immunity to competitors' efforts to lure them away.[13] Their loyalty is also difficult to dislodge and often requires a considerable negative experience to get them to re-evaluate the service provider.[14] Consequently, they are considerably more tolerant of mistakes than the average customer.[15]

■ 11.5   Building a relationship marketing strategy

Before a company begins to design and implement a relationship marketing strategy it has to have some fundamental building blocks in place. Without these any relationship marketing strategy has a high likelihood of failure.[16]

For starters, there has to be a *good level of quality* in the core service that is being offered. There is little point in designing relationship marketing strategies for inferior services, since there is little likelihood that there will be a core group of customers interested in forming a lasting relationship.

11.5.1   Market segmentation

Additionally, it is fundamental that the marketer can *identify and segment the customer base*. Until a few years ago this was a challenging task for most mass consumer services companies. However, data capture and manipulation technology ease this considerably. The loyalty cards issued by UK high street supermarkets would not deliver the benefits to consumers and supermarkets if there was not a sophisticated technological infrastructure supporting the scheme.

Segmentation is not a new marketing tool. However, we would suggest that the development of a winning relationship marketing strategy in services requires the marketer to go beyond the traditional approach where markets are segmented along the lines of (geo)demographics, behaviour and possibly psychographic variables.

The purpose of the segmentation is to design and deliver a service tailored for the segment. In tailoring the service, a company should attempt to quantify the value of

Most profitable customers

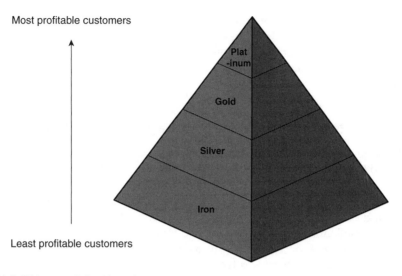

Least profitable customers

Figure 11.4 CLV segmentation hierarchy

a particular customer/segment. This involves estimating customer lifetime value (see Chapter 10 for a fuller explanation). By doing so, the company is then able to determine the value of the relationship and, further, the value it can afford to put into any benefits designed to foster the relationship.

In addition, it will help shape the relationship marketing strategy as the company designs programmes for moving customers from less profitable to more profitable segments.

This analysis of customer lifetime value may highlight the fact that it is not profitable for the company to meet or exceed the expectations of all of its customers. Indeed it has been suggested that in some cases the service provider might need to 'fire' customers.[17] Many UK high street banks have recently segmented their personal banking customer base to provide more 'privileges' for their high net worth individuals. These customers have a personal banker whom they can contact at any time (during business hours) with any request relating to their banking: no call centres for them. Those with whom the bank is less interested in maintaining a relationship, on the other hand, will experience a significantly less responsive operation, one that asks them to be more involved in their own service delivery.

11.5.2 Monitoring the relationship

Finally, a successful relationship marketing strategy needs to have a robust means of monitoring and evaluating the relationship over time. Customer satisfaction studies are helpful in this regard (see Chapter 12 for a fuller discussion). Once again the evaluation programme should be designed with the particular segment in mind. So British Airways regularly takes premium customers away for a 'workshop' weekend. They go to an exotic location, customers take their partners and in addition to the fact-finding on the part of the company there are lots of opportunities for British Airways to deliver a 'wow' factor – famous after-dinner speakers, first to trial new cars, premiere tickets, etc., all of which help to cement the relationship. The company would not consider doing this for its economy passengers.

The company should actively seek feedback and be responsive to this feedback. Remember in relationships the evaluation should appear more like a dialogue than a monologue.

11.5.3 Customer relationship management (CRM) systems

Indeed, the whole approach to monitoring and evaluating customers' services experience should be undertaken in a radically different way to the traditional approach to market research.

In the late 1990s a whole new industry sector developed out of the market research industry and computer software industry. Some companies in these industries saw that many organizations had a need to understand and monitor their customers' behaviour in real time (or as near to this as possible). So there was a desire for this type of system, and now there was technology that could deliver it.

CRM systems (see Table 11.1) are designed to keep a history of all contacts a customer has had with the service provider. So even in mass marketed services where there is little chance that customers will be 'served' by the same employee in the service company on repeated occasions, the company can pick up with the customer where they last left off. Gone are the days of customers having to explain everything from scratch because they happen to make contact with a different employee.

Table 11.1 Common CRM applications

Data collection
Data analysis
Sales force automation
Marketing automation
Call centre automation

Early proponents of such CRM systems considered their implementation would deliver a competitive advantage. Such rewards were often short-lived since such systems were easy to copy. More frequently the expected benefits were never realized. Since many failed to realize that it was not the possession of a CRM system that would deliver the advantage, it was what was done with the information that such systems generated. The CRM system is only a tool to drive the strategy, it does not design, and can only help deliver the strategy.

11.6 Relationship marketing strategies

With the key building blocks of relationship marketing in place, the company is ready to design its relationship strategy. Leonard Berry and A. Parasuraman[18] have developed a framework to assist in the design of relationship strategies. This framework depicts four levels of bond that the service provider can deploy: financial, social, customization and structural.

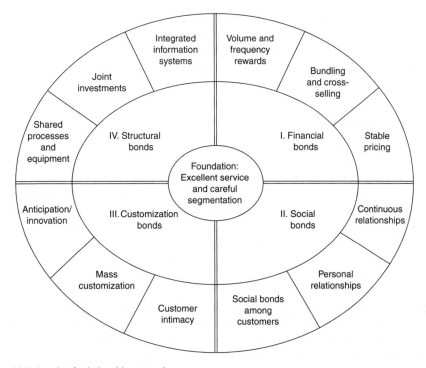

Figure 11.5 Levels of relationship strategies
Source: Zeithaml *et al.* (2006).[5] Reprinted with permission from the authors

11.6.1   Financial bonds

For many, this type of bond represents the starter pack in terms of building customer relationships. Basically the customer is incentivized with reduced prices over time for remaining with the company. Or some sort of volume discount can be offered – for taking a larger share of the customer's business or merely increasing the volume or value of the business that is done. We do not have to look far to find examples of this type of bond – no claims discounts offered by the insurance companies, frequent flyer programmes offered by most of the large airlines, coffee shops that offer to stamp loyalty cards so that a free cup of coffee is given after a certain number have been bought.

In 2004 more than 50 million loyalty cards were issued in the UK – promising discounts, special prizes and exotic holidays for points collected. Eighteen million households include someone with a Boots Advantage Card, 12 million contain a Nectar Card and another 11 million have a Tesco Clubcard, which means that a substantial number of households have more than one card. However, many regard such loyalty card schemes as little more than a clumsy form of price promotion.[19]

These types of programmes are relatively easy to introduce and may even result in some short-term profit improvement. However, they are easily copied – the successful ones nearly always are. So if this is the only plank of a relationship strategy it is unlikely to result in raising retention/loyalty.[20] Further, through time, if financial bonds are used ubiquitously they come to be expected as part of the core service.

Sometimes the financial bond is linked to driving purchases in other markets. Cross-selling and bundling of services are the principle tools used. So mortgage providers will also try to sell household and buildings insurance. And many airlines and hotel chains have preferential rates arranged with car hire companies.

11.6.2   Social bonds

Companies seek to build more intimate relationships through social or interpersonal bonds. The customer is no longer faceless (sometimes even nameless). He is a 'client', 'partner' and in some cases even a 'stakeholder'. Historically this has been predominantly practised in business-to-business services. The advertising agency account manager will be charged by his or her agency with having a strong bond with the marketing director of the client company. The account manager will be expected to socialize with the client and listen to their worries. In return, the client is not expected to complain when the agency delivers late and over-budget.

Increasingly the use of CRM systems has enabled mass consumer services to approach the levels of social bonding previously considered out of reach. But companies rarely make use of the information collected to form social bonds.

Sometimes the social bond is not between the customer and the service employee but is formed between customers. These are the relationships that bind them to the service provider. So the health club that organizes social events at the club is attempting to get customers closer to one another.

11.6.3   Customization bonds

The service provider is attempting to create these type of bonds when it customizes the service that is delivered to particular groups of customers: in other words, the provider tailor-makes the service to the needs of the customer. In the arena of business-to-business services, the service provider may have no alternative other than to customize its offering. Consider the accountancy firm or the commercial law practice: the service they offer one particular client is unlikely to be identical to that offered to any other. The customer becomes bonded to the service provider through this customization. For many such services there is often a high cost for the customer of switching to another service provider. So where customizing the service becomes de facto a necessary component of service delivery, the service provider should also be monitoring the relationship to ensure the customer remains positively predisposed to the company.

Mass consumer marketing companies have also been trying to customize their offerings. This is known as mass customization, or one-to-one marketing.[21] There are reports of a bicycle manufacturer in China offering 80 000 different specifications on one model. In the UK customers using Tesco.com, the Internet shopping site from the high street retailer, will find that the site captures their shopping history and the next time the customer goes to shop online, their customized basket of goods will be offered for them to tailor. The site will also intelligently suggest both new and established products that the customer might like to try based on their known shopping behaviour.

11.6.4   Structural bonds

As with customization, these type of bonds are more prevalent in business-to-business markets. Structural bonds often occur where the services offered by the service provider are designed into the systems or processes of the client company. An example would be a research company that designs a system to gather electronic point of sale (EPOS) from every cash register of a high street retailer, and then feeds this information back in virtual real time to the retailer and their suppliers to ensure stores have the right stock on the shelves.

However, some companies that are serving the general public are also building structural bonds into their service delivery, although in many cases these are reserved for their business-to-business segments. British Airways offers its Executive Club holders the ability not only to book online (which would not be regarded as a structural bond these days), it also allows customers to check-in and select a seat online.

As with customization bonds, the service provider must monitor customers' perceptions of the service experience to make sure that they remain satisfied with the service they have received (see Chapter 12 for a fuller discussion of evaluation).

Summary

In the recent past there has been a paradigm shift in marketing practice from transactional marketing to relationship marketing. While customer acquisition remains important, increased efforts and resources are devoted to holding on to the customer a company has.

As a precursor to the development of a relationship strategy, service providers must establish a good quality service, develop a segmented customer base (preferably using a segmentation strategy that includes some measure of customer equity) and monitor/evaluate customer experience.

With these in place, a relationship strategy can be designed using a combination of financial, social, customization and structural bonds, all of which have the potential for improving the profitability of the service provider.

References

1 Page, M *et al.* (1997) 'Before they leave, switch on the light: knowing the value of keeping customers', *Journal of Targeting, Measurement, and Analysis for Marketing*, **5** (3), 232–246.
2 Reichheld, F F and Sasser Jr, W E (1990) 'Zero defections: quality comes to services', *Harvard Business Review*, Sep.–Oct., 105–111.
3 Reichheld, F F (1994) 'Loyalty and the renaissance of marketing', *Marketing Management*, **2** (4), 24–28.
4 Reichheld, F F (1996) *The Loyalty Effect*. Cambridge, MA: Harvard Business School.
5 Zeithaml, V A, Bitner, M J and Gremier, D D (2006) *Services Marketing: Integrating Customer Focus Across the Organization*, 5th edn. New York: McGraw-Hill.
6 Reichheld (1996), op. cit.
7 A Report by Bain & Co. (1996), cited in Reichheld, *The Loyalty Effect*.
8 Morgan, R M and Hunt, S D (1994) 'The commitment–trust theory of relationship marketing', *Journal of Marketing*, **58**, 20–38.

9 Priluck, R (2003) 'Relationship marketing can mitigate product and service failures', *Journal of Services Marketing*, **17** (1), 37–51.

10 Gwinner, K P, Gremler, D D and Bitner, M J (1998) 'Relational benefits in service industries: the customer's perspective', *Journal of the Academy of Marketing Science*, **26** (2), 101–114.

11 Bove, L L and Johnson, L W (2000) 'A customer-service relationship model', *International Journal of Service Industry Management*, **11** (5), 491–511.

12 Bendapudi, N and Leone, R P (2001) 'How to lose your star performer without losing customers, too', *Harvard Business Review*, November, 104–115.

13 Dick, A S and Basu, K (1994) 'Customer loyalty: toward an integrated conceptual framework', *Journal of the Academy of Marketing Science*, **22** (2), 99–113.

14 Ennew, C T and Binks, M R (1996) 'The impact of service quality and service characteristics on customer retention: small businesses and their banks in the UK', *British Journal of Management*, **7**, 219–230.

15 Hennig-Thurau, T and Klee, A (1997) 'The impact of customer satisfaction and relationship quality on customer retention: a critical reassessment and model development', *Psychology and Marketing*, **14** (8), 737–764.

16 Zeithaml *et al.*, op. cit.

17 Zeithaml, V A, Rust, R T and Lemon, K N (2001) 'The customer pyramid: creating and servicing profitable customers', *California Management Review*, **43** (4), 118–142.

18 Berry, L and Parasuraman, A (1991) *Marketing Services*. New York: Free Press, pp. 136–142.

19 Jamieson, A (2005) 'House of Cards', *The Scotsman*, 11 August, 31–32.

20 Dowling, G R and Uncles, M (1997) 'Do customer loyalty programs really work?', *Sloan Management Review*, Summer, 71–82.

21 Peppers, D and Rogers, M (1999) *The One-to-One Marketing Manager*. New York: Currency/Doubleday.

12

Monitoring and evaluating the service

☐ Introduction

The greater part of this book has been devoted to the various elements needed for the creation of a quality service. If all these components are in place, then the service provider will be hoping that trialists of the service will become loyalists.

In other words, the organization will be looking to attract customers who will engage with it over some time. In the previous chapter on relationship marketing, we explored strategies that an organization might employ to boost retention and generate loyalty.

Whether a relationship marketing approach is being followed or not, one of the key ways in which an organization will continue to succeed is by monitoring and evaluating the service that it currently provides.

On the premise that the service has been designed to satisfy those who consume it, a useful starting point in service evaluation is to monitor customer satisfaction.

Customer complaints are also a useful source of information. The primary aim in understanding complaints is of course to recover the customer. But the information should also be fed back into the service evaluation system to be used strategically to improve future service delivery.

■ 12.1 Customer satisfaction evaluation

What does 'satisfaction' mean? The concept itself is an abstract one. The achievement of satisfaction can be a complex and precarious process. The roles played in the service encounter by service personnel and consumers contribute to this. In the same way that totally satisfied customers are hard to find, the totally dissatisfied customer is also an

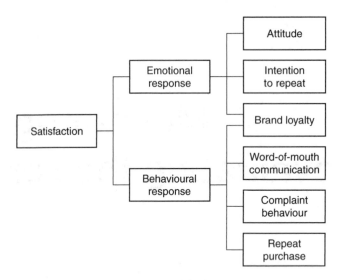

Figure 12.1 Behavioural and emotional responses to satisfaction

elusive creature. While one should understand the extent of customer satisfaction (i.e. how much customers are satisfied), it is perhaps more important to understand the underlying cause of the satisfaction/dissatisfaction.

In general, the response to a satisfactory experience will contain both emotional and behavioural elements (Figure 12.1). So customer satisfaction will result in positive emotional states. These, in turn, mediate the response between customer satisfaction and behavioural responses – positive word of mouth, no complaint behaviour and repeat purchase.

12.1.1   What is satisfaction?

The model used to explain the occurrence of satisfaction is known as the expectancy-disconfirmation model (Figure 12.2). It was first proposed by Oliver in 1977[1] and has subsequently been tested in a variety of different industries.

The model suggests that satisfaction is dependent on customers' expectations, and their perceptions of performance in relation to those expectations. One implication of this model is that to secure satisfaction, management need not (and indeed should not) focus exclusively on improving its performance. Resources should also be devoted to

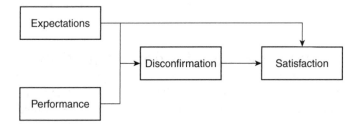

Figure 12.2 Expectancy-disconfirmation model of consumer satisfaction

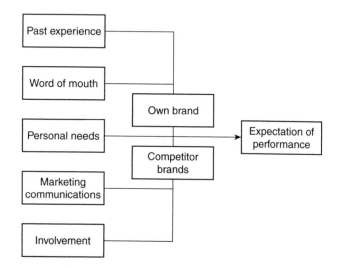

Figure 12.3 Antecedents of expectations

managing customer expectations. As Peters and Austin state: 'Managing expectations is all about under-promising and over-delivering.'[2]

12.1.2 Customer expectations

There are five key factors that influence a customer's expectations: previous experience; personal recommendation; personal needs; marketing communications; and the level of involvement in the purchase (Figure 12.3). Research suggests that the most important of these factors in shaping expectations are the consumer's past experience of the service and what other people say about it.

Customers tend to complain less about services than products even though they are more likely to be dissatisfied with services. One reason why they do not complain as much comes from the active part that they play in specifying the service. If a trip to the hairdresser results in a bad haircut, who is to say that it is because of the hairdresser's incompetence? It may be that the client did not communicate clearly enough what he or she wanted.

Prior to using a service, consumers may have in mind four different scenarios of the service that they might experience:

- The ideal
- The anticipated
- The deserved
- The minimum tolerable.

The consumer can expect any of these (Figure 12.4). As we have seen, expectations shape satisfaction. If the 'minimum tolerable' is expected then this or anything better may lead to satisfaction. Equally, anyone expecting the 'ideal' will be dissatisfied with anything less.

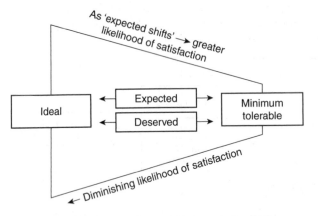

1. The closer 'expected' expectations are to the 'minimum tolerable' the greater the likelihood of satisfaction.
2. Satisfied customers can appear anywhere on the spectrum. What determines their position is the position of 'expected' outcome.

Figure 12.4 Impact of expectations on satisfaction

Sometimes customers have a view about what they 'deserve', even if these are set at a low level. For instance, patients may believe that at the very least they 'deserve' to return from surgery alive. (This may also be the minimum tolerable.) If a customer has a strong idea of what he or she deserves, perhaps formed from a guarantee, or previous usage, then expectations will be set at that level. Expectations will be more firmly held and will probably result in greater levels of dissatisfaction if the service fails to deliver.

The 'deserved' outcome can also modify expectations downwards, e.g. if a builder is instructed to build a house that must be finished in two months, then the level of workmanship that the customer receives is likely to suffer from corner-cutting as the builder struggles to meet the deadline. If the customer realizes the constraints that they have forced the builder to work to, then their 'deserved' outcome should be set at a low level.

What the customer believes he or she deserves may, however, still be lower than his or her 'anticipated' or expected outcome. If this arises then the customer will be dissatisfied. He or she may have chosen not to believe what the builder told him or her at the outset about the most likely consequences of the tight schedule, choosing instead to expect the outcome to be better than the picture painted.

Parasuraman, Zeithaml and Berry[3] define a narrower band for expectations. They describe a 'zone of tolerance' between adequate service provision and the desired service provision (Figure 12.5). This zone expands and contracts. It can also remain

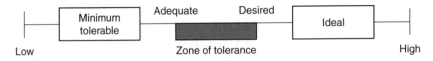

Figure 12.5 Levels of expectations
Source: Based on Parasuraman *et al.* (1990)[3]

unchanged in magnitude, while moving up or down the spectrum. It varies according to the service and to the individual customer. More recently, it has been shown that expectations and the zone of tolerance can fluctuate *during* service consumption.[4,5] Further, satisfaction with individual encounters will affect satisfaction with the overall experience.[6] Consequently, operations managers have an important role in managing expectations *during* service delivery. It is particularly important to manage this satisfactorily at early stages in the process since these encounters have been shown to influence customers' thresholds of tolerance at a later stage in service delivery.

12.1.3 Employee satisfaction

Of course in many service organizations employees play a customer-facing role and their behaviour is a key determinant of customer satisfaction. These employees in turn need to be satisfied. Research has highlighted the variables that are important in determining employee satisfaction[7] (see Table 12.1).

Table 12.1 Factors needed for satisfied employees, listed in order of importance

Supervisor support
Team support
Other departments support
Effectiveness of the technology
Organizational commitment

Source: Sergeant (2000)[7]

12.1.4 Service fairness

Recently the concept of service 'fairness' has been proposed as a determinant of customer satisfaction.[8] Fairness can be broken down into three components – **outcome** fairness, which is the quality of the core service offering; **procedural** fairness, which is concerned with service delivery, i.e. whether it was timely; and **interactional** fairness, which is concerned with the customer's relationships with the service deliverer. Each of these has been found to contribute independently to satisfaction. But it is outcome fairness that is the most critical in understanding a customer's satisfaction response, whereas it is in the areas of process and procedural fairness that the service provider can more easily exceed customers' expectations.[9]

12.1.5 Measuring satisfaction

A variety of research mechanisms can be deployed to measure customer satisfaction. One valuable piece of research would be a study that segmented service attributes into satisfiers, dissatisfiers and criticals.[10] In measuring this, the service provider would gain a clearer understanding of how to allocate operational resources to deliver satisfaction.

Satisfiers are those elements of service delivery which, when performed beyond what the consumer considers adequate, have a positive impact on perceptions. Yet when they are neither in evidence nor well performed, they do not depress perceptions of service quality. These are often elements of service delivery that the customer does not expect. For example, regular users of a particular car hire company may consider performance beyond the adequate if the next time they ring to book a car the receptionist remembers their individual preference for car model, collection and delivery details, etc. However, if none of this happens, it will not result in customers having lower perceptions of service quality.

Dissatisfiers are those elements of service delivery which when performed at a level below that which the consumer believes to be adequate will result in dissatisfaction. But any performance above that level that the consumer considers to be adequate, will have little impact on perceptions of service quality. So, to continue with our example of car hire, if the customer has arranged for the car to be at his or her office at 5 pm, and the car is delivered at 7 pm, then this is likely to result in dissatisfaction. If, on the other hand, the car is delivered at 3 pm, this is not likely to raise perceptions of service quality if the customer is in no position to use the car before 5 pm.

Criticals are those factors that can act as both satisfiers and dissatisfiers. Good performance on these factors can improve perceptions of service quality, and conversely, poor performance can detract from it. So, for example, if empathy is a critical factor, then polite service may raise perceptions of service quality and impolite service may depress them.

A common technique used to measure satisfaction is a quantitative satisfaction survey based on multi-attribute attitude analyses.

12.1.6   Satisfaction survey

Suppose that MBA students as they join a Masters course are asked to describe the factors that influenced their choice of educational establishment. Their list would probably contain the dimensions in the left-hand column of Table 12.2.

Table 12.2 A multi-attribute expectation/satisfaction matrix

Attribute	Pre-consumption expectations			Service experience score			Post-consumption satisfaction		
	(1)	(2)	(3) ((1)×(2))	(4)	(5)	(6) ((4)×(5))	(7)	(8)	(9) ((7)×(8))
Reputation	5	5	25	4	5	20	4	4	16
Standard of lecturing	4	4	16	5	5	25	5	4	20
Quality of materials	3	3	9	2	3	6	2	3	6
Sports facilities	2	2	4	3	4	12	3	3	9
Location	1	2	2	1	2	2	1	3	3
Expectation score			56*			65			
Satisfaction score									54

*Maximum possible score = 75 (where the individual gives each attribute in column 2 a score of 5)

They are then asked to rank the list of attributes:

Most important = 5
Least important = 1

This is shown for a hypothetical student in column 1, Table 12.2. (Note that if the list had contained eight attributes and not five, then the scale would have been: Most important = 8, Least important = 1 and so on.)

Finally, they are asked to state the degree of importance that each holds for them. Using, for example, the following scale:

Very important	5
Fairly important	4
Neither important or unimportant	3
Fairly unimportant	2
Very unimportant	1

These scores are in column 2 in Table 12.2.

The validity of using an importance scale has been called into question because of the ambiguity and somewhat imprecise meaning of the word. Wilkie and Pessemier[11] and Oliver[12] suggest instead that each attribute should be measured on the semantic differential that suits the word best, e.g. good–bad, attractive–unattractive. This may be true for academic works; however, if different attributes have different scales the questionnaire becomes more complex and difficult to administer. The choice between the two methods should be based on the depth of diagnostic information required from the survey.

In this case the student had an *Expectation score* of 56 out of a possible score of 75. This maximum would occur where the student had given an importance rating of 5 to each of the variables.

The same two questions are asked at the end of the MBA course to give a *Revised expectation score* or a *Service experience score* (columns 4 and 5). In situations where the service takes some time to consume, this revised score must be calculated since experience of the service will often change what it takes to make the customer satisfied. In this case the student took up sport during the course and so its importance increased and its ranked position rose. Notice that his expectations have now been revised upwards to 65.

Finally, to compute a *satisfaction score*, the following two questions are asked of the same list of attributes:

Q1   A ranking of the attributes (column 7, Table 12.2):
      Most important = 5
      Least important = 1

Q2   How did the service perform against expectations (column 8, Table 12.2)?

A lot better than expected	5
A little better than expected	4
Just as expected	3

| A little worse than expected | 2 |
| A lot worse than expected | 1 |

Models have been developed where the respondents have instead been asked to discuss their degree of satisfaction. As in the following scale:

Q3   The degree of satisfaction.

Very satisfied	5
Fairly satisfied	4
Neither satisfied nor dissatisfied	3
Fairly dissatisfied	2
Very dissatisfied	1

Many writers prefer the earlier scale. This is because, on the one hand, this scale has been shown to be independent of the level of expectations, and at the same time to be highly correlated with satisfaction.[13] However, in many senses it is more important that the service results in satisfaction than that it lives up to expectations. Indeed the earlier scale tends to ignore the possibility of expectations being revised during the service process.

The satisfaction score for this student is 54. He is therefore dissatisfied. To achieve satisfaction the score has to be equal to, or greater than, the expectation score.

However, the validity of this somewhat blunt approach to the measurement of satisfaction has recently been questioned. We have previously discussed the relevance of measuring expectations in the context of services. Furthermore, concentrating solely on outcome satisfaction and failing to measure satisfaction during the process of consumption may result in inaccurate readings of customers' attitudes.[14] This is particularly true if you believe that after consumption cognitive dissonance will be evident.

Finally, the usefulness of the information provided by these satisfaction studies has also been questioned. What is the meaning of any recorded difference between Expectations and Performance? What is the difference between 80% of your customers being 'very satisfied' and 70% of them being 'very satisfied'? These surveys cannot say, for example, how much more likely a 'satisfied' customer is to switch than a 'very satisfied' customer. So in quantitative studies companies are simultaneously recording high satisfaction ratings and declining loyalty[15] and high switching behaviour among satisfied customers.[16]

In an attempt to provide more powerful satisfaction data, it has been suggested that emotional responses to the service performance and the quality of the satisfaction should also be captured.[17,18]

■ 12.2   Customer complaints

12.2.1   Dissatisfied customers: what do they do?

Until fairly recently there was a general perception that customers unhappy with a service were less likely to complain than when they were unhappy with a product.[19] But recent research suggests that whereas for FMCG products complaints are made by only 4% of those who are unhappy with the product, this rises to 50% with consumer services and an astonishing 75% in business-to-business services.[20] Within the services sector, dissatisfied consumers complain in varying proportions. The cost of the service and the extent of the social involvement have been shown to be positively correlated with complaining behaviour.[21] Over 80% of dissatisfied consumers complain to supermarkets, credit card and cable companies, whereas, just over 30% complain to their GP or dentist (Figure 12.6).

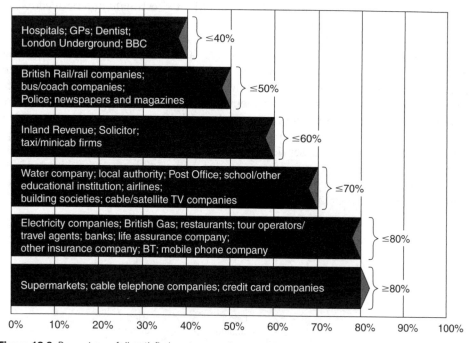

Figure 12.6 Percentage of dissatisfied customers who complain
Source: Consumers' Association (1998)[22]

However, dissatisfied customers are not likely to keep the bad news to themselves. At the same time as deciding not to buy the service again they are probably spreading the bad news.

Customer complaints are actually helpful to the organization for several reasons. First, they give the organization a chance to recover its original customer. Indeed, there is some evidence to suggest that customers whose complaints lead to a successful recovery of the service experience end up more satisfied than those customers who found the initial service encounter satisfactory. It also diminishes the risk of bad publicity, either from personal word-of-mouth communication or in more damaging leaks through the press to the general public, and it provides information that should be useful for development of the service.

Historically, companies have shied away from the whole issue of customer complaints, preferring instead to devote resources to generating business. Retaining business through service recovery is still not widespread. However, while we would suggest that the handling of complaints should be resourced, it has been shown that even those customers who had their complaints satisfactorily resolved were more likely to switch service provider than those who had not been dissatisfied in the first place.[23] Perhaps this is because it is estimated that more than 50% of those who do complain feel worse about their services delivery experience *after* they have complained.[24]

12.2.2   Who complains?

Research has shown that those consumers who do complain about the service they receive tend to be the loyal users of the service. In terms of numbers, they represent only a tiny fraction of the total number of dissatisfied customers. Bell and Zemke[25] estimate that only 4% complain, and Dube and Maute[26] estimate that between 5 and 10% of dissatisfied customers complain.

A great deal of research has been carried out to establish the characteristics of those who complain. Zemke and Bell[27] and Warland, Hermann and Willits[28] found them to be predominantly young women, who were intellectually, socially and economically upmarket. Perhaps they complain more because they are less daunted by confrontation. Perhaps it is because their expectations are higher than for many other groups of consumers. There is certainly evidence to support this latter view. Studies have found that these consumers are the ones most likely to be unhappy about the performance of the services that they purchase.[29,30]

Of the three possible outcomes of poor service delivery (illustrated in Figure 12.7) – not upset, upset/complain and upset/no complaint – it has been found that the two groups that were furthest apart demographically were the upset/complain and the

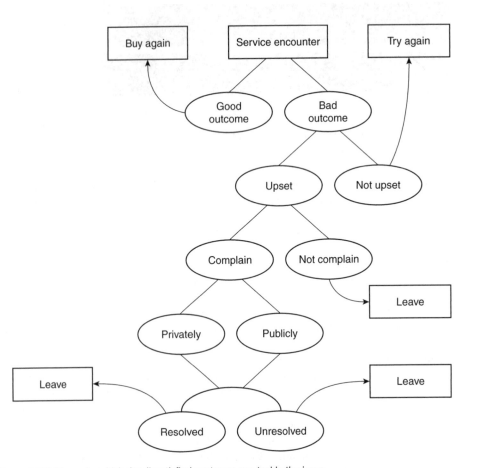

Figure 12.7 Means by which the dissatisfied customer can tackle the issue

upset/no complaint. Those that were not upset tended to be the older, more conservative members of society.[31]

12.2.3   To whom do they complain?

Complain to the service provider

There are a number of options open to the customer who decides to complain (Table 12.3). He or she can go back to the company and complain to them. This is, in fact, the most likely first course of action. Best and Andreasen,[32] found that, on the whole, sellers have a virtual monopoly on complaints handling. The company imposes its own standards, sets the resolutions and decides on any level of compensation.

The unhappy customer can complain in private, e.g. by writing a letter of complaint, or in public, e.g. by creating a scene on the premises.[33] The public complaint is most feared by those companies that do not provide a good service in the first place, or do not have a good complaints handling procedure. Customers sometimes choose to air their grievances publicly in the belief that they are more likely to have them satisfactorily resolved by behaving in this manner in front of other customers.

Successful resolution of complaints by the company also reduces the risk of attracting the attention of the legislature or even the voluntary consumer watchdog. The vociferously negative comments of the *London Evening Standard*'s commuter watchdog no doubt played a part in the establishment of the Passenger's Charter. Had there been no cause for complaint there would have been no watchdog. Had there been no watchdog there would have been less incentive to change.

Complain to a consumer watchdog

So instead of approaching the offending company, the consumer can take a complaint to an organization that has been set up to protect or promote consumers' interests. Some of these organizations deal with all kinds of problems and enquiries, e.g. the Citizens Advice Bureau, which receives public funding, and the Consumers' Association, which has no grants or subsidies from government or industry. There are also industry-specific bodies, e.g. OFGAS for the gas industry, OFFER for the electricity industry, or Greenpeace for the environment. The first two were set up when these industries were privatized. They were given statutory powers to protect consumers' interests. The smaller ones rely on voluntary help and fund-raising for their existence. If these organizations cannot resolve the complaint by conciliation then, in some cases, the aggrieved customer can seek redress through arbitration.

Table 12.3 What the dissatisfied customer can do

Complain to seller
Write or phone manufacturer
Write or phone the head office
Write or phone trade association
Contact Trading Standards Officer
Consult Citizens Advice Bureau
Consult a solicitor
Write or phone Office of Fair Trading

Take legal action

If dissatisfied consumers find no joy through any of the above channels they must then resort to the final method of redress and take legal action.

In England, Wales and Northern Ireland, the **Supply of Goods and Services Act 1982** requires a supplier of a service acting in the course of business to carry out that service:

- with reasonable care and skill
- in a reasonable time (if there is no specific time agreed) and
- for a reasonable charge (if no fixed price was set in advance).

Any goods or parts fitted as part of the contract must be:

- of satisfactory quality
- fit for their purpose and
- as described.

These terms apply unless they have been excluded or varied in the contract governing the supply of services, in which case there are strict limits on the circumstances in which, and the extent to which, an exclusion or variation will be effective (the **Unfair Contract Terms Act 1977** [the Consumers' Association believes that it was as a result of their campaigning that this act was passed][34] and the **Unfair Terms in Consumer Contracts Regulations 1999**).

Whilst the 1982 Act is not applicable in Scotland, Scots common law imposes similar standards of care.

In addition to this basic premise, there are a number of (predominantly consumer-focused) rules, regulations and watchdogs ready to champion the consumer's cause. For example, financial services (the **Financial Services and Markets Act 2000**), banking (the **Mortgage Code** and others) and law (**Professional Ethics** and **The Law Society**) are all tightly regulated.

Remedies

Cancellation: If a supplier of a service materially breaches the conditions of a contract (for example by completely failing to carry out the work ordered) the consumer is likely to have a choice either to affirm the contract (i.e., treat it as still in existence) and claim compensation from the trader for failure to carry out what was agreed or rescind (i.e., cancel) the contract. However, unlike buying goods, it is not as easy for a consumer to reject the whole job and ask for all their money back unless they can show that the workmanship was so poor they got no benefit from it at all.

Work not done on time: When work is not completed on time or within a reasonable time, the consumer may write to the trader to make time 'of the essence of the contract'. This means that the consumer has set a specific date for the work to be finished, after which he or she will consider the trader to be in breach of contract and will be free to get other estimates, have the work completed by another trader, and hold the original company responsible for the costs. The consumer may have to go to court as a last resort to recover these costs. The consumer may also be entitled to compensation for the delay if it has caused him or her a lot of inconvenience, for example in taking extended periods off work to wait in for contractors.

Work not satisfactory: It is usually considered reasonable to give the trader a chance to put things right, and it is worth bearing in mind that the amount of compensation the consumer can claim for shoddy work could be affected if he or she unreasonably refuses to allow the trader an opportunity to make amends. Accordingly, the consumer should (i) inform the trader what he or she is not happy with straight away, and confirm it in writing with a list of the specific problems to be sorted out, and (ii) set a deadline for this work to be done, and give notice that after this time he or she will have no alternative but to get quotes from another contractor and consider suing in County Court for the remedial costs.

Unauthorized work: If the consumer has agreed certain work and the trader goes ahead with additional work without authorization, the consumer does not have to pay for the extra work. However, more practical solutions may be to:

- Accept the need for extra work and pay if it seems reasonable
- Ask the trader to undo the work
- Negotiate a price for the work taking into account the fact it was unauthorized
- In some circumstances, if the trader refuses to release the goods – e.g. the car he or she has done repairs to – the consumer may have to pay under protest and take legal action for compensation.

Withholding payment: If the consumer is not happy with work, he or she may want to consider withholding some of the payment until the work has been completed to his or her satisfaction. In these circumstances the consumer must tell the trader what he or she is doing and why. In the absence of any contractual right to withhold payment the trader may consider this to be a breach of contract by the consumer.

Ultimately it will be for the courts to decide whether or not a breach of contract has occurred and the redress, in the form of damages (compensation) or otherwise, to which a consumer might be entitled.

A claim can generally be pursued though the courts for up to six years after the services have been rendered, providing it can be shown that the problem was due to the work not being carried out properly or the goods or materials used not being of satisfactory quality.

12.2.4 Why do they complain?

Consumers complain because they are dissatisfied. They are dissatisfied because their expectations are not met, and obviously the higher their prepurchase expectations, the more likely they are to be dissatisfied. This is why a key role for communications in service marketing is the management of expectations. To understand more fully why they complain, we have to examine the reasons why their expectations may be unfulfilled.

Miscommunication on a customer's part is only one reason why expectations may not be fulfilled (Figure 12.8). Some of these factors are within the control of the service provider, some are not. It is certainly up to the provider to reduce the likelihood of miscommunication or misinterpretation by making the service clearly understood. It is also the responsibility of the company to ensure both that it clearly understands a client's instructions, and that the client clearly understands what will be delivered. Service providers should take the lead in designing initiatives to reduce these problems.

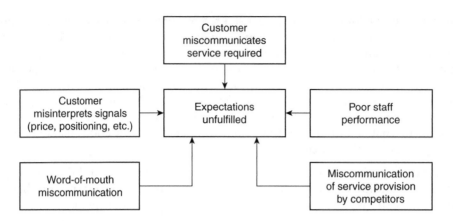

Figure 12.8 Major causes of unfulfilled expectations

However, it is not only prepurchase expectations that condition whether or not a complaint is made. It is also the expectation of the likely outcome from complaining. If consumers expect to achieve something by complaining then they are much more likely to complain. Some psychologists would go even further, by suggesting that even if there is no possibility of rectifying the situation, it is still best to express anger, in order to accept the dissatisfaction.[35] Indeed, recent research has suggested that anger is the dominant emotional response to poor service and that this (as opposed to dissatisfaction) is the major determining factor in terms of a consumer's propensity to complain/repurchase.[36]

The average consumer would probably not take this advice too seriously, no matter how beneficial it may be to them psychologically. They are much more likely to weigh up all the costs and benefits associated with complaining. Their emotional well-being will be only one factor. If they perceive the benefits to outweigh the costs then they will complain. Table 12.4 lists the factors that help fashion the costs and benefits of complaining.

Table 12.4 The costs and benefits of complaining

Costs	Inconvenience	Special trip to complain Form-filling, letter writing Forgo service during complaint process
	Uncertainty	Difficulty finding correct complaint procedure No indication of the action that will be taken
	Unpleasant	Treated rudely, have to hassle Feel guilty, embarrassed
Benefits	Emotional	Chance to assert rights, chance to vent anger, receive an apology
	Functional	Refund, replacement, repair
	Altruistic	Other customers prevented from experiencing dissatisfaction Would feel guilty about not complaining
	Product improvement	Organization would improve its offering

Source: Based on Richins (1990)[36]

Table 12.5 Major sources of complaining

	Transport	Freight	Motor repair	Travel agents	Holidays	Entertainment	Insurance	Banking	Utilities	Telecoms
Substandard service	32	45	66	24	31	29	30	39	30	37
Non-delivery completion	12	12	5	13	9	8	12	3	4	4
Misleading selling	27	16	12	40	44	27	34	36	40	34
Poor complaint handing	7	8	10	8	5	4	9	9	7	9
Unfair terms	8	3	–	6	4	5	11	9	4	5
Safety	1	9	–	–	–	16	–	–	4	–
Pricing	13	7	5	8	6	9	4	4	10	11

Source: Biswell (2004)[37]

12.2.5   What do they complain about?

Customers complain about different problems in different industries (Table 12.5). In banking, account errors are the biggest source of complaints, whereas in air travel, cancellations and flight delays generate the most complaints. Even within an industry, there will be varying weaknesses from different service companies. Each operator should have an understanding of its own weaknesses, and those of their main competitors.

Once again, some service sectors appear to be better than others at handling customer complaints. So although supermarkets received the highest proportion of complaints, they were also the best at satisfactorily resolving them. However, the picture for life and other insurance companies is not as positive, with less than 30% of complainants being satisfied with how their complaint was handled (Figure 12.9).

One of the main reasons for this is that nearly all problems that occur with products can be openly demonstrated and discussed. If a car does not start, it does not start. If a vacuum cleaner fails to clean carpets then this too can be demonstrated. Whereas, who is actually to blame for problems that arise in the consumption of services, where what constitutes satisfactory is often open to judgement and debate. Even where the complaint is justified, service providers may still feel that their own position is also quite defensible. This often relates to verbal and non-verbal signals from the consumer that the service provider attempts to interpret. Communication is a transactional process.

Imagine a company rings a courier in a panic. It desperately needs to get a document to Paris the following day. The courier goes to extraordinary lengths to see that it gets there, and this results in some extra costs. When the company receives the invoice it is outraged by the price. The service provider misinterpreted the signals about urgency from the company.

A large party in a restaurant spends a long time deciding what they want to eat, apparently preferring to chat with fellow diners. They do not appear to be in any hurry, or to want an attentive waiting staff. When the bill arrives they leave no tip, saying that they were disappointed with the time that they spent waiting for their food.

These are two examples of service scenarios where the service provider would feel that the complaint was unjustified. However, the customer would feel that the service provider was to blame for having misjudged the customers' requirements.

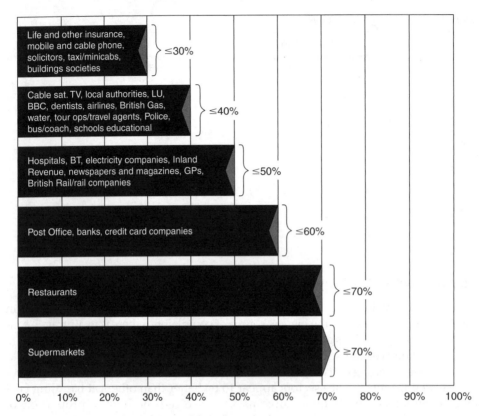

Figure 12.9 Percentage of complaints satisfactorily resolved
Source: Consumers' Association[22]

12.3   Service recovery

Successful complaints handling is one strategy for what has come to be known today as service recovery.[38] This is where the organization treats dissatisfied customers in such a way that they leave the service experience feeling positively disposed towards the service provider and willing to engage with the organization in future transactions. Service recovery can take place where the service provider operates a comprehensive guarantee. It also occurs where the organization that is not working to any specified guarantee meets or exceeds the expectations of the complaining customer in the way in which it handles a complaint.

The distinguishing characteristics of services mean that it is often more difficult to recover an unsatisfactory experience. Simultaneity of production and consumption means that it is not always possible to undo or re-do the service. Consider a poor concert performance, or a disappointing swimming lesson. The heterogeneous nature of many services means that some failure is inevitable. However, the high level of customer involvement, whilst sometimes contributing to service mistakes, can also present good opportunities for service recovery. The findings of research have suggested that employee behaviour (as opposed to problems caused by faulty systems or policies) is one of the most difficult types of failure to recover from.[39]

In addition to recovering specific service failures, a strategic recovery system should be built into the service process because:[40]

- Failure in one area can often precipitate service breakdown in other areas
- Unattended failures tend to recur
- Failures tend to decrease customer confidence
- Recovery tends to have a positive halo effect.

There are two basic parts to any such service recovery system. The first is the transactional element that relates to the recovery of the specific experience. The second is the way in which information from this complaint is used by the organization (see later section in this chapter on effective complaint handling).

Note, however, that efforts to recover potential defectors should not be treated uniformly. Organizations should base their offers on the potential profitability of individual customers (see discussion on customer segmentation and profitability in Chapter 11).[41]

The severity of the service failure conditions both the strength of the negative reaction and the customer's expectation for service recovery.[42] Dissatisfaction with the service can also become more intense if the complainant does not feel that the complaint is being handled appropriately. This individual is already in an irritable frame of mind and therefore staff need to be trained to handle the situation sensitively. Ideally, these employees should be empowered to take decisions about the best course of action. However, many companies find this an uncomfortable suggestion believing that the employee will always err on the side of the customer, and perhaps be over-generous with any compensation. Other companies take a more progressive view, as Jan Carlzon CEO of SAS said:

> What's the danger of giving away too much? Are you worried about an over-satisfied customer? That's not much of a worry. You can forget about an over-satisfied customer, but an unsatisfied customer is one of the most expensive problems you can have ... the danger is not that employees will give away too much. It's that they won't give away anything because they don't dare.[43]

If the empowerment of front-line employees is not possible, then senior management themselves must be prepared to play an active part in the resolution of complaints. Top management involvement usually goes down well with customers, because customers like to deal with those who have the power and confidence to act on their behalf. They should be called in at the slightest hint that the customer might be dissatisfied with the way a complaint is being handled.

A recent empirical study suggests that from the complainant's viewpoint the most important aspect of service recovery is for the organization to accept responsibility for the problem (even if in approximately one-third of complaints, the customer is in fact responsible). The empowerment of front-line staff to resolve complaints was the next most important factor. Receiving an apology was the least impressive recovery strategy. A personal apology either face to face or by telephone was preferred to that of a written one.[44]

The same study also found evidence to suggest that the way an organization recovers is situation-specific. So, however well it has performed in the past, and consequently has satisfied the customer, none of this will have any bearing on a customer's satisfaction with service recovery procedures.

12.4   Effective complaint-handling procedures

Companies that take a pragmatic view will accept that they can make mistakes. They will recognize that customers will occasionally have a better idea of the way that the service should be delivered. Indeed a dearth of complaints is more often a danger signal than a cause for celebration. It is to the organization's advantage to encourage customers to air their views, and it should set up a complaint-handling procedure that does just that. As the President of world-wide quality at American Express says, 'the formula that I use is: better complaint handling equals higher customer satisfaction, equals higher brand loyalty, equals higher profitability'.[45]

When designing a complaint-handling system, it can often be difficult to strike the right balance between making the system easily accessible, and making it too accessible. The organization wants to encourage users to make justifiable complaints, but it is counterproductive to set up a complaints procedure that creates the impression that the organization is expecting lots of complaints. This usually means that the service provider does not believe that it is offering a good service. Customers will very quickly pick this up, and begin to start looking for problems. It would be much more productive to provide a better service in the first place.

Historically, dealing with customer complaints was considered a second-rate occupation for marketing professionals. It was much more stimulating and glamorous to be developing new products and advertising campaigns. Customer complaint-handling was regarded as a maintenance function and a cost centre to the business.

Fortunately nowadays, many companies take a more enlightened view. They incorporate complaints handling into their strategic mix, and call it Customer Service or Customer Care. Until the late 1990s it was common practice in those companies to staff these operations with marketing personnel, thereby allowing them to experience first-hand the voices of consumers. There is an old management saying, 'If you're going to be a general, you have to remember what its like to be a private.' The organization benefits in several ways by staffing customer service with these employees. It raises the profile of the department in the company. It makes a statement to all employees about the importance that the company attaches to the resolution of complaints. In doing so, it communicates the significance of providing a quality service, and finally, it generally also leads to improvements in the way that complaints are handled. Employees charged with complaint-handling will often make suggestions about the powers they need to do the job well, and ways in which the department could be run more effectively. However, more recently there has been a trend towards outsourcing this function to call centres.

12.4.1   The benefits of effective complaint-handling

Companies that devote resources to an effective complaints procedure benefit in many ways:

- They are given a second chance to make good their relationship with a dissatisfied customer.
- Adverse word-of-mouth publicity is avoided.
- They will understand what would improve their current service.

- They will know where their operations problems lie.
- Employees may be motivated to provide a better-quality service.

To make the best use of a customer service department it is not enough to deal expediently with each complaint as it is received. Naturally, this is all that the aggrieved customer is interested in. Initially, it should also be what interests the company most.

There are many examples of companies who have gone to extraordinary lengths to try to please a dissatisfied customer: most of them are American. As a nation, the United States seems to be more clued up to the benefits of dealing with complaints effectively. Americans can be less reticent about going 'over the top' in an overt attempt to keep a customer.

However, in addition to dealing with complaints, the company should also attempt to learn from its mistakes. It does this by putting in place management information systems that enable customer service staff to record every complaint that is made and then to report these complaints (Figure 12.10). Management must be able to identify the cause of complaints if it is to aid the development of the service. For example, it has been estimated that British banks spend more than twice what they

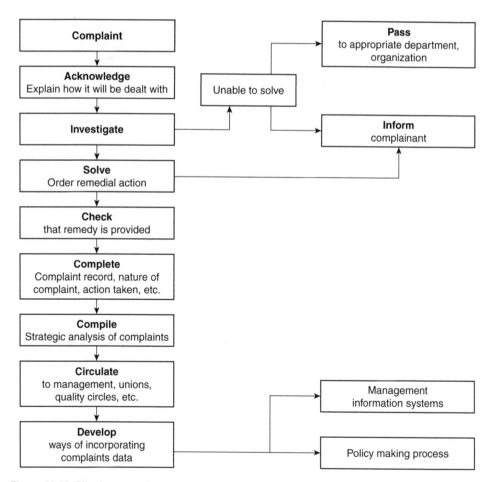

Figure 12.10 Effective complaints-handling process

ought to in order to operate their service. This is because their procedures are so error-prone that they continually lose documents and waste precious time and money tracking them down, or regenerating them. This problem came to light because customer complaints were monitored. Knowing the source of the problem, all they need to do is deal with it. As Einstein said, 'The formulation of a problem is far more essential than a solution'.[46]

The success of a complaint management process can also be examined by checking complaining data against satisfaction and retention. This is illustrated in Figure 12.11 using data adapted from a survey of hotel guests.[47] The first diagram shows an organization's complaint resolution performance. In this case, 25% of customers have a problem with the service. Only half of those report the problem, and of those that do, 30% remain unresolved.

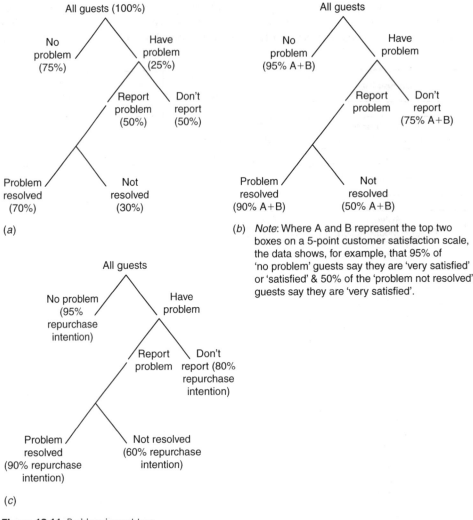

(b) *Note*: Where A and B represent the top two boxes on a 5-point customer satisfaction scale, the data shows, for example, that 95% of 'no problem' guests say they are 'very satisfied' or 'satisfied' & 50% of the 'problem not resolved' guests say they are 'very satisfied'.

Figure 12.11 Problem impact tree
Source: Rust *et al.* (1995)[47]

The Problem Impact Tree shown in Figure 12.11(*b*) displays satisfaction data from the same customers. The letters A and B represent the top two points on a five-point satisfaction rating scale. Among customers with a problem, satisfaction falls from 90% for those whose problem is resolved to 50% for those whose problem remains unresolved. In this case, satisfaction in the 'problem resolved' category is almost as high as for those in the 'no problem' category.

Customers who do not report a problem also end up with relatively low levels of satisfaction (75%). But they are not as low as those whose complaints remain unresolved (50%).

Complaint management also affects customer retention. Once again, Figure 12.11 illustrates the serious implications of not resolving complaints satisfactorily. If retention data is not available, then 'intention to repeat' survey data can be used. Combining satisfaction and retention data with complaint management information enables management to calculate the value of guiding the customer down different branches of the Problem Impact Tree. This will help the organization maximize its resources to greatest effect.

12.5   Guarantees

12.5.1   The provision of guarantees

The function of the guarantee is that it reduces risk to consumers both before and after purchase. It also conveys a powerful marketing message and helps to shape customers' expectations of a quality service. In reducing risk, the guarantee often diminishes much of the ambiguity often associated with service provision. However, ambiguity often arises from the intangible nature of the service, and the more intangible the service, the more difficult it is to provide guarantees (Figure 12.12).

For example, it is easy for a cobbler to guarantee to repair shoes in 24 hours or to provide the service free of charge. The smart cobbler should rarely find himself working for nothing. If he expects to turn round all shoes in a 24-hour period, then once he has taken on all that he can manage in this time, he can just refuse to accept any more under the conditions of the guarantee.

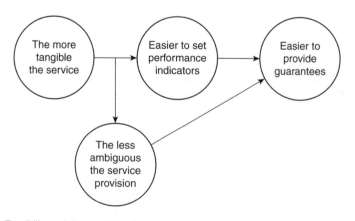

Figure 12.12 Tangibility and the provision of guarantees

It is more difficult for a tutor to guarantee the results of her students. There are many intangible aspects of such a service, and not all of these are under the control of the tutor. This is not to say that those responsible for providing services with some intangibility should not provide guarantees. Indeed, guarantees have been developed for services as intangible as education, and driving instruction.[48] In both cases, free additional instruction was offered to those who did not successfully complete their course. However, too often those who provide the more intangible services shelter behind the shield of difficulty when it comes to the provision of guarantees. Note that offering guarantees against service failure is not nearly as powerful as guaranteeing customer satisfaction.[49]

Many companies operating in competitive markets use guarantees as a positioning tool. They use it as a means of differentiating themselves from the competition, e.g. when Thomson Holidays first offered 'No surcharges guaranteed' it was the first tour operator to do this. However, the uniqueness of this benefit was short-lived. Like so many service developments, it was easily copied. Note also that this particular guarantee only applied to one aspect of the service.

Sometimes companies adopt a more all-embracing approach. Instead of providing a specific guarantee, they guarantee total customer satisfaction. We can probably all think of services that provide 'satisfaction guaranteed'. Whether or not we believe them is another matter. Many such companies attach no meaning to these statements, using them merely as a form of words intended to convey a quality service. But if they do, then as we have already stated this type of guarantee is more powerful than one guarding more specifically against service failure.

12.5.2   Designing a guarantee

Guarantees can be either explicit or implicit. The latter are earned by the service provider and are not created overnight. Such guarantees are often held by up-market hotels and restaurants.

There are several factors/questions that an organization should consider when deciding whether or not to offer a guarantee:[50]

- Can the company afford to offer one? This in turn is related to ...
- The company's quality and performance standards: if these are relatively low, there may be significant costs associated with offering a guarantee.
- What are the risk perceptions associated with offering one?
- Do competitors offer one? If so is it against what kind of factor?
- Should it be unconditional, or against a specific aspect of the service?
- Will it be a monetary or non-monetary response?
- What is the hassle-free process by which customer can invoke the guarantee?

The all-embracing guarantee of the sort described earlier is in fact not the best type of guarantee that a company can offer. The best guarantees meet the criteria summarized in Table 12.6.

Easy to understand

The guarantee should be as short and simple as possible. It should be written in clear, plain English to help prevent any ambiguity from creeping in. The ideal is to

Table 12.6 Qualities of the ideal guarantee

Easy to understand
Easy to invoke
Unconditional
Credible
Focused on customer needs
Meaningful (significant penalty of payout)
Provide clear performance standards

think of an advertising endline; normally only one sentence in length, and with the intention of being highly memorable.

Easy to invoke

Companies are often fearful of making guarantees easy to invoke because they are frightened of the potential cost. They can see the benefits of offering guarantees to consumers, but cannot see what benefits are to be gained by making them easy to invoke.

Unconditional

For the same reasons that it is important to make it easy for dissatisfied customers to complain, it is best to make the guarantee as unconditional as possible. This type of guarantee communicates to staff and customers that the service provider believes in the quality of their offering. Naturally, it is only sensible to offer such a guarantee if the service is a quality one.

Credible

To provide a guarantee that customers regard as incredible casts doubt on everything that the company does. Driving schools that guarantee learner drivers will pass first time are making unbelievable promises. The learner will know that there are many factors affecting whether or not they pass the driving test that are outside the control of the instructor, e.g. the nerves of the learner, or the mood of the test examiner. A table of pass rates relative to other driving schools would probably prove more credible, and would serve the main purpose of providing a guaranteed risk reduction.

Focused on customer needs

A guarantee should be guaranteeing aspects of service that are important to customers. It should not be focusing on what the company regards as important, or on what the company thinks customers regard as important.

Enlightened service providers should have identified those aspects of their service that are critically important to customers, not only to aid the design of a guarantee, but also to enable them to design a quality service.

Meaningful (with significant penalties or payouts)

The guarantee is not meaningful if the penalties that accrue to the provider, or the levels of compensation paid to the customer, are insignificant. In both these cases there is little incentive for the company to improve its service offering. Most dissatisfied customers will not take the trouble to complain. Even if they did, the company would not suffer high payout costs and so is less likely to work on service improvements.

Provide clear performance standards

Employees should know the targets they are trying to meet. The achievement of these standards generally denotes the provision of a good service. So, the pizza company that guarantees to deliver within a given time, states what the company regards as the maximum time that a customer should have to wait for a pizza. This guarantee gives kitchen and waiting staff clear performance standards.

12.6   Customer defections

We have previously suggested that organizations should attempt to minimize customer defections. However, it has been suggested that the best management processes do not attempt to eliminate all defections.[51] Some customers will defect regardless of what a company does to tempt them to stay. Furthermore, attempting a zero defections strategy is likely to represent an inefficient use of resources.

A good defections management programme will attempt to identify those who have or are about to leave. However, it is not always easy to identify those customers who are about to defect. It is easier in those services where a contractual agreement is in place. In such industries, customers may begin to complain, or suggest that a competitor is offering a lower price, as the original contract approaches its renewal.

In consumer services, building a database that records purchase frequencies and values will help pinpoint potential defectors. Such a database is relatively easy to establish in services where reservations or appointments are necessary. Another means of capturing the information is to design a loyalty card or frequent purchase programme where customers are rewarded for their loyalty. The service operator can then spot customers whose purchase frequency has declined. Or those who buy with the same frequency but purchase less at each occasion. Both are indicators that the customer may be about to defect.

Summary

In this chapter we have discussed a number of ways in which the organization can attempt to understand and learn from its customers' experiences. We have looked at gathering information on customer satisfaction and from customer complaints. We have also considered that an information feedback loop should also be present in any guarantee process. Invocation of guarantees and increased complaining behaviour can be potential predictors of customer defections. But where possible it is probably more reliable to try to anticipate potential defections through database modelling of consumer purchasing patterns.

The benefit of building such management information systems into the service process is that the service provider can continue to learn and develop the service offering in ways that are likely to result in continuing to satisfy customers.

References

1   Oliver, R (1977) 'Effect of expectation and disconfirmation on postexposure product evaluation: an alternative interpretation', *Journal of Applied Psychology*, **62**, August, 480–486.

2   Peters, T and Austin, N (1985) *A Passion for Excellence*. New York: Random House.

3   Parasuraman, A, Zeithaml, V A and Berry, L L (1990) *Delivering Quality Service*. New York: Free Press.

4   Johnson, R (1995) 'The zone of tolerance exploring the relationship between service transactions and satisfaction with the overall service', *International Journal of Service Management*, **6** (2), 46–61.

5   Cottam, A (1998) *The Experiential Nature of Service Consumption: An Investigation of the Formation of Customer Satisfaction*. Unpublished PhD thesis, University of Manchester Institute of Science and Technology.

6   Johnson, R, op. cit.

7   Sergeant, A (2000) 'When do customer contact employees satisfy customers?', *Journal of Service Research*, **3** (1), 18–34.

8   Clemmer, E C and Schneider, B (1996) 'Fair service', in *Advances in Services Marketing and Management*, **5**, 109–126.

9   Winsted, K F (2000) Service behaviours that lead to satisfied customers', *European Journal of Marketing*, **34** (3), 399–417.

10 Johnson, R and Lyth, D (1988) 'Service quality: integrating customer expectations and operational capability', *Proceedings of the QUIS Symposium*, University of Karlstad, Sweden, August.

11 Wilkie, W L and Pessemier, E A (1973) 'Issues in marketing's use of multiattribute attitude models', *Journal of the Market Research Society*, **x**, 428–441.

12 Oliver R L (1980) 'Product dissatisfaction as a function of prior expectation and subsequent disconfirmation: new evidence', in Day R L and Hunt, H K (eds), *New Dimensions of Consumer Satisfaction and Complaining Behaviour*. Bloomington, IN: Indiana University Press.

13 Warland, R H, Hermann, R O and Willits, J (1975) 'Dissatisfied customers: who gets upset and who takes action', *Journal of Consumer Affairs*, **9**.

14 Miller, J (1977) 'Studying satisfaction: modifying models, eliciting expectations, posing problems and making meaningful measurement', in Hunt, K (ed.), *Conceptualization and Measurement of Customer Satisfaction and Dissatisfaction*. Cambridge, MA: Marketing Science Institute.

15 Griel, H (1993) 'Zufriendene Kunden als Markenwelchsler', *Absatzwirtschaft*, **36** (2), 90–94.

16 Riecheld, F F and Aspinall, K (1994) 'Building high-loyalty business systems', *Journal of Retail Banking*, **15**, 421–429.

17 Casado Diaz, A N and Mas Ruiz, F J (2002) 'The consumer's reaction to delays in service', *International Journal of Service Industry Management*, **13** (2), 118–140.

18 Cottam, op. cit.

19 Consumers' Association (1998) *Consumer Complaints Survey*.

20 Goodman, J. (1999) 'Basic facts on customer complaint behaviour and the impact of service on the bottom line', in speech to 7th Annual Quality Service Conference, St Pete Beach, USA.

21 McCole, P (2004) 'Dealing with complaints in services', *International Journal of Contemporary Hospitality Management*, **16** (6), 345–354.

22 Consumers' Association (1998) *Handled with Care? Consumer Complaints 1991–1997*. Policy Report, London: Consumers' Association.

23 Bolton, R N and Bronkhurst, T M (1995) 'The relationship between customer complaints and subsequent exit behaviour', in Kardes, F and Sujan, M (eds), *Advances in Consumer Behaviour* 22. Boston, MA: Association for Consumer Research.

24 Naylor, G (2003) 'The complaining customer: a service provider's best friend', *Journal of Consumer Satisfaction, Dissatisfaction and Complaining Behaviour*, **16**, 241–248.

25 Bell, C R and Zemke, R (1988) 'Do service procedures tie employees' hands?', *Personnel Journal*, September, 76–83.

26 Dube, L and Maute, M (1996) 'The antecedents of brand switching, brand loyalty, and verbal responses to service failures', in Swartz, T, Bowen, D and Brown, S (eds), *Advances in Services Marketing and Management*, **5**, 127–151.

27 Zemke, R and Bell, C (1990) 'Do service procedures tie employees' hands?' *Personnel Journal*, September, 76–83.

28 Warland *et al.*, op. cit.

29 Miller, op. cit.

30 Best, A and Andreasen, A R (1977) 'Consumer response to unsatisfactory purchases: a survey of perceiving defects, voicing complaints and obtaining redress', *Law and Society Review*, November, 701–742.

31 Warland *et al.*, op. cit.

32 Best and Andreasen, op. cit.

33 Day, R L and Landon, E L (1977) 'Towards a theory of complaining behaviour', in Woodside, A G, Sheth, J N and Bennett, P D (eds), *Consumer and Industrial Buying Behaviour*. New York: Elsevier, pp. 425–437.

34 Holmes, A (1992) Quote in a letter from Ashley Holmes of the Consumers' Association.

35 Kubler-Ross, E (1969) *On Death and Dying*. London: Macmillan.

36 Richins, M (1990) 'Consumer perceptions of costs and benefits associated with complaining', in Hunt, H K and Day, R L (eds), *Refining Concepts and Measures of Consumer Satisfaction and Complaining Behaviour*. Bloomington, IN: Indiana University Press, pp. 50–53.

37 Biswell, K (2004) *Consumer Effectiveness Report: Customer Complaints Data*. London: Consumer Policy Unit, British Standards Institution.

38 Hart, G, Heskett, J and Sasser, W E (1990) 'The profitable art of service recovery', *Harvard Business Review*, July–Aug., 148–156.

39 Hoffman, K D *et al.* (1995) 'Tracking service failures and employee service recovery efforts', *Journal of Services Marketing*, **9** (2), 49–61.

40 Duffy, J A (2000) 'Service recovery', in Fitzsimmons, J A and Fitzsimmons, M J (eds), *New Service Development: Creating Memorable Experiences*. Thousand Oaks, CA: Sage.

41 Brown, S *et al.* (1996) 'Service recovery: its value and limitations as a retail strategy', *International Journal of Service Industry Management*, **7** (5), 32–46.

42 Duffy, op. cit.

43 Carlzon, J (1989) *Moments of Truth*. New York: Harper & Row.

44 Bosoff, C and Leong, J (1997) 'Empowerment, attribution and apologising as dimensions of service recovery', *International Journal of Service Industry Management*, **9**, 21–47.

45 Sellers, P (1988) 'How to handle customers' gripes', *Fortune*, 24 October.

46 Einstein, A (1954) *Ideas and Options*. New York: Crown.

47 Rust, R T *et al.* (1995) 'Making complaints a management tool', *Marketing Management*, **1** (3), 30–45.

48 Heskett, J L *et al.* (1990) *Service Breakthroughs: Changing the Rules of the Game*. New York: Free Press.

49 Ostrom, A L and Hart, C (2000) 'Service guarantees', in Schwartz, T A and Iacobucci, D (eds), *Handbook of Services Marketing and Management*. Thousand Oaks, CA: Sage.

50 Ibid.

51 Kurtz, D L and Clow, K E (1998) *Services Marketing*. Chichester: Wiley.

Index